W9-ANA-693

AMERICAN FORECLOSURE

Everything U Need to Know... ™

about

PREVENTING & BUYING

TREVOR RHODES, CEO OF AMERUSA

McGraw Hill

New York   Chicago   San Francisco   Lisbon
London   Madrid   Mexico City   Milan   New Delhi
San Juan   Seoul   Singapore   Sydney   Toronto

Trademarks: EUNTK, EUNTK.com, Everything U Need to Know... and the Everything U Need to Know... horseshoe bar logo, are all trademarks or registered trademarks of the EUNTK Corporation and may not be used without written permission. All other trademarks are the property of their respective owners.

Disclaimer: While the publisher and the author have used their best efforts in preparing this book, they make no representations or warranties with respect to the accuracy or completeness of the contents. Neither the publisher nor author shall be liable for any loss of profit or commercial damages, including but not limited to special, incidental, consequential or other damages. If legal advice or other expert assistance is required, it is strongly recommended that the services of a competent and experienced professional should be sought.

McGraw-Hill books are available at special quantity discounts to use as premiums and sales promotions, or for use in corporate training programs. For more information, please write to the Director of Special Sales, Professional Publishing, McGraw-Hill, Two Penn Plaza, New York, NY 10121-2298. Or contact your local bookstore.

For information about any of the other Everything U Need to Know... products and services, visit www.EUNTK.com. If you have questions or comments, please email them to feedback@euntk.com.

Available through book retailers nationwide.

McGraw-Hill Director, Business Editorial: Mary Glenn
EUNTK Managing Editor: Tomas Mureika
CD-ROM Software: TailoredApplication.com
Index: ProfessionalIndexing.com

This book is printed on acid-free paper.

To my wife, Lisa—
For her love and support during the good times and...
the bad.

In memory of

Sharon Petelle, Morris Rotenberg, James Adair,
Edmund Pikulinski, Edward Zbikowski, Jr.,
and Gillian Gobo

Acknowledgments

This *American Foreclosure* volume from **Everything U Need to Know... (EUNTK)** would not be possible without the support and assistance from the following companies and individuals: AmerUSA.net, Four Squared Images, Banning Lumber & Millwork, Jane Pikulinksi, Helen Cameron, Sophie Chilinski, Edward Zbikowski Sr., Craig Petelle, Tommy Petelle, Mark & Terry Banning, Daniel Shupe, John, Sharon & Amy Pikulinski, Jon Adair, Mike Adair, Barbara McPherson, David McPherson, Daniel, Rosemary, Lauren & Brandon Lester.

Table of Contents

Everything U Need to Know...™

Chapter 6: Foreclosure Prevention, Part I: Lender Communication.....................191

Chapter 7: Foreclosure Prevention, Part II:
Making the Most Out of Your Money...............................229

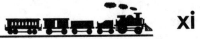

[Appendices continue on following page]

Introduction

Back in 2005 – about three years prior to the first printing of this **"Everything U Need to Know..."** volume – everyone in the mortgage industry with a three-digit IQ knew exactly where the real estate market was headed. And if not, they were too greedy to care. The initial design for this series was prepared in 2006 and submitted to publishers in early 2007, long before the mainstream news media and even the President of the United States began seriously addressing the real estate market crash caused primarily by the mortgage industry. (Sure, we could add many other factors into the equation, but it is an indisputable fact that the over-inflated property values – coupled with the riskiest mortgage programs ever written – are *right at the forefront*).

It all began in the 1990s with **a surge of sub-prime mortgage lenders** and their **highly volatile loan products that were designed to entice and confuse borrowers and qualify almost anyone.** *These products yielded lenders and loan officers an enormous amount of money* (upwards of thousands of dollars per loan). With a payday like that, you can see how the greed easily took precedence over borrower education and awareness.

And where were the state and federal government regulators to protect you and the process? *The loan disclosures meant to inform you were but meager attempts, buried among dozens of pages that borrowers were never encouraged to read.* **Most of the loan officers couldn't even decipher or explain their contents.** As your hand cramped signing dozens of pages, the common response heard industry-wide was the typical espousal, *"Don't worry, these are just standard forms that are required."*

Unfortunately, most consumers were unaware of the consequences of their actions in accepting such ridiculous terms (i.e., short-term adjustable rates that were fixed for only two or three years... which then adjust as much as 2% higher each year thereafter!). **And so here we are, facing astronomical numbers of**

real estate foreclosures across the country... *a good environment for those with money to invest, but a bad one for most of us, who suddenly find ourselves facing tenancy as opposed to homeownership.*

American Foreclosure **is designed as a two-pronged book, designed to educate parties on both sides of the situation:** for those who need a way of *preventing* foreclosure (or at least some good, honest advice on realistic options – without enduring further pain and suffering from foreclosure prevention scams) and for those who are interested in *buying* foreclosures, but who are unsure of how to begin and which steps must be taken to stay on the correct path so that they, too, don't fall prey to the real estate crisis at hand.

And on a very personal note to the homeowner in need of help: This volume from the **"Everything U Need to Know..."** series is backed by not only an author who is an experienced real estate professional, licensed mortgage broker and Chief Executive Officer of a credit reporting agency, but also **someone who lost his first home to foreclosure** – *experiencing firsthand the financial, marital and emotional stresses that invariably accompany the process.* *American Foreclosure* was carefully crafted at this personal experience level, in order to enlighten, comfort and empower you to face your own housing emergency.

But enough of this self-help guru nonsense; let's introduce you to the world of the **"American Foreclosure."** And don't worry – as dry as this topic can sometimes be, we've done our best to keep it stimulating, interesting, rewarding and educational throughout this book. We want to tell you **"Everything U Need to Know..."** – but that doesn't mean it has to be a dreadful experience! So relax and enjoy this volume!

And if you ever need further assistance, **check out the official website for this entire series** at **www.EUNTK.com** – for discussion groups, laws and statutes, other subjects in the series, plus a whole lot more... *for the absolute easiest way there is to learn* **"Everything U Need to Know..."**

Chapter 1

American Foreclosure:
Understanding Both Sides of the Story

This Chapter Discusses:

★ **What Is Foreclosure?**
★ **The Homeowner Side**
★ **The Investor Side**

The first thing you need to understand about an **American Foreclosure** is that – like most things in life – *there are two sides to every story*. In the case of **foreclosures**, there are always two parties with opposing interests – **those that want to prevent their homes from being repossessed** and **those that seek to invest in purchasing properties at the lowest possible cost.**

This volume of **"Everything U Need to Know..."** is deliberately presented for both these audiences – **No matter which side of the field you're on, being aware of what the other side can and can't do is undeniably** *invaluable knowledge* **to have** as you prepare either your defense or offense.

So for those of you facing foreclosure on your home, consider the parts of this book addressed to investors *not* as insensitivity to your stressful situation – but, instead, *as a means to how you may be able to use that knowledge to your best advantage!*

What Is Foreclosure?

Most of you are probably aware of the basic concept behind foreclosure, but – for many – it may be necessary to provide a brief overview before continuing any further. *And it can't hurt even the seasoned pro to make sure we're all playing with the same deck of cards.* **The best way to explain foreclosure is to equate it to financing an automobile and then having it repossessed.** *The premise is the same.* Whether it's a vehicle or real estate, *the lender who lent you the money to finance it also had you agree to allow them to use it as collateral to guarantee you would pay back what is owed, plus interest.*

In the case of *foreclosure,* **the lender essentially has a right to sell your home if you default (fail to make payments).** *Once the lender initiates the foreclosure process, there are a total of four possible outcomes depending upon your reaction* (later chapters will provide step-by-step detail about the entire process, as well as specific state-by-state guidelines):

☆ The Four Possible Outcomes of the Foreclosure Process:

- ♦ **You can reinstate the loan by paying off all of your missed payments** (including penalties, interest and fees) **during the reinstatement period determined by your state's law.**
- ♦ **You can sell the property to a third party prior to paying off what is owed and avoid having a foreclosure appear on your credit report.** *This must happen within a prescribed number of days* (as determined by your state) *before your property is scheduled to be sold at a public auction.*
- ♦ **Your property** *is sold* **at a public auction.**
- ♦ **The lender takes possession of the property** – either *through an agreement with you before the public auction* or *during the public auction by submitting the highest bid* **in order to buy it.**

The Homeowner Side

Needless to say (regardless of the outcome), this is an unbelievably stressful time for any homeowner. Facing foreclosure causes a tremendous amount of fear and strain, but *there are many reasonable solutions and strategies as discussed throughout this book to assist you in determining which path is best for you.* Ironically, **you'll probably find the most beneficial attribute of this essential volume to be the insight into the Investors' Side** of the story and *their* **rights** and **likely incentives for their actions…**

By addressing both sides of the story, *American Foreclosure* **will enable you to become better equipped to handle your situation.** After all, before going into battle you must *"know thy (thine) enemy,"* right? **The irony here is that the investor can actually be a life saving ally.** So *don't dismiss or ignore the other side of the story when it may actually be able to help you* **improve your chances of surviving** such turbulent times.

The Investor Side

Yes, the goal of a real estate investor is to make money, naturally. But **before you begin investing, you should familiarize yourself with the homeowner's perception and the challenges they face** (not only *to strategize your approach on how to best find and invest in foreclosures*, but *to learn to do so with dignity and compassion*). **As an investor,** *you* **have the ability to save someone from further pain and suffering** – unlike most predators out there seeking to make a killing *regardless of the cost* to the other side. Not to sound too cliché, but instead of pouring salt in an open wound, **you can** *still* **profit and actually provide a bandage both at the same time!**

Chapter 2

Before You Miss Your First Payment: The Advice *No One Else* Will Give You!

This Chapter Discusses:

★ **Assessing Your Financial Situation**

★ **Lining Up a More Reasonable Home**

★ **Letting Go of Nonessential Debt**

Caution!: *This chapter really hits the ground running,* right out of the gate – **because it's intended for those who either are current on their home loan payments** (fearing they may not be able to sustain them for too much longer) **or have just missed their first payment, but may have the ability to catch up** (by either liquidating assets or getting assistance from friends or family).

If you are behind on your loan by more than one month and don't have the cash reserves to bring it current – or if you are unemployed – you may want to skip ahead to **Chapter 3** *to begin the road to recovery* **by first understanding the foreclosure process.** Subsequent chapters will then help guide you to reasonable and realistic options that are readily available to you for preventing (or, at least, delaying) your lender from foreclosing.

Assessing Your Financial Situation

Let's be honest – *most of the time, you can see financial hardship* somewhere on the horizon *well before it gets too hard to handle.* There is **nothing better than being prepared** – so, ideally, you've discovered this book while things are a little easier to manage. ***Because* as soon *as you start falling behind,* your options become increasingly limited** *as your situation progressively worsens*.

The **one problem** you need to be concerned about **is the impact a foreclosure can have on your credit rating** – *and unless you already have another home lined up, you definitely don't need a foreclosure appearing on your credit file for all the other potential lenders to see*. Even **falling** *merely two months* **behind on a mortgage can prove to be detrimental when trying to buy** *(or even rent)* **another home.** And – let's face it – once you've savored the experience of being a homeowner, it's difficult to resign and become a tenant.

Of course, there are those that will debate **the economics behind** *renting versus buying*, **but it's an indisputable fact that "the quintessential American dream" involves owning your own home** – so *let's do what must be done* to keep you living that dream, seeing as **it's always better to be your own landlord** instead of a tenant who must abide by the terms of someone else's lease agreement.

The first step before doing anything else **is to honestly assess your current financial situation.**

Ask Yourself:

> ➤ *After paying your bills and living expenses each month, do you have* **at least 10%** *of your monthly income left over for retirement/savings?*

If the answer is no, then you've got to face facts and admit there's a serious crunch going on which needs to be alleviated – so consider one of *four options*.

☆ Four Possible Options for Alleviating a Housing Crunch:

- Buy a **less expensive home**;
- Allow some of your **nonessential bills** to fall by the wayside;
- **Refinance** – *if* your current rate and term is significantly above current interest rates (i.e., greater than 2%) – but there's more to it than that… **You also need to assess the property's taxes, insurance and utilities,** because – regardless of what the principal and interest payments are on your home loan – your **ancillary payments** may also be a big part of the problem; or;
- **Get a roommate** to share the expenses (granted, this is an unreasonable and unrealistic option for most).

You can obviously determine for yourself which choice you are willing to make. For the purposes of this chapter, **there are usually only two "ideal" options**:

☆ Option 1: Move On

List your home for sale and *buy a less expensive one.*

☆ Option 2: Hunker Down

Hold on tight to your home, but *let go of some of your debt.*

The other remaining two options are seldom effective in the long run, since refinancing only works if you have an extraordinarily high interest rate that can be lowered by at least 2% or more, depending on your needs. And **don't bother taking out a second mortgage or home equity loan to keep you afloat,** because in most cases *it will only delay the inevitable.* Finally, as far as **finding a roommate**: *this is probably the last headache you want right now* – it's best not to depend on anyone other than yourself or your spouse, so **budget accordingly.**

Lining Up a More Reasonable Home

If you are struggling to keep your payments on time each month and know for a fact there are more reasonably priced homes in your community worth purchasing, **don't be afraid to have the foresight to realize you can't continue to barely make ends meet**. Sure, the adjustment may create a little heartache at home, but *it's much better to face facts and act now than to struggle to the point of becoming so far past due that you can no longer buy another home for several more years.*

If you feel the crunch coming on, you should contact a loan officer at a local reputable lending institution and see about getting pre-qualified to purchase a less expensive home. As long as they give you the okay to proceed, *you should immediately begin looking for a new home* **and list your current one for sale with a licensed real estate agent;** *this is* **without a doubt** *a good option.*

Don't list your current house *"for sale by owner."* **Lenders feel more comfortable** if your primary residence is listed in **MLS** (the **Multiple Listing Service** *used by real estate agents to advertise to other agents* that your property is for sale). This way, **it doesn't look like the less expensive property you are trying to buy will be used as an investment property as opposed to your new primary residence.** Of course, any experienced loan officer should tell you this, but in case they don't, **you** *definitely* **want your home in MLS!**

If you're worried about *disclosing enough income to qualify for both homes at the same time,* **most lenders offer** *"stated" or "no income" programs* **to accommodate such a maneuver and juggle both payments.**

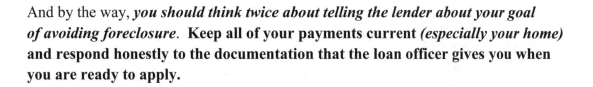
And by the way, *you should think twice about telling the lender about your goal of avoiding foreclosure*. **Keep all of your payments current** *(especially your home)* **and respond honestly to the documentation that the loan officer gives you when you are ready to apply.**

It's quite possible your current home will not sell. In which case, *you may have to let it go* – as discussed later in **Chapter 8** – because **you certainly don't want to overextend your cash reserves on two mortgages.**

The important thing to keep in mind is that *you will have a home that you can afford to manage!* It may not be the home you've always dreamed of (or have become accustomed to), but at least it will be there for you *a lot longer*.

Again, keep your existing home loan current until you close on the new one! *The last thing you need is the lender ordering a verification of your current loan* days before closing – only to find out that you didn't make the last payment. *Believe it or not, this happens a lot – and it can be a* **major** *deal breaker!*

TIP

Letting Go of Nonessential Debt

Okay, so if the local lenders in town can't pre-qualify you to buy another home, then the second option is to *just let 'em go, Tex!*

Tally up those *"nonessential bills"* **– such as credit cards, retail cards, gasoline cards and medical collections** *(not to be confused with medical insurance)* **– and determine which ones you can afford to keep; the ones you can't** *– just toss 'em for now.*

Quite frankly, *you don't need credit cards to maintain your lifestyle.* **Cash living has always been best – most debit check cards offer the convenience and buying protection of major credit cards** without having to endure unreasonable finance charges.

It's more important to have a home for yourself and your family than to keep paying on high interest credit cards and nonessential bills!

Just **be sure you budget yourself to hold on to your essential bills** – such as *insurance, groceries* and *automobile loans.* **These are needed** to maintain your health, your job and a modest existence.

In case you're wondering about **filing for bankruptcy**, *it's strongly discouraged and often unnecessary* – unless you absolutely need to delay foreclosure (as discussed in **Chapter 11**) and/or have substantial assets that are not protected and can easily be found and levied. **Credit is a game that can easily be won when you are taught the correct way to play.** *Bankruptcy* – on the other hand – *can be equated to forfeiting…* when you may only be a few points behind.

And what about **credit counseling programs**, you ask? *Profit or non-profit, credit counseling programs will* **probably** *not be able to do you much good.* Despite what you may have heard, **credit counseling still has a negative impact on your credit worthiness and doesn't help your immediate situation,** *because you will have to make payments to all creditors proportionately* (you'll be lucky to see any savings).

If maintaining your unsecured debt requires this much attention, you may just want to *think about letting 'em go.* Your creditors will close your accounts as soon as you enter a credit counseling program anyway. **Many consumers have had greater success by simply letting go.** Not only did they *save more cash,* but they eventually had a better chance at repairing their credit (one creditor at a time).

For more information, please reference the ***American Credit Repair*** volume, which **discusses this topic and other debt help services in greater detail** and **provides better alternatives for handling your personal finances.**

Don't worry about your credit rating when trying to save your home, just worry about saving your home! As soon as you get a handle on your cash flow, you can then take the necessary steps to begin repairing your credit. For now, learning how to survive without plastic playing cards and other nonessential obligations will be a *great* step in the right direction.

TIP

By the way, **letting go means *exactly* that**: *You* never *make another payment toward the nonessential debts* you determine you can live without. Regardless of the settlement offers that may be extended to you, **you should never make another payment** (not one penny) **until you are able to comfortably manage a place to live**. Even the **Federal Housing Administration** advises on its website, *"Delay payments on credit cards and other unsecured debt until you have paid your mortgage."*

So let's recap this very important introductory chapter for those who are still **current with their home payments... but feel the crunch coming on the horizon.**

☆ A Review of Your Two Options Before Missing Your First Payment:

- *If you are barely able to keep paying your home loan on time and can qualify to buy a less expensive home, go for it.* **This is the best option** unless your financial crisis is only temporary.
- **If you are unable to buy another home or can't find a less expensive one,** *stop paying your unsecured nonessential bills* **to help manage your home loan.**

Remember: *The worst thing you can do is lose your current home without having another one lined up to take its place!*

Whenever possible, **it's much better to be a homeowner than a tenant.** And *don't worry about your credit rating right now; just keep paying your home and other secured obligations on time.* **Credit cards and other "nonessential" unsecured obligations mentioned before should be of little importance to you at this point.**

Chapter 3

Understanding the Foreclosure Process, Part I: The Loan Documents Defined

This Chapter Discusses:

★ **Promissory Note**
★ **Mortgage**
★ **Deed of Trust**

It's obviously important to understand the underlying documents that permit a lender to take possession of your home. **These simple legal instruments are** *drafted to empower them (not you!)* – so their money and investors are protected in accordance with the laws of your state. With that being said, you can **expect each state to have its own set of laws and procedures** that a lender must follow to initiate and complete the foreclosure process.

The **details of each state** are presented in **Chapter 5**. But don't jump ahead, because you must first become familiar with the documents you probably filed away and forgot you ever signed. While they may not have seemed to be that important at the time, **they are very powerful legal instruments that need to be understood** *before* **you try to save your home.**

Promissory Note

Just like it sounds, a *promissory note* is a **promise to repay the money you borrowed to buy your home.**

First off – *yes, you actually promised to pay the money back* – **except this promise is not a mere handshake**; it has been cured in concrete and reinforced with cold hard legal steel. In other words, **it's nearly impossible to break**!

The **promissory note** is **designed to clearly outline the terms of the loan** and contains **seven primary components** you should understand.

The Seven Primary Components of a Promissory Note:

☆ Principal

This is the ***total amount of money you borrowed from the lender.***
For example: If you bought a $500,000 house and provided a down payment of $50,000 plus your closing costs (e.g., lender fees, taxes, insurance), then your principal balance would be $450,000.

For those of you that refinanced, the principal would be the total amount of the refinanced loan – which most likely included your closing costs and any cash you may have taken out of the property for debt consolidation (home improvements or even vacationing across the country in the new family truckster).

☆ Interest

…As if you don't already know what this is, right? **The promissory note will undoubtedly list** *how much the lender is entitled to receive for lending you their money.*

Interest rates are calculated annually (365 days, to be exact) and will be *fixed, adjustable* or *based on margin* (interest rates that are determined by adding a fixed rate on top of an index – such as prime, treasury notes, etc.).

You typically hear this margin approach with home equity line advertisements from banks (i.e., prime + 1% or prime - 1 %).

★ Term

This part *stipulates how much time you have to repay the loan – which is usually indicated as a pre-specified number of months.* **For example**: A 30-year mortgage would be listed as 360 months. (And if you thought *that* was a long time to repay a debt, some lenders are now offering loans with terms based upon 40+ years!)

★ Payment

On most loans, *this figure is comprised of the principal and interest as referenced earlier* – **it does not include your taxes and insurance, which are subject to change every year**.

In addition to specifying the payment amount, **this section will also indicate when the final payment is due**. If the note is for a *"balloon mortgage"* (one that requires a single final lump sum to be paid after a certain amount of time has passed), **then the total amount due on the final payment will also be stated here.**

★ Security

Most promissory notes used in a real estate transaction have **the property being purchased or refinanced held as collateral to guarantee the repayment of the loan**. This part *entitles the lender to sell the property to pay off the loan if you should stop making payments*.

★ Acceleration

This is an **important clause** that obviously **makes things a little easier for the lender if you don't make a payment.** *As soon as you fail to make a payment, this clause allows the lender to accelerate the loan by demanding the entire amount, including principal and interest.* This is clearly stated so they don't have to try to collect for each missed payment – a convenient way of avoiding a lengthy and painstaking legal process.

★ Negotiability

As you may have already experienced in the past, **lenders buy and sell loans all of the time.** In fact, *selling a loan is how a lender frees up extra cash to fund more loans*. You can **learn more about the ways in which lenders profit** by reading *American Mortgage* from **Everything U Need to Know...** This clause contained within a promissory note simply *solidifies this right for the lender*.

A **sample promissory note is provided on the next three pages** for your review. This particular note is intended for a 30-year mortgage that has installment payments (monthly payments). *If you already have a mortgage and didn't discard your loan documents* (yes, there are some Americans that actually toss 'em aside – never to be seen again until a copy is provided by the lender's process server when it's time to foreclose!), *you may want to actually read what you've signed.* **Not all promissory notes are the same!**

Promissory Note

PROMISSORY NOTE

_____, _____   _____, _____
       [Date]   [City]   [State]

_____
              [Property Address]

1. BORROWER'S PROMISE TO PAY

In return for a loan that I have received, I promise to pay U.S. $_____ (this amount is called "Principal"), plus interest, to the order of the Lender. The Lender is _____.
I will make all payments under this Note in the form of cash, check or money order.

I understand that the Lender may transfer this Note. The Lender or anyone who takes this Note by transfer and who is entitled to receive payments under this Note is called the "Note Holder."

2. INTEREST

Interest will be charged on unpaid principal until the full amount of Principal has been paid. I will pay interest at a yearly rate of _____%.

The interest rate required by this Section 2 is the rate I will pay both before and after any default described in Section 6(B) of this Note.

3. PAYMENTS

(A) Time and Place of Payments

I will pay principal and interest by making a payment every month.

I will make my monthly payment on the _____ day of each month beginning on _____, _____. I will make these payments every month until I have paid all of the principal and interest and any other charges described below that I may owe under this Note. Each monthly payment will be applied as of its scheduled due date and will be applied to interest before Principal. If, on _____, 20___. I still owe amounts under this Note, I will pay those amounts in full on that date, which is called the "Maturity Date."

I will make my monthly payments at _____
or at a different place if required by the Note Holder.

(B) Amount of Monthly Payments

My monthly payment will be in the amount of U.S. $_____.

4. BORROWER'S RIGHT TO PREPAY

I have the right to make payments of Principal at any time before they are due. A payment of Principal only is known as a "Prepayment." When I make a Prepayment, I will tell the Note Holder in writing that I am doing so. I may not designate a payment as a Prepayment if I have not made all the monthly payments due under the Note.

I may make a full Prepayment or partial Prepayments without paying a Prepayment charge. The Note Holder will use my Prepayments to reduce the amount of Principal that I owe under this Note. However, the Note Holder may apply my Prepayment to the accrued and unpaid interest on the Prepayment amount, before applying my Prepayment to reduce the Principal amount of the Note. If I make a partial Prepayment, there will be no changes in the due date or in the amount of my monthly payment unless the Note Holder agrees in writing to those changes.

5. LOAN CHARGES

If a law, which applies to this loan and which sets maximum loan charges, is finally interpreted so that the interest or other loan charges collected or to be collected in connection with this loan exceed the permitted limits, then: (a) any such loan charge shall be reduced by the amount necessary to reduce the charge to the permitted limit; and (b) any sums already collected from me which exceeded permitted limits will be refunded to me. The Note Holder may choose to make this refund by reducing the Principal I owe under this Note or by making a direct payment to me. If a refund reduces Principal, the reduction will be treated as a partial Prepayment.

6. BORROWER'S FAILURE TO PAY AS REQUIRED

(A) Late Charge for Overdue Payments

If the Note Holder has not received the full amount of any monthly payment by the end of _____ calendar days after the date it is due, I will pay a late charge to the Note Holder. The amount of the charge will be ____% of my overdue payment of principal and interest. I will pay this late charge promptly but only once on each late payment.

Everything U Need to Know...™

Promissory Note

(B) Default

If I do not pay the full amount of each monthly payment on the date it is due, I will be in default.

(C) Notice of Default

If I am in default, the Note Holder may send me a written notice telling me that if I do not pay the overdue amount by a certain date, the Note Holder may require me to pay immediately the full amount of Principal which has not been paid and all the interest that I owe on that amount. That date must be at least 30 days after the date on which the notice is mailed to me or delivered by other means.

(D) No Waiver By Note Holder

Even if, at a time when I am in default, the Note Holder does not require me to pay immediately in full as described above, the Note Holder will still have the right to do so if I am in default at a later time.

(E) Payment of Note Holder's Costs and Expenses

If the Note Holder has required me to pay immediately in full as described above, the Note Holder will have the right to be paid back by me for all of its costs and expenses in enforcing this Note to the extent not prohibited by applicable law. Those expenses include, for example, reasonable attorneys' fees.

7. GIVING OF NOTICES

Unless applicable law requires a different method, any notice that must be given to me under this Note will be given by delivering it or by mailing it by first class mail to me at the Property Address above or at a different address if I give the Note Holder a notice of my different address.

Any notice that must be given to the Note Holder under this Note will be given by delivering it or by mailing it by first class mail to the Note Holder at the address stated in Section 3(A) above or at a different address if I am given a notice of that different address.

8. OBLIGATIONS OF PERSONS UNDER THIS NOTE

If more than one person signs this Note, each person is fully and personally obligated to keep all of the promises made in this Note, including the promise to pay the full amount owed. Any person who is a guarantor, surety or endorser of this Note is also obligated to do these things. Any person who takes over these obligations, including the obligations of a guarantor, surety or endorser of this Note, is also obligated to keep all of the promises made in this Note. The Note Holder may enforce its rights under this Note against each person individually or against all of us together. This means that any one of us may be required to pay all of the amounts owed under this Note.

9. WAIVERS

I and any other person who has obligations under this Note waive the rights of Presentment and Notice of Dishonor. "Presentment" means the right to require the Note Holder to demand payment of amounts due. "Notice of Dishonor" means the right to require the Note Holder to give notice to other persons that amounts due have not been paid.

10. UNIFORM SECURED NOTE

This Note is a uniform instrument with limited variations in some jurisdictions. In addition to the protections given to the Note Holder under this Note, a Mortgage, Deed of Trust, or Security Deed (the "Security Instrument"), dated the same date as this Note, protects the Note Holder from possible losses which might result if I do not keep the promises which I make in this Note. That Security Instrument describes how and under what conditions I may be required to make immediate payment in full of all amounts I owe under this Note. Some of those conditions are described as follows:

Lender may require immediate payment in full of all Sums Secured by this Security Instrument if all or any part of the Property, or if any right in the Property, is sold or transferred without Lender's prior written permission. If Borrower is not a natural person and a beneficial interest in Borrower is sold or transferred without Lender's prior written permission, Lender also may require immediate payment in full. However, this option shall not be exercised by Lender if such exercise is prohibited by Applicable Law.

If Lender requires immediate payment in full under this Section 18, Lender will give me a notice which states this requirement. The notice will give me at least 30 days to make the required payment. The 30-day period will begin on the date the notice is given to me in the manner required by Section 15 of this Security Instrument. If I do not make the required payment during that period, Lender may act to enforce its rights under this Security Instrument without giving me any further notice or demand for payment.

Promissory Note

WITNESS THE HAND(S) AND SEAL(S) OF THE UNDERSIGNED.

_____(Seal)
                -Borrower

_____(Seal)
                -Borrower

_____(Seal)
                -Borrower

[Sign Original Only]

Now before moving on to either of the next set of documents, it's important to understand (once again) that *each state is different*. **Some states (jurisdictions) will use a *mortgage* and others a *deed of trust*.** So to save you a little reading time and in the event you don't already know, we have included **a chart depicting each state's most commonly used security instrument for a primary residence**.

Note: You are about to discover that a ***deed of trust* contains a *power of sale clause*** (a lender-friendly attribute defined later in this chapter) and that a ***mortgage* typically does not**. For that reason, you'll see the following chart mention a few states that prefer to use a **"Mortgage (with a Power of Sale clause)."** But don't worry – even though it may be a little confusing – it will come together as you continue reading.

Each State's Most Commonly Used Security Instrument for a Primary Residence

Alabama	Deed of Trust
Alaska	Deed of Trust
Arizona	Deed of Trust
Arkansas	Deed of Trust
California	Deed of Trust
Colorado	Deed of Trust
Connecticut	Mortgage
Delaware	Mortgage
District of Columbia	Deed of Trust
Florida	Mortgage
Georgia	Security Deed (Deed of Trust)
Hawaii	Deed of Trust
Idaho	Deed of Trust
Illinois	Mortgage
Indiana	Mortgage
Iowa	Mortgage
Kansas	Mortgage
Kentucky	Mortgage
Louisiana	Mortgage
Maine	Mortgage
Maryland	Mortgage (with a Power of Sale clause)
Massachusetts	Mortgage (with a Power of Sale clause)
Michigan	Deed of Trust
Minnesota	Mortgage (with a Power of Sale clause)
Mississippi	Mortgage (with a Power of Sale clause)
Missouri	Deed of Trust

Montana	Deed of Trust
Nebraska	Deed of Trust
Nevada	Deed of Trust
New Hampshire	Mortgage (with a Power of Sale clause)
New Jersey	Mortgage
New Mexico	Mortgage
New York	Mortgage
North Carolina	Mortgage (with a Power of Sale clause)
North Dakota	Mortgage
Ohio	Mortgage
Oklahoma	Mortgage (with a Power of Sale clause)
Oregon	Deed of Trust
Pennsylvania	Mortgage
Rhode Island	Mortgage (with a Power of Sale clause)
South Carolina	Mortgage
South Dakota	Deed of Trust
Tennessee	Deed of Trust
Texas	Deed of Trust
Utah	Deed of Trust
Vermont	Mortgage
Virginia	Mortgage (with a Power of Sale clause)
Washington	Deed of Trust
West Virginia	Deed of Trust
Wisconsin	Mortgage
Wyoming	Deed of Trust

Mortgage

A *mortgage* is a lengthy security instrument used by the lender to publicly record a legal claim against your property in exchange for lending you money. This is *how the lender protects itself in case you fail to abide by the terms of the promissory note.*

Both the mortgage and the promissory note are recorded together at the county recorder's office. Each of these documents can then be viewed by the general public at any time – this is why they are called *public records.*

The **mortgage requires two parties to sign** – *the mortgagor (the borrower)* **and** *the mortgagee (the lender).* The **mortgagor could consist of one or more persons or entities** (e.g., spouse, partner, corporation); the **same goes for the mortgagee, although it is** *typically* **one company or investor** lending you the money. (Sometimes, home sellers even offer their own financing.)

We realize **it can get confusing when trying to remember if the mortgagor is the borrower or lender. Try associating the last** *"or"* **in** *mortgagor* **with the** *"or"* **in** *borrower.* If that doesn't work, then *mark this page*. Even professionals in the industry get these two mixed up once in a while…!

Here are some **relevant terms and conditions of a mortgage** that are worth noting**:**

The Relevant Terms and Conditions of a Mortgage:

★ Mortgagee's Name and Address

The *investor or company (lender) who lends the money* that is secured by your home.

★ County Recorder Information

The *county office that received and recorded the mortgage into public record,* making special note of the date, time and recording fee.

This is **usually stamped on the top right of the document,** unless your copy was given to you prior to the recording (i.e., you received a copy of the mortgage at the closing table or anytime before the official filing of the mortgage).

★ Date of Execution

The *date that the document was signed by you,* the mortgagor.

★ Mortgagor(s) Name and Address

The *individual(s) or entity borrowing the money.*

★ Legal Description

This includes *what the county deems to be the official description of your property's location,* such as the lot, tract number and block.

★ Principal Amount of the Loan

The *total amount of money being borrowed from the mortgagee* **(lender).**

★ Acknowledgment

Simple *language stating that the mortgagor (borrower) was in no way coerced and willingly signed the mortgage.*

A copy of an actual mortgage is shown on the next fifteen pages. *If you can access a copy of your own mortgage, we would suggest reading it instead of the one provided in this chapter.* **If not, you can always contact you county recorder's office and retrieve a copy for a nominal fee.**

Otherwise, enjoy! This **sample mortgage** is packed *chock-full* of stimulating legal rhetoric…

Mortgage

After Recording Return To:

_____

_____

_____

_____

SAMPLE

_____ **[Space Above This Line for Recording Data]** _____

MORTGAGE

DEFINITIONS

Words used in multiple sections of this document are defined below and other words are defined in Sections 3, 11, 13, 18, 20 and 21. Certain rules regarding the usage of words used in this document are also provided in Section 16.

(A) "Security Instrument" means this document, which is dated _____, _____, together with all Riders to this document.

(B) "Borrower" is _____. Borrower is the mortgagor under this Security Instrument.

(C) "Lender" is _____. Lender is a _____ organized and existing under the laws of _____. Lender's address is _____ _____. Lender is the mortgagee under this Security Instrument.

(D) "Note" means the promissory note signed by Borrower and dated _____, _____. The Note states that Borrower owes Lender _____ Dollars (U.S. $_____) plus interest. Borrower has promised to pay this debt in regular Periodic Payments and to pay the debt in full not later than _____.

(E) "Property" means the property that is described below under the heading "Transfer of Rights in the Property."

(F) "Loan" means the debt evidenced by the Note, plus interest, any prepayment charges and late charges due under the Note, and all sums due under this Security Instrument, plus interest.

(G) "Riders" means all Riders to this Security Instrument that are executed by Borrower. The following Riders are to be executed by Borrower [check box as applicable]:

☐ Adjustable Rate Rider	☐ Condominium Rider	☐ Second Home Rider
☐ Balloon Rider	☐ Planned Unit Development Rider	☐ Other(s) [specify] _____
☐ 1-4 Family Rider	☐ Biweekly Payment Rider	

Mortgage

(H) **"Applicable Law"** means all controlling applicable federal, state and local statutes, regulations, ordinances and administrative rules and orders (that have the effect of law) as well as all applicable final, non-appealable judicial opinions.

(I) **"Community Association Dues, Fees, and Assessments"** means all dues, fees, assessments and other charges that are imposed on Borrower or the Property by a condominium association, homeowners association or similar organization.

(J) **"Electronic Funds Transfer"** means any transfer of funds, other than a transaction originated by check, draft, or similar paper instrument, which is initiated through an electronic terminal, telephonic instrument, computer, or magnetic tape so as to order, instruct, or authorize a financial institution to debit or credit an account. Such term includes, but is not limited to, point-of-sale transfers, automated teller machine transactions, transfers initiated by telephone, wire transfers, and automated clearinghouse transfers.

(K) **"Escrow Items"** means those items that are described in Section 3.

(L) **"Miscellaneous Proceeds"** means any compensation, settlement, award of damages, or proceeds paid by any third party (other than insurance proceeds paid under the coverages described in Section 5) for: (i) damage to, or destruction of, the Property; (ii) condemnation or other taking of all or any part of the Property; (iii) conveyance in lieu of condemnation; or (iv) misrepresentations of, or omissions as to, the value and/or condition of the Property.

(M) **"Mortgage Insurance"** means insurance protecting Lender against the nonpayment of, or default on, the Loan.

(N) **"Periodic Payment"** means the regularly scheduled amount due for (i) principal and interest under the Note, plus (ii) any amounts under Section 3 of this Security Instrument.

(O) **"RESPA"** means the Real Estate Settlement Procedures Act (12 U.S.C. §2601 et seq.) and its implementing regulation, Regulation X (24 C.F.R. Part 3500), as they might be amended from time to time, or any additional or successor legislation or regulation that governs the same subject matter. As used in this Security Instrument, "RESPA" refers to all requirements and restrictions that are imposed in regard to a "federally related mortgage loan" even if the Loan does not qualify as a "federally related mortgage loan" under RESPA.

(P) **"Successor in Interest of Borrower"** means any party that has taken title to the Property, whether or not that party has assumed Borrower's obligations under the Note and/or this Security Instrument.

TRANSFER OF RIGHTS IN THE PROPERTY

This Security Instrument secures to Lender: (i) the repayment of the Loan, and all renewals, extensions and modifications of the Note; and (ii) the performance of Borrower's covenants and agreements under this Security Instrument and the Note. For this purpose, Borrower does hereby mortgage, grant and convey to Lender, the following described property located in the

_____ of _____:

   [Type of Recording Jurisdiction]   [Name of Recording Jurisdiction]

which currently has the address of _____

                                               [Street]

_____, Florida _____ ("Property Address"):

     [City]   [Zip Code]

Everything U Need to Know...

Mortgage

TOGETHER WITH all the improvements now or hereafter erected on the property, and all easements, appurtenances, and fixtures now or hereafter a part of the property. All replacements and additions shall also be covered by this Security Instrument. All of the foregoing is referred to in this Security Instrument as the "Property."

BORROWER COVENANTS that Borrower is lawfully seised of the estate hereby conveyed and has the right to mortgage, grant and convey the Property and that the Property is unencumbered, except for encumbrances of record. Borrower warrants and will defend generally the title to the Property against all claims and demands, subject to any encumbrances of record.

THIS SECURITY INSTRUMENT combines uniform covenants for national use and non-uniform covenants with limited variations by jurisdiction to constitute a uniform security instrument covering real property.

UNIFORM COVENANTS. Borrower and Lender covenant and agree as follows:

1. Payment of Principal, Interest, Escrow Items, Prepayment Charges, and Late Charges. Borrower shall pay when due the principal of, and interest on, the debt evidenced by the Note and any prepayment charges and late charges due under the Note. Borrower shall also pay funds for Escrow Items pursuant to Section 3. Payments due under the Note and this Security Instrument shall be made in U.S. currency. However, if any check or other instrument received by Lender as payment under the Note or this Security Instrument is returned to Lender unpaid, Lender may require that any or all subsequent payments due under the Note and this Security Instrument be made in one or more of the following forms, as selected by Lender: (a) cash; (b) money order; (c) certified check, bank check, treasurer's check or cashier's check, provided any such check is drawn upon an institution whose deposits are insured by a federal agency, instrumentality, or entity; or (d) Electronic Funds Transfer.

Payments are deemed received by Lender when received at the location designated in the Note or at such other location as may be designated by Lender in accordance with the notice provisions in Section 15. Lender may return any payment or partial payment if the payment or partial payments are insufficient to bring the Loan current. Lender may accept any payment or partial payment insufficient to bring the Loan current, without waiver of any rights hereunder or prejudice to its rights to refuse such payment or partial payments in the future, but Lender is not obligated to apply such payments at the time such payments are accepted. If each Periodic Payment is applied as of its scheduled due date, then Lender need not pay interest on unapplied funds. Lender may hold such unapplied funds until Borrower makes payment to bring the Loan current. If Borrower does not do so within a reasonable period of time, Lender shall either apply such funds or return them to Borrower. If not applied earlier, such funds will be applied to the outstanding principal balance under the Note immediately prior to foreclosure. No offset or claim which Borrower might have now or in the future against Lender shall relieve Borrower from making payments due under the Note and this Security Instrument or performing the covenants and agreements secured by this Security Instrument.

2. Application of Payments or Proceeds. Except as otherwise described in this Section 2, all payments accepted and applied by Lender shall be applied in the following order of priority: (a) interest due under the Note; (b) principal due under the Note; (c) amounts due under Section 3.

Mortgage

Such payments shall be applied to each Periodic Payment in the order in which it became due. Any remaining amounts shall be applied first to late charges, second to any other amounts due under this Security Instrument, and then to reduce the principal balance of the Note.

If Lender receives a payment from Borrower for a delinquent Periodic Payment which includes a sufficient amount to pay any late charge due, the payment may be applied to the delinquent payment and the late charge. If more than one Periodic Payment is outstanding, Lender may apply any payment received from Borrower to the repayment of the Periodic Payments if, and to the extent that, each payment can be paid in full. To the extent that any excess exists after the payment is applied to the full payment of one or more Periodic Payments, such excess may be applied to any late charges due. Voluntary prepayments shall be applied first to any prepayment charges and then as described in the Note.

Any application of payments, insurance proceeds, or Miscellaneous Proceeds to principal due under the Note shall not extend or postpone the due date, or change the amount, of the Periodic Payments.

3. Funds for Escrow Items. Borrower shall pay to Lender on the day Periodic Payments are due under the Note, until the Note is paid in full, a sum (the "Funds") to provide for payment of amounts due for: (a) taxes and assessments and other items which can attain priority over this Security Instrument as a lien or encumbrance on the Property; (b) leasehold payments or ground rents on the Property, if any; (c) premiums for any and all insurance required by Lender under Section 5; and (d) Mortgage Insurance premiums, if any, or any sums payable by Borrower to Lender in lieu of the payment of Mortgage Insurance premiums in accordance with the provisions of Section 10. These items are called "Escrow Items." At origination or at any time during the term of the Loan, Lender may require that Community Association Dues, Fees, and Assessments, if any, be escrowed by Borrower, and such dues, fees and assessments shall be an Escrow Item. Borrower shall promptly furnish to Lender all notices of amounts to be paid under this Section. Borrower shall pay Lender the Funds for Escrow Items unless Lender waives Borrower's obligation to pay the Funds for any or all Escrow Items. Lender may waive Borrower's obligation to pay to Lender Funds for any or all Escrow Items at any time. Any such waiver may only be in writing. In the event of such waiver, Borrower shall pay directly, when and where payable, the amounts due for any Escrow Items for which payment of Funds has been waived by Lender and, if Lender requires, shall furnish to Lender receipts evidencing such payment within such time period as Lender may require. Borrower's obligation to make such payments and to provide receipts shall for all purposes be deemed to be a covenant and agreement contained in this Security Instrument, as the phrase "covenant and agreement" is used in Section 9. If Borrower is obligated to pay Escrow Items directly, pursuant to a waiver, and Borrower fails to pay the amount due for an Escrow Item, Lender may exercise its rights under Section 9 and pay such amount and Borrower shall then be obligated under Section 9 to repay to Lender any such amount. Lender may revoke the waiver as to any or all Escrow Items at any time by a notice given in accordance with Section 15 and, upon such revocation, Borrower shall pay to Lender all Funds, and in such amounts, that are then required under this Section 3.

Lender may, at any time, collect and hold Funds in an amount (a) sufficient to permit Lender to apply the Funds at the time specified under RESPA, and (b) not to exceed the maximum amount a lender can require under RESPA. Lender shall estimate the amount of Funds due on the basis of current data and reasonable estimates of expenditures of future Escrow Items or otherwise in accordance with Applicable Law.

SAMPLE

Mortgage

The Funds shall be held in an institution whose deposits are insured by a federal agency, instrumentality, or entity (including Lender, if Lender is an institution whose deposits are so insured) or in any Federal Home Loan Bank. Lender shall apply the Funds to pay the Escrow Items no later than the time specified under RESPA. Lender shall not charge Borrower for holding and applying the Funds, annually analyzing the escrow account, or verifying the Escrow Items, unless Lender pays Borrower interest on the Funds and Applicable Law permits Lender to make such a charge. Unless an agreement is made in writing or Applicable Law requires interest to be paid on the Funds, Lender shall not be required to pay Borrower any interest or earnings on the Funds. Borrower and Lender can agree in writing, however, that interest shall be paid on the Funds. Lender shall give to Borrower, without charge, an annual accounting of the Funds as required by RESPA.

If there is a surplus of Funds held in escrow, as defined under RESPA, Lender shall account to Borrower for the excess funds in accordance with RESPA. If there is a shortage of Funds held in escrow, as defined under RESPA, Lender shall notify Borrower as required by RESPA, and Borrower shall pay to Lender the amount necessary to make up the shortage in accordance with RESPA, but in no more than 12 monthly payments. If there is a deficiency of Funds held in escrow, as defined under RESPA, Lender shall notify Borrower as required by RESPA, and Borrower shall pay to Lender the amount necessary to make up the deficiency in accordance with RESPA, but in no more than 12 monthly payments.

Upon payment in full of all sums secured by this Security Instrument, Lender shall promptly refund to Borrower any Funds held by Lender.

4. Charges; Liens. Borrower shall pay all taxes, assessments, charges, fines, and impositions attributable to the Property which can attain priority over this Security Instrument, leasehold payments or ground rents on the Property, if any, and Community Association Dues, Fees, and Assessments, if any. To the extent that these items are Escrow Items, Borrower shall pay them in the manner provided in Section 3.

Borrower shall promptly discharge any lien which has priority over this Security Instrument unless Borrower: (a) agrees in writing to the payment of the obligation secured by the lien in a manner acceptable to Lender, but only so long as Borrower is performing such agreement; (b) contests the lien in good faith by, or defends against enforcement of the lien in, legal proceedings which in Lender's opinion operate to prevent the enforcement of the lien while those proceedings are pending, but only until such proceedings are concluded; or (c) secures from the holder of the lien an agreement satisfactory to Lender subordinating the lien to this Security Instrument. If Lender determines that any part of the Property is subject to a lien which can attain priority over this Security Instrument, Lender may give Borrower a notice identifying the lien. Within 10 days of the date on which that notice is given, Borrower shall satisfy the lien or take one or more of the actions set forth above in this Section 4.

Lender may require Borrower to pay a one-time charge for a real estate tax verification and/or reporting service used by Lender in connection with this Loan.

5. Property Insurance. Borrower shall keep the improvements now existing or hereafter erected on the Property insured against loss by fire, hazards included within the term "extended coverage," and any other hazards including, but not limited to, earthquakes and floods, for which Lender requires insurance. This insurance shall be maintained in the amounts (including deductible levels) and for the periods that Lender requires. What Lender requires pursuant to the preceding sentences can change during the term of the Loan. The insurance carrier providing the insurance shall be chosen by Borrower subject to Lender's right to disapprove Borrower's choice, which right

Mortgage

shall not be exercised unreasonably. Lender may require Borrower to pay, in connection with this Loan, either: (a) a one-time charge for flood zone determination, certification and tracking services; or (b) a one-time charge for flood zone determination and certification services and subsequent charges each time remappings or similar changes occur which reasonably might affect such determination or certification. Borrower shall also be responsible for the payment of any fees imposed by the Federal Emergency Management Agency in connection with the review of any flood zone determination resulting from an objection by Borrower.

If Borrower fails to maintain any of the coverages described above, Lender may obtain insurance coverage, at Lender's option and Borrower's expense. Lender is under no obligation to purchase any particular type or amount of coverage. Therefore, such coverage shall cover Lender, but might or might not protect Borrower, Borrower's equity in the Property, or the contents of the Property, against any risk, hazard or liability and might provide greater or lesser coverage than was previously in effect. Borrower acknowledges that the cost of the insurance coverage so obtained might significantly exceed the cost of insurance that Borrower could have obtained. Any amounts disbursed by Lender under this Section 5 shall become additional debt of Borrower secured by this Security Instrument. These amounts shall bear interest at the Note rate from the date of disbursement and shall be payable, with such interest, upon notice from Lender to Borrower requesting payment.

All insurance policies required by Lender and renewals of such policies shall be subject to Lender's right to disapprove such policies, shall include a standard mortgage clause, and shall name Lender as mortgagee and/or as an additional loss payee. Lender shall have the right to hold the policies and renewal certificates. If Lender requires, Borrower shall promptly give to Lender all receipts of paid premiums and renewal notices. If Borrower obtains any form of insurance coverage, not otherwise required by Lender, for damage to, or destruction of, the Property, such policy shall include a standard mortgage clause and shall name Lender as mortgagee and/or as an additional loss payee.

In the event of loss, Borrower shall give prompt notice to the insurance carrier and Lender. Lender may make proof of loss if not made promptly by Borrower. Unless Lender and Borrower otherwise agree in writing, any insurance proceeds, whether or not the underlying insurance was required by Lender, shall be applied to restoration or repair of the Property, if the restoration or repair is economically feasible and Lender's security is not lessened. During such repair and restoration period, Lender shall have the right to hold such insurance proceeds until Lender has had an opportunity to inspect such Property to ensure the work has been completed to Lender's satisfaction, provided that such inspection shall be undertaken promptly. Lender may disburse proceeds for the repairs and restoration in a single payment or in a series of progress payments as the work is completed. Unless an agreement is made in writing or Applicable Law requires interest to be paid on such insurance proceeds, Lender shall not be required to pay Borrower any interest or earnings on such proceeds. Fees for public adjusters, or other third parties, retained by Borrower shall not be paid out of the insurance proceeds and shall be the sole obligation of Borrower. If the restoration or repair is not economically feasible or Lender's security would be lessened, the insurance proceeds shall be applied to the sums secured by this Security Instrument, whether or not then due, with the excess, if any, paid to Borrower. Such insurance proceeds shall be applied in the order provided for in Section 2.

If Borrower abandons the Property, Lender may file, negotiate and settle any available insurance claim and related matters. If Borrower does not respond within 30 days to a notice from

Mortgage

Lender that the insurance carrier has offered to settle a claim, then Lender may negotiate and settle the claim. The 30-day period will begin when the notice is given. In either event, or if Lender acquires the Property under Section 22 or otherwise, Borrower hereby assigns to Lender (a) Borrower's rights to any insurance proceeds in an amount not to exceed the amounts unpaid under the Note or this Security Instrument, and (b) any other of Borrower's rights (other than the right to any refund of unearned premiums paid by Borrower) under all insurance policies covering the Property, insofar as such rights are applicable to the coverage of the Property. Lender may use the insurance proceeds either to repair or restore the Property or to pay amounts unpaid under the Note or this Security Instrument, whether or not then due.

6. Occupancy. Borrower shall occupy, establish, and use the Property as Borrower's principal residence within 60 days after the execution of this Security Instrument and shall continue to occupy the Property as Borrower's principal residence for at least one year after the date of occupancy, unless Lender otherwise agrees in writing, which consent shall not be unreasonably withheld, or unless extenuating circumstances exist which are beyond Borrower's control.

7. Preservation, Maintenance and Protection of the Property; Inspections. Borrower shall not destroy, damage or impair the Property, allow the Property to deteriorate or commit waste on the Property. Whether or not Borrower is residing in the Property, Borrower shall maintain the Property in order to prevent the Property from deteriorating or decreasing in value due to its condition. Unless it is determined pursuant to Section 5 that repair or restoration is not economically feasible, Borrower shall promptly repair the Property if damaged to avoid further deterioration or damage. If insurance or condemnation proceeds are paid in connection with damage to, or the taking of, the Property, Borrower shall be responsible for repairing or restoring the Property only if Lender has released proceeds for such purposes. Lender may disburse proceeds for the repairs and restoration in a single payment or in a series of progress payments as the work is completed. If the insurance or condemnation proceeds are not sufficient to repair or restore the Property, Borrower is not relieved of Borrower's obligation for the completion of such repair or restoration.

Lender or its agent may make reasonable entries upon and inspections of the Property. If it has reasonable cause, Lender may inspect the interior of the improvements on the Property. Lender shall give Borrower notice at the time of or prior to such an interior inspection specifying such reasonable cause.

8. Borrower's Loan Application. Borrower shall be in default if, during the Loan application process, Borrower or any persons or entities acting at the direction of Borrower or with Borrower's knowledge or consent gave materially false, misleading, or inaccurate information or statements to Lender (or failed to provide Lender with material information) in connection with the Loan. Material representations include, but are not limited to, representations concerning Borrower's occupancy of the Property as Borrower's principal residence.

9. Protection of Lender's Interest in the Property and Rights Under this Security Instrument. If (a) Borrower fails to perform the covenants and agreements contained in this Security Instrument, (b) there is a legal proceeding that might significantly affect Lender's interest in the Property and/or rights under this Security Instrument (such as a proceeding in bankruptcy, probate, for condemnation or forfeiture, for enforcement of a lien which may attain priority over this Security Instrument or to enforce laws or regulations), or (c) Borrower has abandoned the Property, then Lender may do and pay for whatever is reasonable or appropriate to protect Lender's interest in the Property and rights under this Security Instrument, including protecting and/or assessing the

Mortgage

value of the Property, and securing and/or repairing the Property. Lender's actions can include, but are not limited to: (a) paying any sums secured by a lien which has priority over this Security Instrument; (b) appearing in court; and (c) paying reasonable attorneys' fees to protect its interest in the Property and/or rights under this Security Instrument, including its secured position in a bankruptcy proceeding. Securing the Property includes, but is not limited to, entering the Property to make repairs, change locks, replace or board up doors and windows, drain water from pipes, eliminate building or other code violations or dangerous conditions, and have utilities turned on or off. Although Lender may take action under this Section 9, Lender does not have to do so and is not under any duty or obligation to do so. It is agreed that Lender incurs no liability for not taking any or all actions authorized under this Section 9.

Any amounts disbursed by Lender under this Section 9 shall become additional debt of Borrower secured by this Security Instrument. These amounts shall bear interest at the Note rate from the date of disbursement and shall be payable, with such interest, upon notice from Lender to Borrower requesting payment.

If this Security Instrument is on a leasehold, Borrower shall comply with all the provisions of the lease. If Borrower acquires fee title to the Property, the leasehold and the fee title shall not merge unless Lender agrees to the merger in writing.

10. Mortgage Insurance. If Lender required Mortgage Insurance as a condition of making the Loan, Borrower shall pay the premiums required to maintain the Mortgage Insurance in effect. If, for any reason, the Mortgage Insurance coverage required by Lender ceases to be available from the mortgage insurer that previously provided such insurance and Borrower was required to make separately designated payments toward the premiums for Mortgage Insurance, Borrower shall pay the premiums required to obtain coverage substantially equivalent to the Mortgage Insurance previously in effect, at a cost substantially equivalent to the cost to Borrower of the Mortgage Insurance previously in effect, from an alternate mortgage insurer selected by Lender. If substantially equivalent Mortgage Insurance coverage is not available, Borrower shall continue to pay to Lender the amount of the separately designated payments that were due when the insurance coverage ceased to be in effect. Lender will accept, use and retain these payments as a non-refundable loss reserve in lieu of Mortgage Insurance. Such loss reserve shall be non-refundable, notwithstanding the fact that the Loan is ultimately paid in full, and Lender shall not be required to pay Borrower any interest or earnings on such loss reserve. Lender can no longer require loss reserve payments if Mortgage Insurance coverage (in the amount and for the period that Lender requires) provided by an insurer selected by Lender again becomes available, is obtained, and Lender requires separately designated payments toward the premiums for Mortgage Insurance. If Lender required Mortgage Insurance as a condition of making the Loan and Borrower was required to make separately designated payments toward the premiums for Mortgage Insurance, Borrower shall pay the premiums required to maintain Mortgage Insurance in effect, or to provide a non-refundable loss reserve, until Lender's requirement for Mortgage Insurance ends in accordance with any written agreement between Borrower and Lender providing for such termination or until termination is required by Applicable Law. Nothing in this Section 10 affects Borrower's obligation to pay interest at the rate provided in the Note.

Mortgage Insurance reimburses Lender (or any entity that purchases the Note) for certain losses it may incur if Borrower does not repay the Loan as agreed. Borrower is not a party to the Mortgage Insurance.

Mortgage

Mortgage insurers evaluate their total risk on all such insurance in force from time to time, and may enter into agreements with other parties that share or modify their risk, or reduce losses. These agreements are on terms and conditions that are satisfactory to the mortgage insurer and the other party (or parties) to these agreements. These agreements may require the mortgage insurer to make payments using any source of funds that the mortgage insurer may have available (which may include funds obtained from Mortgage Insurance premiums).

As a result of these agreements, Lender, any purchaser of the Note, another insurer, any reinsurer, any other entity, or any affiliate of any of the foregoing, may receive (directly or indirectly) amounts that derive from (or might be characterized as) a portion of Borrower's payments for Mortgage Insurance, in exchange for sharing or modifying the mortgage insurer's risk, or reducing losses. If such agreement provides that an affiliate of Lender takes a share of the insurer's risk in exchange for a share of the premiums paid to the insurer, the arrangement is often termed "captive reinsurance." Further:

(a) Any such agreements will not affect the amounts that Borrower has agreed to pay for Mortgage Insurance, or any other terms of the Loan. Such agreements will not increase the amount Borrower will owe for Mortgage Insurance, and they will not entitle Borrower to any refund.

(b) Any such agreements will not affect the rights Borrower has – if any – with respect to the Mortgage Insurance under the Homeowners Protection Act of 1998 or any other law. These rights may include the right to receive certain disclosures, to request and obtain cancellation of the Mortgage Insurance, to have the Mortgage Insurance terminated automatically, and/or to receive a refund of any Mortgage Insurance premiums that were unearned at the time of such cancellation or termination.

11. Assignment of Miscellaneous Proceeds; Forfeiture. All Miscellaneous Proceeds are hereby assigned to and shall be paid to Lender.

If the Property is damaged, such Miscellaneous Proceeds shall be applied to restoration or repair of the Property, if the restoration or repair is economically feasible and Lender's security is not lessened. During such repair and restoration period, Lender shall have the right to hold such Miscellaneous Proceeds until Lender has had an opportunity to inspect such Property to ensure the work has been completed to Lender's satisfaction, provided that such inspection shall be undertaken promptly. Lender may pay for the repairs and restoration in a single disbursement or in a series of progress payments as the work is completed. Unless an agreement is made in writing or Applicable Law requires interest to be paid on such Miscellaneous Proceeds, Lender shall not be required to pay Borrower any interest or earnings on such Miscellaneous Proceeds. If the restoration or repair is not economically feasible or Lender's security would be lessened, the Miscellaneous Proceeds shall be applied to the sums secured by this Security Instrument, whether or not then due, with the excess, if any, paid to Borrower. Such Miscellaneous Proceeds shall be applied in the order provided for in Section 2.

In the event of a total taking, destruction, or loss in value of the Property, the Miscellaneous Proceeds shall be applied to the sums secured by this Security Instrument, whether or not then due, with the excess, if any, paid to Borrower.

In the event of a partial taking, destruction, or loss in value of the Property in which the fair market value of the Property immediately before the partial taking, destruction, or loss in value is equal to or greater than the amount of the sums secured by this Security Instrument immediately before the partial taking, destruction, or loss in value, unless Borrower and Lender otherwise agree

Mortgage

in writing, the sums secured by this Security Instrument shall be reduced by the amount of the Miscellaneous Proceeds multiplied by the following fraction: (a) the total amount of the sums secured immediately before the partial taking, destruction, or loss in value divided by (b) the fair market value of the Property immediately before the partial taking, destruction, or loss in value. Any balance shall be paid to Borrower.

In the event of a partial taking, destruction, or loss in value of the Property in which the fair market value of the Property immediately before the partial taking, destruction, or loss in value is less than the amount of the sums secured immediately before the partial taking, destruction, or loss in value, unless Borrower and Lender otherwise agree in writing, the Miscellaneous Proceeds shall be applied to the sums secured by this Security Instrument whether or not the sums are then due.

If the Property is abandoned by Borrower, or if, after notice by Lender to Borrower that the Opposing Party (as defined in the next sentence) offers to make an award to settle a claim for damages, Borrower fails to respond to Lender within 30 days after the date the notice is given, Lender is authorized to collect and apply the Miscellaneous Proceeds either to restoration or repair of the Property or to the sums secured by this Security Instrument, whether or not then due. "Opposing Party" means the third party that owes Borrower Miscellaneous Proceeds or the party against whom Borrower has a right of action in regard to Miscellaneous Proceeds.

Borrower shall be in default if any action or proceeding, whether civil or criminal, is begun that, in Lender's judgment, could result in forfeiture of the Property or other material impairment of Lender's interest in the Property or rights under this Security Instrument. Borrower can cure such a default and, if acceleration has occurred, reinstate as provided in Section 19, by causing the action or proceeding to be dismissed with a ruling that, in Lender's judgment, precludes forfeiture of the Property or other material impairment of Lender's interest in the Property or rights under this Security Instrument. The proceeds of any award or claim for damages that are attributable to the impairment of Lender's interest in the Property are hereby assigned and shall be paid to Lender.

All Miscellaneous Proceeds that are not applied to restoration or repair of the Property shall be applied in the order provided for in Section 2.

12. Borrower Not Released; Forbearance By Lender Not a Waiver. Extension of the time for payment or modification of amortization of the sums secured by this Security Instrument granted by Lender to Borrower or any Successor in Interest of Borrower shall not operate to release the liability of Borrower or any Successors in Interest of Borrower. Lender shall not be required to commence proceedings against any Successor in Interest of Borrower or to refuse to extend time for payment or otherwise modify amortization of the sums secured by this Security Instrument by reason of any demand made by the original Borrower or any Successors in Interest of Borrower. Any forbearance by Lender in exercising any right or remedy including, without limitation, Lender's acceptance of payments from third persons, entities or Successors in Interest of Borrower or in amounts less than the amount then due, shall not be a waiver of or preclude the exercise of any right or remedy.

13. Joint and Several Liability; Co-signers; Successors and Assigns Bound. Borrower covenants and agrees that Borrower's obligations and liability shall be joint and several. However, any Borrower who co-signs this Security Instrument but does not execute the Note (a "co-signer"): (a) is co-signing this Security Instrument only to mortgage, grant and convey the co-signer's interest in the Property under the terms of this Security Instrument; (b) is not personally obligated to pay the sums secured by this Security Instrument; and (c) agrees that Lender and any other Borrower can

Mortgage

agree to extend, modify, forbear or make any accommodations with regard to the terms of this Security Instrument or the Note without the co-signer's consent.

Subject to the provisions of Section 18, any Successor in Interest of Borrower who assumes Borrower's obligations under this Security Instrument in writing, and is approved by Lender, shall obtain all of Borrower's rights and benefits under this Security Instrument. Borrower shall not be released from Borrower's obligations and liability under this Security Instrument unless Lender agrees to such release in writing. The covenants and agreements of this Security Instrument shall bind (except as provided in Section 20) and benefit the successors and assigns of Lender.

14. Loan Charges. Lender may charge Borrower fees for services performed in connection with Borrower's default, for the purpose of protecting Lender's interest in the Property and rights under this Security Instrument, including, but not limited to, attorneys' fees, property inspection and valuation fees. In regard to any other fees, the absence of express authority in this Security Instrument to charge a specific fee to Borrower shall not be construed as a prohibition on the charging of such fee. Lender may not charge fees that are expressly prohibited by this Security Instrument or by Applicable Law.

If the Loan is subject to a law which sets maximum loan charges, and that law is finally interpreted so that the interest or other loan charges collected or to be collected in connection with the Loan exceed the permitted limits, then: (a) any such loan charge shall be reduced by the amount necessary to reduce the charge to the permitted limit; and (b) any sums already collected from Borrower which exceeded permitted limits will be refunded to Borrower. Lender may choose to make this refund by reducing the principal owed under the Note or by making a direct payment to Borrower. If a refund reduces principal, the reduction will be treated as a partial prepayment without any prepayment charge (whether or not a prepayment charge is provided for under the Note). Borrower's acceptance of any such refund made by direct payment to Borrower will constitute a waiver of any right of action Borrower might have arising out of such overcharge.

15. Notices. All notices given by Borrower or Lender in connection with this Security Instrument must be in writing. Any notice to Borrower in connection with this Security Instrument shall be deemed to have been given to Borrower when mailed by first class mail or when actually delivered to Borrower's notice address if sent by other means. Notice to any one Borrower shall constitute notice to all Borrowers unless Applicable Law expressly requires otherwise. The notice address shall be the Property Address unless Borrower has designated a substitute notice address by notice to Lender. Borrower shall promptly notify Lender of Borrower's change of address. If Lender specifies a procedure for reporting Borrower's change of address, then Borrower shall only report a change of address through that specified procedure. There may be only one designated notice address under this Security Instrument at any one time. Any notice to Lender shall be given by delivering it or by mailing it by first class mail to Lender's address stated herein unless Lender has designated another address by notice to Borrower. Any notice in connection with this Security Instrument shall not be deemed to have been given to Lender until actually received by Lender. If any notice required by this Security Instrument is also required under Applicable Law, the Applicable Law requirement will satisfy the corresponding requirement under this Security Instrument.

16. Governing Law; Severability; Rules of Construction. This Security Instrument shall be governed by federal law and the law of the jurisdiction in which the Property is located. All rights and obligations contained in this Security Instrument are subject to any requirements and limitations of Applicable Law. Applicable Law might explicitly or implicitly allow the parties to

Mortgage

agree by contract or it might be silent, but such silence shall not be construed as a prohibition against agreement by contract. In the event that any provision or clause of this Security Instrument or the Note conflicts with Applicable Law, such conflict shall not affect other provisions of this Security Instrument or the Note which can be given effect without the conflicting provision.

As used in this Security Instrument: (a) words of the masculine gender shall mean and include corresponding neuter words or words of the feminine gender; (b) words in the singular shall mean and include the plural and vice versa; and (c) the word "may" gives sole discretion without any obligation to take any action.

17. Borrower's Copy. Borrower shall be given one copy of the Note and of this Security Instrument.

18. Transfer of the Property or a Beneficial Interest in Borrower. As used in this Section 18, "Interest in the Property" means any legal or beneficial interest in the Property, including, but not limited to, those beneficial interests transferred in a bond for deed, contract for deed, installment sales contract or escrow agreement, the intent of which is the transfer of title by Borrower at a future date to a purchaser.

If all or any part of the Property or any Interest in the Property is sold or transferred (or if Borrower is not a natural person and a beneficial interest in Borrower is sold or transferred) without Lender's prior written consent, Lender may require immediate payment in full of all sums secured by this Security Instrument. However, this option shall not be exercised by Lender if such exercise is prohibited by Applicable Law.

If Lender exercises this option, Lender shall give Borrower notice of acceleration. The notice shall provide a period of not less than 30 days from the date the notice is given in accordance with Section 15 within which Borrower must pay all sums secured by this Security Instrument. If Borrower fails to pay these sums prior to the expiration of this period, Lender may invoke any remedies permitted by this Security Instrument without further notice or demand on Borrower.

19. Borrower's Right to Reinstate After Acceleration. If Borrower meets certain conditions, Borrower shall have the right to have enforcement of this Security Instrument discontinued at any time prior to the earliest of: (a) five days before sale of the Property pursuant to any power of sale contained in this Security Instrument; (b) such other period as Applicable Law might specify for the termination of Borrower's right to reinstate; or (c) entry of a judgment enforcing this Security Instrument. Those conditions are that Borrower: (a) pays Lender all sums which then would be due under this Security Instrument and the Note as if no acceleration had occurred; (b) cures any default of any other covenants or agreements; (c) pays all expenses incurred in enforcing this Security Instrument, including, but not limited to, reasonable attorneys' fees, property inspection and valuation fees, and other fees incurred for the purpose of protecting Lender's interest in the Property and rights under this Security Instrument; and (d) takes such action as Lender may reasonably require to assure that Lender's interest in the Property and rights under this Security Instrument, and Borrower's obligation to pay the sums secured by this Security Instrument, shall continue unchanged. Lender may require that Borrower pay such reinstatement sums and expenses in one or more of the following forms, as selected by Lender: (a) cash; (b) money order; (c) certified check, bank check, treasurer's check or cashier's check, provided any such check is drawn upon an institution whose deposits are insured by a federal agency, instrumentality or entity; or (d) Electronic Funds Transfer. Upon reinstatement by Borrower, this Security Instrument and obligations secured hereby shall remain fully effective as if no acceleration had occurred. However, this right to reinstate shall not apply in the case of acceleration under Section 18.

Mortgage

SAMPLE

20. Sale of Note; Change of Loan Servicer; Notice of Grievance. The Note or a partial interest in the Note (together with this Security Instrument) can be sold one or more times without prior notice to Borrower. A sale might result in a change in the entity (known as the "Loan Servicer") that collects Periodic Payments due under the Note and this Security Instrument and performs other mortgage loan servicing obligations under the Note, this Security Instrument, and Applicable Law. There also might be one or more changes of the Loan Servicer unrelated to a sale of the Note. If there is a change of the Loan Servicer, Borrower will be given written notice of the change which will state the name and address of the new Loan Servicer, the address to which payments should be made and any other information RESPA requires in connection with a notice of transfer of servicing. If the Note is sold and thereafter the Loan is serviced by a Loan Servicer other than the purchaser of the Note, the mortgage loan servicing obligations to Borrower will remain with the Loan Servicer or be transferred to a successor Loan Servicer and are not assumed by the Note purchaser unless otherwise provided by the Note purchaser.

Neither Borrower nor Lender may commence, join, or be joined to any judicial action (as either an individual litigant or the member of a class) that arises from the other party's actions pursuant to this Security Instrument or that alleges that the other party has breached any provision of, or any duty owed by reason of, this Security Instrument, until such Borrower or Lender has notified the other party (with such notice given in compliance with the requirements of Section 15) of such alleged breach and afforded the other party hereto a reasonable period after the giving of such notice to take corrective action. If Applicable Law provides a time period which must elapse before certain action can be taken, that time period will be deemed to be reasonable for purposes of this paragraph. The notice of acceleration and opportunity to cure given to Borrower pursuant to Section 22 and the notice of acceleration given to Borrower pursuant to Section 18 shall be deemed to satisfy the notice and opportunity to take corrective action provisions of this Section 20.

21. Hazardous Substances. As used in this Section 21: (a) "Hazardous Substances" are those substances defined as toxic or hazardous substances, pollutants, or wastes by Environmental Law and the following substances: gasoline, kerosene, other flammable or toxic petroleum products, toxic pesticides and herbicides, volatile solvents, materials containing asbestos or formaldehyde, and radioactive materials; (b) "Environmental Law" means federal laws and laws of the jurisdiction where the Property is located that relate to health, safety or environmental protection; (c) "Environmental Cleanup" includes any response action, remedial action, or removal action, as defined in Environmental Law; and (d) an "Environmental Condition" means a condition that can cause, contribute to, or otherwise trigger an Environmental Cleanup.

Borrower shall not cause or permit the presence, use, disposal, storage, or release of any Hazardous Substances, or threaten to release any Hazardous Substances, on or in the Property. Borrower shall not do, nor allow anyone else to do, anything affecting the Property (a) that is in violation of any Environmental Law, (b) which creates an Environmental Condition, or (c) which, due to the presence, use, or release of a Hazardous Substance, creates a condition that adversely affects the value of the Property. The preceding two sentences shall not apply to the presence, use, or storage on the Property of small quantities of Hazardous Substances that are generally recognized to be appropriate to normal residential uses and to maintenance of the Property (including, but not limited to, hazardous substances in consumer products).

Borrower shall promptly give Lender written notice of (a) any investigation, claim, demand, lawsuit or other action by any governmental or regulatory agency or private party involving the Property and any Hazardous Substance or Environmental Law of which Borrower has actual

Mortgage

knowledge, (b) any Environmental Condition, including but not limited to, any spilling, leaking, discharge, release or threat of release of any Hazardous Substance, and (c) any condition caused by the presence, use or release of a Hazardous Substance which adversely affects the value of the Property. If Borrower learns, or is notified by any governmental or regulatory authority, or any private party, that any removal or other remediation of any Hazardous Substance affecting the Property is necessary, Borrower shall promptly take all necessary remedial actions in accordance with Environmental Law. Nothing herein shall create any obligation on Lender for an Environmental Cleanup.

NON-UNIFORM COVENANTS. Borrower and Lender further covenant and agree as follows:

22. Acceleration; Remedies. Lender shall give notice to Borrower prior to acceleration following Borrower's breach of any covenant or agreement in this Security Instrument (but not prior to acceleration under Section 18 unless Applicable Law provides otherwise). The notice shall specify: (a) the default; (b) the action required to cure the default; (c) a date, not less than 30 days from the date the notice is given to Borrower, by which the default must be cured; and (d) that failure to cure the default on or before the date specified in the notice may result in acceleration of the sums secured by this Security Instrument, foreclosure by judicial proceeding and sale of the Property. The notice shall further inform Borrower of the right to reinstate after acceleration and the right to assert in the foreclosure proceeding the non-existence of a default or any other defense of Borrower to acceleration and foreclosure. If the default is not cured on or before the date specified in the notice, Lender at its option may require immediate payment in full of all sums secured by this Security Instrument without further demand and may foreclose this Security Instrument by judicial proceeding. Lender shall be entitled to collect all expenses incurred in pursuing the remedies provided in this Section 22, including, but not limited to, reasonable attorneys' fees and costs of title evidence.

23. Release. Upon payment of all sums secured by this Security Instrument, Lender shall release this Security Instrument. Borrower shall pay any recordation costs. Lender may charge Borrower a fee for releasing this Security Instrument, but only if the fee is paid to a third party for services rendered and the charging of the fee is permitted under Applicable Law.

24. Attorneys' Fees. As used in this Security Instrument and the Note, attorneys' fees shall include those awarded by an appellate court and any attorneys' fees incurred in a bankruptcy proceeding.

25. Jury Trial Waiver. The Borrower hereby waives any right to a trial by jury in any action, proceeding, claim, or counterclaim, whether in contract or tort, at law or in equity, arising out of or in any way related to this Security Instrument or the Note.

Everything U Need to Know...

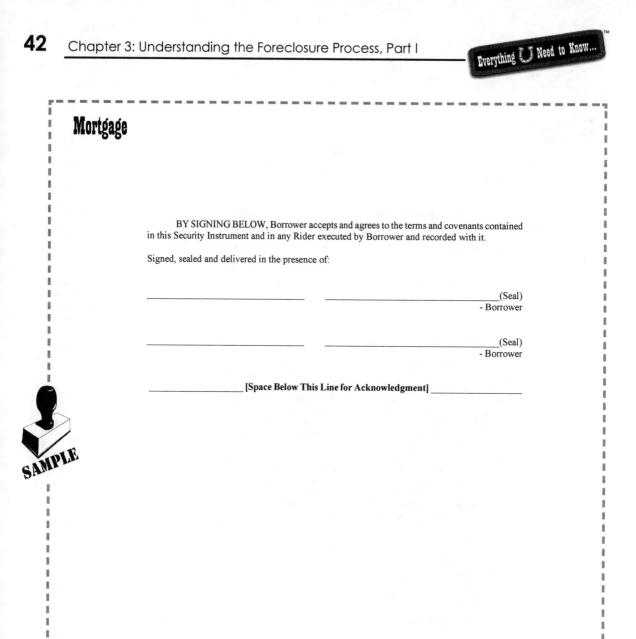

Mortgage

BY SIGNING BELOW, Borrower accepts and agrees to the terms and covenants contained in this Security Instrument and in any Rider executed by Borrower and recorded with it.

Signed, sealed and delivered in the presence of:

_____   _____(Seal)
                                                                                - Borrower

_____   _____(Seal)
                                                                                - Borrower

_____ **[Space Below This Line for Acknowledgment]** _____

SAMPLE

Deed of Trust

If you are in a state that *uses a deed of trust in lieu of a mortgage* to secure a lender's interest in your property in case of default, then you need to be aware that **this lengthy security instrument actually involves** *three separate parties*. "Huh," did you say? **Yes** – and these three are defined as follows:

The Three Parties to a Deed of Trust:

★ Trustor

The *borrower who signed the promissory note and owns the home.* (The **rare exception to this** would be **someone else acting as the trustor**, because he or she offered his or her property as collateral for your loan.)

★ Beneficiary

This is just a *different word for lender*. The investor or entity lending the money would be the one to benefit.

★ Trustee

This is an independent party *who officially retains title to the property until you either finish making all of your payments, sell the property or stop making your payments.* **When you default on a loan secured by a deed of trust, the beneficiary (lender) has the right to request the trustee to foreclose on the property and sell it by conducting a public auction. The proceeds of the sale will then benefit the lender** – hence the term *beneficiary*.

Following are the *relevant terms and conditions* worth noting about a *deed of trust*… (If you compare these against the mortgage section, you'll notice that they are very similar):

The Relevant Terms and Conditions of a Deed of Trust:

☆ Lender's Name and Address

The *investor or company who lends the money* that is secured by your home.

☆ County Recorder Information

Including *date, time and fee paid to record the deed of trust into the public record.*

This is **usually stamped on the top right of the document**, unless your copy was given to you at the closing table or anytime before the filing of the deed of trust.

☆ Date of Execution

The *date that the document was signed by the trustor* (borrower).

☆ Trustor(s) Name and Address

The *individual(s) or entity borrowing the money.*

☆ Beneficiary

The *name of the lender.*

☆ Trustee

The *name of the individual or entity holding the title to the property being pledged as collateral* for repayment of the loan.

★ Legal Description of Property

This includes *what the county deems to be the official description of your property's location,* such as the lot, tract number and block.

★ Principal Amount of the Loan

The *total amount of money being borrowed* from the lender.

★ Power of Sale Clause

This is *the most powerful component of a deed of trust,* because **it legally allows a lender the means to take control of the property and sell it without having to go to court.**

★ Acknowledgment

Simple *language stating that the borrower* (the trustor) *was in no way coerced and willingly signed the deed of trust.*

A **sample deed of trust for a traditional loan has been provided on the next sixteen pages**. As stated earlier in the mortgage section, *if you have the ability to retrieve a copy of your own deed of trust, your time would be better spent reviewing yours* – unless your curiosity compels you to compare it against the one provided here. Keep in Mind: **Not every deed of trust will be the same,** *especially when comparing different lenders.*

Everything U Need to Know...™

Deed of Trust

After Recording Return To:

_____

_____

_____

_____

SAMPLE

_____[Space Above This Line For Recording Data]_____

DEED OF TRUST

DEFINITIONS

Words used in multiple sections of this document are defined below and other words are defined in Sections 3, 11, 13, 18, 20 and 21. Certain rules regarding the usage of words used in this document are also provided in Section 16.

(A) **"Security Instrument"** means this document, which is dated _____, _____, together with all Riders to this document.

(B) **"Borrower"** is _____.
Borrower is the trustor under this Security Instrument.

(C) **"Lender"** is _____.
Lender is a _____ organized and existing under the laws of_____. Lender's address is _____
_____. Lender is the beneficiary under this Security Instrument.

(D) **"Trustee"** is _____.

(E) **"Note"** means the promissory note signed by Borrower and dated _____, _____. The Note states that Borrower owes Lender _____
Dollars (U.S. $_____) plus interest. Borrower has promised to pay this debt in regular Periodic Payments and to pay the debt in full not later than
_____.

(F) **"Property"** means the property that is described below under the heading "Transfer of Rights in the Property."

(G) **"Loan"** means the debt evidenced by the Note, plus interest, any prepayment charges and late charges due under the Note, and all sums due under this Security Instrument, plus interest.

Deed of Trust

(H) **"Riders"** means all Riders to this Security Instrument that are executed by Borrower. The following Riders are to be executed by Borrower [check box as applicable]:

☐ Adjustable Rate Rider   ☐ Condominium Rider   ☐ Second Home Rider
☐ Balloon Rider   ☐ Planned Unit Development Rider   ☐ Other(s) [specify]

☐ 1-4 Family Rider   ☐ Biweekly Payment Rider

(I) **"Applicable Law"** means all controlling applicable federal, state and local statutes, regulations, ordinances and administrative rules and orders (that have the effect of law) as well as all applicable final, non-appealable judicial opinions.

(J) **"Community Association Dues, Fees, and Assessments"** means all dues, fees, assessments and other charges that are imposed on Borrower or the Property by a condominium association, homeowners association or similar organization.

(K) **"Electronic Funds Transfer"** means any transfer of funds, other than a transaction originated by check, draft, or similar paper instrument, which is initiated through an electronic terminal, telephonic instrument, computer, or magnetic tape so as to order, instruct, or authorize a financial institution to debit or credit an account. Such term includes, but is not limited to, point-of-sale transfers, automated teller machine transactions, transfers initiated by telephone, wire transfers, and automated clearinghouse transfers.

(L) **"Escrow Items"** means those items that are described in Section 3.

(M) **"Miscellaneous Proceeds"** means any compensation, settlement, award of damages, or proceeds paid by any third party (other than insurance proceeds paid under the coverages described in Section 5) for: (i) damage to, or destruction of, the Property; (ii) condemnation or other taking of all or any part of the Property; (iii) conveyance in lieu of condemnation; or (iv) misrepresentations of, or omissions as to, the value and/or condition of the Property.

(N) **"Mortgage Insurance"** means insurance protecting Lender against the nonpayment of, or default on, the Loan.

(O) **"Periodic Payment"** means the regularly scheduled amount due for (i) principal and interest under the Note, plus (ii) any amounts under Section 3 of this Security Instrument.

(P) **"RESPA"** means the Real Estate Settlement Procedures Act (12 U.S.C. §2601 et seq.) and its implementing regulation, Regulation X (24 C.F.R. Part 3500), as they might be amended from time to time, or any additional or successor legislation or regulation that governs the same subject matter. As used in this Security Instrument, "RESPA" refers to all requirements and restrictions that are imposed in regard to a "federally related mortgage loan" even if the Loan does not qualify as a "federally related mortgage loan" under RESPA.

(Q) **"Successor in Interest of Borrower"** means any party that has taken title to the Property, whether or not that party has assumed Borrower's obligations under the Note and/or this Security Instrument.

Deed of Trust

TRANSFER OF RIGHTS IN THE PROPERTY

This Security Instrument secures to Lender: (i) the repayment of the Loan, and all renewals, extensions and modifications of the Note; and (ii) the performance of Borrower's covenants and agreements under this Security Instrument and the Note. For this purpose, Borrower irrevocably grants and conveys to Trustee, in trust, with power of sale, the following described property located in the _____ of _____:

[Type of Recording Jurisdiction]   [Name of Recording Jurisdiction]

which currently has the address of _____

[Street]

_____, California _____ ("Property Address"):

[City]   [Zip Code]

TOGETHER WITH all the improvements now or hereafter erected on the property, and all easements, appurtenances, and fixtures now or hereafter a part of the property. All replacements and additions shall also be covered by this Security Instrument. All of the foregoing is referred to in this Security Instrument as the "Property."

BORROWER COVENANTS that Borrower is lawfully seised of the estate hereby conveyed and has the right to grant and convey the Property and that the Property is unencumbered, except for encumbrances of record. Borrower warrants and will defend generally the title to the Property against all claims and demands, subject to any encumbrances of record.

THIS SECURITY INSTRUMENT combines uniform covenants for national use and non-uniform covenants with limited variations by jurisdiction to constitute a uniform security instrument covering real property.

UNIFORM COVENANTS. Borrower and Lender covenant and agree as follows:
1. **Payment of Principal, Interest, Escrow Items, Prepayment Charges, and Late Charges.** Borrower shall pay when due the principal of, and interest on, the debt evidenced by the Note and any prepayment charges and late charges due under the Note. Borrower shall also pay funds for Escrow Items pursuant to Section 3. Payments due under the Note and this Security Instrument shall be made in U.S. currency. However, if any check or other instrument received by Lender as payment under the Note or this Security Instrument is returned to Lender unpaid, Lender may require that any or all subsequent payments due under the Note and this Security Instrument be made in one or more of the following forms, as selected by Lender: (a) cash; (b) money order; (c) certified check, bank check, treasurer's check or cashier's check, provided any such check is drawn upon an institution whose deposits are insured by a federal agency, instrumentality, or entity; or (d) Electronic Funds Transfer.

Payments are deemed received by Lender when received at the location designated in the Note or at such other location as may be designated by Lender in accordance with the notice provisions in Section 15. Lender may return any payment or partial payment if the payment or partial payments are insufficient to bring the Loan current. Lender may accept any payment or partial payment insufficient to bring the Loan current, without waiver of any rights hereunder or

Deed of Trust

prejudice to its rights to refuse such payment or partial payments in the future, but Lender is not obligated to apply such payments at the time such payments are accepted. If each Periodic Payment is applied as of its scheduled due date, then Lender need not pay interest on unapplied funds. Lender may hold such unapplied funds until Borrower makes payment to bring the Loan current. If Borrower does not do so within a reasonable period of time, Lender shall either apply such funds or return them to Borrower. If not applied earlier, such funds will be applied to the outstanding principal balance under the Note immediately prior to foreclosure. No offset or claim which Borrower might have now or in the future against Lender shall relieve Borrower from making payments due under the Note and this Security Instrument or performing the covenants and agreements secured by this Security Instrument.

    2.   Application of Payments or Proceeds. Except as otherwise described in this Section 2, all payments accepted and applied by Lender shall be applied in the following order of priority: (a) interest due under the Note; (b) principal due under the Note; (c) amounts due under Section 3. Such payments shall be applied to each Periodic Payment in the order in which it became due. Any remaining amounts shall be applied first to late charges, second to any other amounts due under this Security Instrument, and then to reduce the principal balance of the Note.

    If Lender receives a payment from Borrower for a delinquent Periodic Payment which includes a sufficient amount to pay any late charge due, the payment may be applied to the delinquent payment and the late charge. If more than one Periodic Payment is outstanding, Lender may apply any payment received from Borrower to the repayment of the Periodic Payments if, and to the extent that, each payment can be paid in full. To the extent that any excess exists after the payment is applied to the full payment of one or more Periodic Payments, such excess may be applied to any late charges due. Voluntary prepayments shall be applied first to any prepayment charges and then as described in the Note.

    Any application of payments, insurance proceeds, or Miscellaneous Proceeds to principal due under the Note shall not extend or postpone the due date, or change the amount, of the Periodic Payments.

    3.   Funds for Escrow Items. Borrower shall pay to Lender on the day Periodic Payments are due under the Note, until the Note is paid in full, a sum (the "Funds") to provide for payment of amounts due for: (a) taxes and assessments and other items which can attain priority over this Security Instrument as a lien or encumbrance on the Property; (b) leasehold payments or ground rents on the Property, if any; (c) premiums for any and all insurance required by Lender under Section 5; and (d) Mortgage Insurance premiums, if any, or any sums payable by Borrower to Lender in lieu of the payment of Mortgage Insurance premiums in accordance with the provisions of Section 10. These items are called "Escrow Items." At origination or at any time during the term of the Loan, Lender may require that Community Association Dues, Fees, and Assessments, if any, be escrowed by Borrower, and such dues, fees and assessments shall be an Escrow Item. Borrower shall promptly furnish to Lender all notices of amounts to be paid under this Section. Borrower shall pay Lender the Funds for Escrow Items unless Lender waives Borrower's obligation to pay the Funds for any or all Escrow Items. Lender may waive Borrower's obligation to pay to Lender Funds for any or all Escrow Items at any time. Any such waiver may only be in writing. In the event of such waiver, Borrower shall pay directly, when and where payable, the amounts due for any Escrow Items for which payment of Funds has been waived by Lender and, if Lender requires, shall furnish to Lender receipts evidencing such payment within such time period as Lender may require. Borrower's obligation to make such payments and to provide receipts shall for all purposes be deemed to be a covenant

Deed of Trust

and agreement contained in this Security Instrument, as the phrase "covenant and agreement" is used in Section 9. If Borrower is obligated to pay Escrow Items directly, pursuant to a waiver, and Borrower fails to pay the amount due for an Escrow Item, Lender may exercise its rights under Section 9 and pay such amount and Borrower shall then be obligated under Section 9 to repay to Lender any such amount. Lender may revoke the waiver as to any or all Escrow Items at any time by a notice given in accordance with Section 15 and, upon such revocation, Borrower shall pay to Lender all Funds, and in such amounts, that are then required under this Section 3.

Lender may, at any time, collect and hold Funds in an amount (a) sufficient to permit Lender to apply the Funds at the time specified under RESPA, and (b) not to exceed the maximum amount a lender can require under RESPA. Lender shall estimate the amount of Funds due on the basis of current data and reasonable estimates of expenditures of future Escrow Items or otherwise in accordance with Applicable Law.

The Funds shall be held in an institution whose deposits are insured by a federal agency, instrumentality, or entity (including Lender, if Lender is an institution whose deposits are so insured) or in any Federal Home Loan Bank. Lender shall apply the Funds to pay the Escrow Items no later than the time specified under RESPA. Lender shall not charge Borrower for holding and applying the Funds, annually analyzing the escrow account, or verifying the Escrow Items, unless Lender pays Borrower interest on the Funds and Applicable Law permits Lender to make such a charge. Unless an agreement is made in writing or Applicable Law requires interest to be paid on the Funds, Lender shall not be required to pay Borrower any interest or earnings on the Funds. Borrower and Lender can agree in writing, however, that interest shall be paid on the Funds. Lender shall give to Borrower, without charge, an annual accounting of the Funds as required by RESPA.

If there is a surplus of Funds held in escrow, as defined under RESPA, Lender shall account to Borrower for the excess funds in accordance with RESPA. If there is a shortage of Funds held in escrow, as defined under RESPA, Lender shall notify Borrower as required by RESPA, and Borrower shall pay to Lender the amount necessary to make up the shortage in accordance with RESPA, but in no more than 12 monthly payments. If there is a deficiency of Funds held in escrow, as defined under RESPA, Lender shall notify Borrower as required by RESPA, and Borrower shall pay to Lender the amount necessary to make up the deficiency in accordance with RESPA, but in no more than 12 monthly payments.

Upon payment in full of all sums secured by this Security Instrument, Lender shall promptly refund to Borrower any Funds held by Lender.

4.   Charges; Liens. Borrower shall pay all taxes, assessments, charges, fines, and impositions attributable to the Property which can attain priority over this Security Instrument, leasehold payments or ground rents on the Property, if any, and Community Association Dues, Fees, and Assessments, if any. To the extent that these items are Escrow Items, Borrower shall pay them in the manner provided in Section 3.

Borrower shall promptly discharge any lien which has priority over this Security Instrument unless Borrower: (a) agrees in writing to the payment of the obligation secured by the lien in a manner acceptable to Lender, but only so long as Borrower is performing such agreement; (b) contests the lien in good faith by, or defends against enforcement of the lien in, legal proceedings which in Lender's opinion operate to prevent the enforcement of the lien while those proceedings are pending, but only until such proceedings are concluded; or (c) secures from the holder of the lien an agreement satisfactory to Lender subordinating the lien to this Security Instrument. If Lender determines that any part of the Property is subject to a lien which

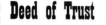
Deed of Trust

can attain priority over this Security Instrument, Lender may give Borrower a notice identifying the lien. Within 10 days of the date on which that notice is given, Borrower shall satisfy the lien or take one or more of the actions set forth above in this Section 4.

Lender may require Borrower to pay a one-time charge for a real estate tax verification and/or reporting service used by Lender in connection with this Loan.

5.   Property Insurance. Borrower shall keep the improvements now existing or hereafter erected on the Property insured against loss by fire, hazards included within the term "extended coverage," and any other hazards including, but not limited to, earthquakes and floods, for which Lender requires insurance. This insurance shall be maintained in the amounts (including deductible levels) and for the periods that Lender requires. What Lender requires pursuant to the preceding sentences can change during the term of the Loan. The insurance carrier providing the insurance shall be chosen by Borrower subject to Lender's right to disapprove Borrower's choice, which right shall not be exercised unreasonably. Lender may require Borrower to pay, in connection with this Loan, either: (a) a one-time charge for flood zone determination, certification and tracking services; or (b) a one-time charge for flood zone determination and certification services and subsequent charges each time remappings or similar changes occur which reasonably might affect such determination or certification. Borrower shall also be responsible for the payment of any fees imposed by the Federal Emergency Management Agency in connection with the review of any flood zone determination resulting from an objection by Borrower.

If Borrower fails to maintain any of the coverages described above, Lender may obtain insurance coverage, at Lender's option and Borrower's expense. Lender is under no obligation to purchase any particular type or amount of coverage. Therefore, such coverage shall cover Lender, but might or might not protect Borrower, Borrower's equity in the Property, or the contents of the Property, against any risk, hazard or liability and might provide greater or lesser coverage than was previously in effect. Borrower acknowledges that the cost of the insurance coverage so obtained might significantly exceed the cost of insurance that Borrower could have obtained. Any amounts disbursed by Lender under this Section 5 shall become additional debt of Borrower secured by this Security Instrument. These amounts shall bear interest at the Note rate from the date of disbursement and shall be payable, with such interest, upon notice from Lender to Borrower requesting payment.

All insurance policies required by Lender and renewals of such policies shall be subject to Lender's right to disapprove such policies, shall include a standard mortgage clause, and shall name Lender as mortgagee and/or as an additional loss payee and Borrower further agrees to generally assign rights to insurance proceeds to the holder of the Note up to the amount of the outstanding loan balance. Lender shall have the right to hold the policies and renewal certificates. If Lender requires, Borrower shall promptly give to Lender all receipts of paid premiums and renewal notices. If Borrower obtains any form of insurance coverage, not otherwise required by Lender, for damage to, or destruction of, the Property, such policy shall include a standard mortgage clause and shall name Lender as mortgagee and/or as an additional loss payee and Borrower further agrees to generally assign rights to insurance proceeds to the holder of the Note up to the amount of the outstanding loan balance.

In the event of loss, Borrower shall give prompt notice to the insurance carrier and Lender. Lender may make proof of loss if not made promptly by Borrower. Unless Lender and Borrower otherwise agree in writing, any insurance proceeds, whether or not the underlying insurance was required by Lender, shall be applied to restoration or repair of the Property, if the

Deed of Trust

restoration or repair is economically feasible and Lender's security is not lessened. During such repair and restoration period, Lender shall have the right to hold such insurance proceeds until Lender has had an opportunity to inspect such Property to ensure the work has been completed to Lender's satisfaction, provided that such inspection shall be undertaken promptly. Lender may disburse proceeds for the repairs and restoration in a single payment or in a series of progress payments as the work is completed. Unless an agreement is made in writing or Applicable Law requires interest to be paid on such insurance proceeds, Lender shall not be required to pay Borrower any interest or earnings on such proceeds. Fees for public adjusters, or other third parties, retained by Borrower shall not be paid out of the insurance proceeds and shall be the sole obligation of Borrower. If the restoration or repair is not economically feasible or Lender's security would be lessened, the insurance proceeds shall be applied to the sums secured by this Security Instrument, whether or not then due, with the excess, if any, paid to Borrower. Such insurance proceeds shall be applied in the order provided for in Section 2.

If Borrower abandons the Property, Lender may file, negotiate and settle any available insurance claim and related matters. If Borrower does not respond within 30 days to a notice from Lender that the insurance carrier has offered to settle a claim, then Lender may negotiate and settle the claim. The 30-day period will begin when the notice is given. In either event, or if Lender acquires the Property under Section 22 or otherwise, Borrower hereby assigns to Lender (a) Borrower's rights to any insurance proceeds in an amount not to exceed the amounts unpaid under the Note or this Security Instrument, and (b) any other of Borrower's rights (other than the right to any refund of unearned premiums paid by Borrower) under all insurance policies covering the Property, insofar as such rights are applicable to the coverage of the Property. Lender may use the insurance proceeds either to repair or restore the Property or to pay amounts unpaid under the Note or this Security Instrument, whether or not then due.

6. Occupancy. Borrower shall occupy, establish, and use the Property as Borrower's principal residence within 60 days after the execution of this Security Instrument and shall continue to occupy the Property as Borrower's principal residence for at least one year after the date of occupancy, unless Lender otherwise agrees in writing, which consent shall not be unreasonably withheld, or unless extenuating circumstances exist which are beyond Borrower's control.

7. Preservation, Maintenance and Protection of the Property; Inspections. Borrower shall not destroy, damage or impair the Property, allow the Property to deteriorate or commit waste on the Property. Whether or not Borrower is residing in the Property, Borrower shall maintain the Property in order to prevent the Property from deteriorating or decreasing in value due to its condition. Unless it is determined pursuant to Section 5 that repair or restoration is not economically feasible, Borrower shall promptly repair the Property if damaged to avoid further deterioration or damage. If insurance or condemnation proceeds are paid in connection with damage to, or the taking of, the Property, Borrower shall be responsible for repairing or restoring the Property only if Lender has released proceeds for such purposes. Lender may disburse proceeds for the repairs and restoration in a single payment or in a series of progress payments as the work is completed. If the insurance or condemnation proceeds are not sufficient to repair or restore the Property, Borrower is not relieved of Borrower's obligation for the completion of such repair or restoration.

Lender or its agent may make reasonable entries upon and inspections of the Property. If it has reasonable cause, Lender may inspect the interior of the improvements on the Property.

Deed of Trust

Lender shall give Borrower notice at the time of or prior to such an interior inspection specifying such reasonable cause.

8. Borrower's Loan Application. Borrower shall be in default if, during the Loan application process, Borrower or any persons or entities acting at the direction of Borrower or with Borrower's knowledge or consent gave materially false, misleading, or inaccurate information or statements to Lender (or failed to provide Lender with material information) in connection with the Loan. Material representations include, but are not limited to, representations concerning Borrower's occupancy of the Property as Borrower's principal residence.

9. Protection of Lender's Interest in the Property and Rights Under this Security Instrument. If (a) Borrower fails to perform the covenants and agreements contained in this Security Instrument, (b) there is a legal proceeding that might significantly affect Lender's interest in the Property and/or rights under this Security Instrument (such as a proceeding in bankruptcy, probate, for condemnation or forfeiture, for enforcement of a lien which may attain priority over this Security Instrument or to enforce laws or regulations), or (c) Borrower has abandoned the Property, then Lender may do and pay for whatever is reasonable or appropriate to protect Lender's interest in the Property and rights under this Security Instrument, including protecting and/or assessing the value of the Property, and securing and/or repairing the Property. Lender's actions can include, but are not limited to: (a) paying any sums secured by a lien which has priority over this Security Instrument; (b) appearing in court; and (c) paying reasonable attorneys' fees to protect its interest in the Property and/or rights under this Security Instrument, including its secured position in a bankruptcy proceeding. Securing the Property includes, but is not limited to, entering the Property to make repairs, change locks, replace or board up doors and windows, drain water from pipes, eliminate building or other code violations or dangerous conditions, and have utilities turned on or off. Although Lender may take action under this Section 9, Lender does not have to do so and is not under any duty or obligation to do so. It is agreed that Lender incurs no liability for not taking any or all actions authorized under this Section 9.

Any amounts disbursed by Lender under this Section 9 shall become additional debt of Borrower secured by this Security Instrument. These amounts shall bear interest at the Note rate from the date of disbursement and shall be payable, with such interest, upon notice from Lender to Borrower requesting payment.

If this Security Instrument is on a leasehold, Borrower shall comply with all the provisions of the lease. If Borrower acquires fee title to the Property, the leasehold and the fee title shall not merge unless Lender agrees to the merger in writing.

10. Mortgage Insurance. If Lender required Mortgage Insurance as a condition of making the Loan, Borrower shall pay the premiums required to maintain the Mortgage Insurance in effect. If, for any reason, the Mortgage Insurance coverage required by Lender ceases to be available from the mortgage insurer that previously provided such insurance and Borrower was required to make separately designated payments toward the premiums for Mortgage Insurance, Borrower shall pay the premiums required to obtain coverage substantially equivalent to the Mortgage Insurance previously in effect, at a cost substantially equivalent to the cost to Borrower of the Mortgage Insurance previously in effect, from an alternate mortgage insurer selected by Lender. If substantially equivalent Mortgage Insurance coverage is not available, Borrower shall continue to pay to Lender the amount of the separately designated payments that were due when the insurance coverage ceased to be in effect. Lender will accept, use and retain

Deed of Trust

these payments as a non-refundable loss reserve in lieu of Mortgage Insurance. Such loss reserve shall be non-refundable, notwithstanding the fact that the Loan is ultimately paid in full, and Lender shall not be required to pay Borrower any interest or earnings on such loss reserve. Lender can no longer require loss reserve payments if Mortgage Insurance coverage (in the amount and for the period that Lender requires) provided by an insurer selected by Lender again becomes available, is obtained, and Lender requires separately designated payments toward the premiums for Mortgage Insurance. If Lender required Mortgage Insurance as a condition of making the Loan and Borrower was required to make separately designated payments toward the premiums for Mortgage Insurance, Borrower shall pay the premiums required to maintain Mortgage Insurance in effect, or to provide a non-refundable loss reserve, until Lender's requirement for Mortgage Insurance ends in accordance with any written agreement between Borrower and Lender providing for such termination or until termination is required by Applicable Law. Nothing in this Section 10 affects Borrower's obligation to pay interest at the rate provided in the Note.

Mortgage Insurance reimburses Lender (or any entity that purchases the Note) for certain losses it may incur if Borrower does not repay the Loan as agreed. Borrower is not a party to the Mortgage Insurance.

Mortgage insurers evaluate their total risk on all such insurance in force from time to time, and may enter into agreements with other parties that share or modify their risk, or reduce losses. These agreements are on terms and conditions that are satisfactory to the mortgage insurer and the other party (or parties) to these agreements. These agreements may require the mortgage insurer to make payments using any source of funds that the mortgage insurer may have available (which may include funds obtained from Mortgage Insurance premiums).

As a result of these agreements, Lender, any purchaser of the Note, another insurer, any reinsurer, any other entity, or any affiliate of any of the foregoing, may receive (directly or indirectly) amounts that derive from (or might be characterized as) a portion of Borrower's payments for Mortgage Insurance, in exchange for sharing or modifying the mortgage insurer's risk, or reducing losses. If such agreement provides that an affiliate of Lender takes a share of the insurer's risk in exchange for a share of the premiums paid to the insurer, the arrangement is often termed "captive reinsurance." Further:

(a) **Any such agreements will not affect the amounts that Borrower has agreed to pay for Mortgage Insurance, or any other terms of the Loan. Such agreements will not increase the amount Borrower will owe for Mortgage Insurance, and they will not entitle Borrower to any refund.**

(b) **Any such agreements will not affect the rights Borrower has - if any - with respect to the Mortgage Insurance under the Homeowners Protection Act of 1998 or any other law. These rights may include the right to receive certain disclosures, to request and obtain cancellation of the Mortgage Insurance, to have the Mortgage Insurance terminated automatically, and/or to receive a refund of any Mortgage Insurance premiums that were unearned at the time of such cancellation or termination.**

11. **Assignment of Miscellaneous Proceeds; Forfeiture.** All Miscellaneous Proceeds are hereby assigned to and shall be paid to Lender.

If the Property is damaged, such Miscellaneous Proceeds shall be applied to restoration or repair of the Property, if the restoration or repair is economically feasible and Lender's security is not lessened. During such repair and restoration period, Lender shall have the right to hold such Miscellaneous Proceeds until Lender has had an opportunity to inspect such Property

Deed of Trust

to ensure the work has been completed to Lender's satisfaction, provided that such inspection shall be undertaken promptly. Lender may pay for the repairs and restoration in a single disbursement or in a series of progress payments as the work is completed. Unless an agreement is made in writing or Applicable Law requires interest to be paid on such Miscellaneous Proceeds, Lender shall not be required to pay Borrower any interest or earnings on such Miscellaneous Proceeds. If the restoration or repair is not economically feasible or Lender's security would be lessened, the Miscellaneous Proceeds shall be applied to the sums secured by this Security Instrument, whether or not then due, with the excess, if any, paid to Borrower. Such Miscellaneous Proceeds shall be applied in the order provided for in Section 2.

In the event of a total taking, destruction, or loss in value of the Property, the Miscellaneous Proceeds shall be applied to the sums secured by this Security Instrument, whether or not then due, with the excess, if any, paid to Borrower.

In the event of a partial taking, destruction, or loss in value of the Property in which the fair market value of the Property immediately before the partial taking, destruction, or loss in value is equal to or greater than the amount of the sums secured by this Security Instrument immediately before the partial taking, destruction, or loss in value, unless Borrower and Lender otherwise agree in writing, the sums secured by this Security Instrument shall be reduced by the amount of the Miscellaneous Proceeds multiplied by the following fraction: (a) the total amount of the sums secured immediately before the partial taking, destruction, or loss in value divided by (b) the fair market value of the Property immediately before the partial taking, destruction, or loss in value. Any balance shall be paid to Borrower.

In the event of a partial taking, destruction, or loss in value of the Property in which the fair market value of the Property immediately before the partial taking, destruction, or loss in value is less than the amount of the sums secured immediately before the partial taking, destruction, or loss in value, unless Borrower and Lender otherwise agree in writing, the Miscellaneous Proceeds shall be applied to the sums secured by this Security Instrument whether or not the sums are then due.

If the Property is abandoned by Borrower, or if, after notice by Lender to Borrower that the Opposing Party (as defined in the next sentence) offers to make an award to settle a claim for damages, Borrower fails to respond to Lender within 30 days after the date the notice is given, Lender is authorized to collect and apply the Miscellaneous Proceeds either to restoration or repair of the Property or to the sums secured by this Security Instrument, whether or not then due. "Opposing Party" means the third party that owes Borrower Miscellaneous Proceeds or the party against whom Borrower has a right of action in regard to Miscellaneous Proceeds.

Borrower shall be in default if any action or proceeding, whether civil or criminal, is begun that, in Lender's judgment, could result in forfeiture of the Property or other material impairment of Lender's interest in the Property or rights under this Security Instrument. Borrower can cure such a default and, if acceleration has occurred, reinstate as provided in Section 19, by causing the action or proceeding to be dismissed with a ruling that, in Lender's judgment, precludes forfeiture of the Property or other material impairment of Lender's interest in the Property or rights under this Security Instrument. The proceeds of any award or claim for damages that are attributable to the impairment of Lender's interest in the Property are hereby assigned and shall be paid to Lender.

All Miscellaneous Proceeds that are not applied to restoration or repair of the Property shall be applied in the order provided for in Section 2.

Deed of Trust

12. **Borrower Not Released; Forbearance By Lender Not a Waiver.** Extension of the time for payment or modification of amortization of the sums secured by this Security Instrument granted by Lender to Borrower or any Successor in Interest of Borrower shall not operate to release the liability of Borrower or any Successors in Interest of Borrower. Lender shall not be required to commence proceedings against any Successor in Interest of Borrower or to refuse to extend time for payment or otherwise modify amortization of the sums secured by this Security Instrument by reason of any demand made by the original Borrower or any Successors in Interest of Borrower. Any forbearance by Lender in exercising any right or remedy including, without limitation, Lender's acceptance of payments from third persons, entities or Successors in Interest of Borrower or in amounts less than the amount then due, shall not be a waiver of or preclude the exercise of any right or remedy.

13. **Joint and Several Liability; Co-signers; Successors and Assigns Bound.** Borrower covenants and agrees that Borrower's obligations and liability shall be joint and several. However, any Borrower who co-signs this Security Instrument but does not execute the Note (a "co-signer"): (a) is co-signing this Security Instrument only to mortgage, grant and convey the co-signer's interest in the Property under the terms of this Security Instrument; (b) is not personally obligated to pay the sums secured by this Security Instrument; and (c) agrees that Lender and any other Borrower can agree to extend, modify, forbear or make any accommodations with regard to the terms of this Security Instrument or the Note without the co-signer's consent.

Subject to the provisions of Section 18, any Successor in Interest of Borrower who assumes Borrower's obligations under this Security Instrument in writing, and is approved by Lender, shall obtain all of Borrower's rights and benefits under this Security Instrument. Borrower shall not be released from Borrower's obligations and liability under this Security Instrument unless Lender agrees to such release in writing. The covenants and agreements of this Security Instrument shall bind (except as provided in Section 20) and benefit the successors and assigns of Lender.

14. **Loan Charges.** Lender may charge Borrower fees for services performed in connection with Borrower's default, for the purpose of protecting Lender's interest in the Property and rights under this Security Instrument, including, but not limited to, attorneys' fees, property inspection and valuation fees. In regard to any other fees, the absence of express authority in this Security Instrument to charge a specific fee to Borrower shall not be construed as a prohibition on the charging of such fee. Lender may not charge fees that are expressly prohibited by this Security Instrument or by Applicable Law.

If the Loan is subject to a law which sets maximum loan charges, and that law is finally interpreted so that the interest or other loan charges collected or to be collected in connection with the Loan exceed the permitted limits, then: (a) any such loan charge shall be reduced by the amount necessary to reduce the charge to the permitted limit; and (b) any sums already collected from Borrower which exceeded permitted limits will be refunded to Borrower. Lender may choose to make this refund by reducing the principal owed under the Note or by making a direct payment to Borrower. If a refund reduces principal, the reduction will be treated as a partial prepayment without any prepayment charge (whether or not a prepayment charge is provided for under the Note). Borrower's acceptance of any such refund made by direct payment to Borrower will constitute a waiver of any right of action Borrower might have arising out of such overcharge.

Deed of Trust

15.   Notices. All notices given by Borrower or Lender in connection with this Security Instrument must be in writing. Any notice to Borrower in connection with this Security Instrument shall be deemed to have been given to Borrower when mailed by first class mail or when actually delivered to Borrower's notice address if sent by other means. Notice to any one Borrower shall constitute notice to all Borrowers unless Applicable Law expressly requires otherwise. The notice address shall be the Property Address unless Borrower has designated a substitute notice address by notice to Lender. Borrower shall promptly notify Lender of Borrower's change of address. If Lender specifies a procedure for reporting Borrower's change of address, then Borrower shall only report a change of address through that specified procedure. There may be only one designated notice address under this Security Instrument at any one time. Any notice to Lender shall be given by delivering it or by mailing it by first class mail to Lender's address stated herein unless Lender has designated another address by notice to Borrower. Any notice in connection with this Security Instrument shall not be deemed to have been given to Lender until actually received by Lender. If any notice required by this Security Instrument is also required under Applicable Law, the Applicable Law requirement will satisfy the corresponding requirement under this Security Instrument.

16.   Governing Law; Severability; Rules of Construction.   This Security Instrument shall be governed by federal law and the law of the jurisdiction in which the Property is located. All rights and obligations contained in this Security Instrument are subject to any requirements and limitations of Applicable Law. Applicable Law might explicitly or implicitly allow the parties to agree by contract or it might be silent, but such silence shall not be construed as a prohibition against agreement by contract. In the event that any provision or clause of this Security Instrument or the Note conflicts with Applicable Law, such conflict shall not affect other provisions of this Security Instrument or the Note which can be given effect without the conflicting provision.

As used in this Security Instrument: (a) words of the masculine gender shall mean and include corresponding neuter words or words of the feminine gender; (b) words in the singular shall mean and include the plural and vice versa; and (c) the word "may" gives sole discretion without any obligation to take any action.

17.   Borrower's Copy. Borrower shall be given one copy of the Note and of this Security Instrument.

18.   Transfer of the Property or a Beneficial Interest in Borrower. As used in this Section 18, "Interest in the Property" means any legal or beneficial interest in the Property, including, but not limited to, those beneficial interests transferred in a bond for deed, contract for deed, installment sales contract or escrow agreement, the intent of which is the transfer of title by Borrower at a future date to a purchaser.

If all or any part of the Property or any Interest in the Property is sold or transferred (or if Borrower is not a natural person and a beneficial interest in Borrower is sold or transferred) without Lender's prior written consent, Lender may require immediate payment in full of all sums secured by this Security Instrument. However, this option shall not be exercised by Lender if such exercise is prohibited by Applicable Law.

If Lender exercises this option, Lender shall give Borrower notice of acceleration. The notice shall provide a period of not less than 30 days from the date the notice is given in accordance with Section 15 within which Borrower must pay all sums secured by this Security Instrument. If Borrower fails to pay these sums prior to the expiration of this period, Lender

Deed of Trust

SAMPLE

may invoke any remedies permitted by this Security Instrument without further notice or demand on Borrower.

      19.   **Borrower's Right to Reinstate After Acceleration.** If Borrower meets certain conditions, Borrower shall have the right to have enforcement of this Security Instrument discontinued at any time prior to the earliest of: (a) five days before sale of the Property pursuant to any power of sale contained in this Security Instrument; (b) such other period as Applicable Law might specify for the termination of Borrower's right to reinstate; or (c) entry of a judgment enforcing this Security Instrument. Those conditions are that Borrower: (a) pays Lender all sums which then would be due under this Security Instrument and the Note as if no acceleration had occurred; (b) cures any default of any other covenants or agreements; (c) pays all expenses incurred in enforcing this Security Instrument, including, but not limited to, reasonable attorneys' fees, property inspection and valuation fees, and other fees incurred for the purpose of protecting Lender's interest in the Property and rights under this Security Instrument; and (d) takes such action as Lender may reasonably require to assure that Lender's interest in the Property and rights under this Security Instrument, and Borrower's obligation to pay the sums secured by this Security Instrument, shall continue unchanged. Lender may require that Borrower pay such reinstatement sums and expenses in one or more of the following forms, as selected by Lender: (a) cash; (b) money order; (c) certified check, bank check, treasurer's check or cashier's check, provided any such check is drawn upon an institution whose deposits are insured by a federal agency, instrumentality or entity; or (d) Electronic Funds Transfer. Upon reinstatement by Borrower, this Security Instrument and obligations secured hereby shall remain fully effective as if no acceleration had occurred. However, this right to reinstate shall not apply in the case of acceleration under Section 18.

      20.   **Sale of Note; Change of Loan Servicer; Notice of Grievance.** The Note or a partial interest in the Note (together with this Security Instrument) can be sold one or more times without prior notice to Borrower. A sale might result in a change in the entity (known as the "Loan Servicer") that collects Periodic Payments due under the Note and this Security Instrument and performs other mortgage loan servicing obligations under the Note, this Security Instrument, and Applicable Law. There also might be one or more changes of the Loan Servicer unrelated to a sale of the Note. If there is a change of the Loan Servicer, Borrower will be given written notice of the change which will state the name and address of the new Loan Servicer, the address to which payments should be made and any other information RESPA requires in connection with a notice of transfer of servicing. If the Note is sold and thereafter the Loan is serviced by a Loan Servicer other than the purchaser of the Note, the mortgage loan servicing obligations to Borrower will remain with the Loan Servicer or be transferred to a successor Loan Servicer and are not assumed by the Note purchaser unless otherwise provided by the Note purchaser.

      Neither Borrower nor Lender may commence, join, or be joined to any judicial action (as either an individual litigant or the member of a class) that arises from the other party's actions pursuant to this Security Instrument or that alleges that the other party has breached any provision of, or any duty owed by reason of, this Security Instrument, until such Borrower or Lender has notified the other party (with such notice given in compliance with the requirements of Section 15) of such alleged breach and afforded the other party hereto a reasonable period after the giving of such notice to take corrective action. If Applicable Law provides a time period which must elapse before certain action can be taken, that time period will be deemed to be reasonable for purposes of this paragraph. The notice of acceleration and opportunity to cure

Deed of Trust

given to Borrower pursuant to Section 22 and the notice of acceleration given to Borrower pursuant to Section 18 shall be deemed to satisfy the notice and opportunity to take corrective action provisions of this Section 20.

21.   Hazardous Substances. As used in this Section 21: (a) "Hazardous Substances" are those substances defined as toxic or hazardous substances, pollutants, or wastes by Environmental Law and the following substances: gasoline, kerosene, other flammable or toxic petroleum products, toxic pesticides and herbicides, volatile solvents, materials containing asbestos or formaldehyde, and radioactive materials; (b) "Environmental Law" means federal laws and laws of the jurisdiction where the Property is located that relate to health, safety or environmental protection; (c) "Environmental Cleanup" includes any response action, remedial action, or removal action, as defined in Environmental Law; and (d) an "Environmental Condition" means a condition that can cause, contribute to, or otherwise trigger an Environmental Cleanup.

Borrower shall not cause or permit the presence, use, disposal, storage, or release of any Hazardous Substances, or threaten to release any Hazardous Substances, on or in the Property. Borrower shall not do, nor allow anyone else to do, anything affecting the Property (a) that is in violation of any Environmental Law, (b) which creates an Environmental Condition, or (c) which, due to the presence, use, or release of a Hazardous Substance, creates a condition that adversely affects the value of the Property. The preceding two sentences shall not apply to the presence, use, or storage on the Property of small quantities of Hazardous Substances that are generally recognized to be appropriate to normal residential uses and to maintenance of the Property (including, but not limited to, hazardous substances in consumer products).

Borrower shall promptly give Lender written notice of (a) any investigation, claim, demand, lawsuit or other action by any governmental or regulatory agency or private party involving the Property and any Hazardous Substance or Environmental Law of which Borrower has actual knowledge, (b) any Environmental Condition, including but not limited to, any spilling, leaking, discharge, release or threat of release of any Hazardous Substance, and (c) any condition caused by the presence, use or release of a Hazardous Substance which adversely affects the value of the Property. If Borrower learns, or is notified by any governmental or regulatory authority, or any private party, that any removal or other remediation of any Hazardous Substance affecting the Property is necessary, Borrower shall promptly take all necessary remedial actions in accordance with Environmental Law. Nothing herein shall create any obligation on Lender for an Environmental Cleanup.

NON-UNIFORM COVENANTS. Borrower and Lender further covenant and agree as follows:

22.   Acceleration; Remedies. Lender shall give notice to Borrower prior to acceleration following Borrower's breach of any covenant or agreement in this Security Instrument (but not prior to acceleration under Section 18 unless Applicable Law provides otherwise). The notice shall specify: (a) the default; (b) the action required to cure the default; (c) a date, not less than 30 days from the date the notice is given to Borrower, by which the default must be cured; and (d) that failure to cure the default on or before the date specified in the notice may result in acceleration of the sums secured by this Security Instrument and sale of the Property. The notice shall further inform Borrower of the right to reinstate after acceleration and the right to bring a court action to assert the non-existence of a default or any other defense of Borrower to acceleration and sale. If the

Deed of Trust

SAMPLE

default is not cured on or before the date specified in the notice, Lender at its option may require immediate payment in full of all sums secured by this Security Instrument without further demand and may invoke the power of sale and any other remedies permitted by Applicable Law. Lender shall be entitled to collect all expenses incurred in pursuing the remedies provided in this Section 22, including, but not limited to, reasonable attorneys' fees and costs of title evidence.

If Lender invokes the power of sale, Lender shall execute or cause Trustee to execute a written notice of the occurrence of an event of default and of Lender's election to cause the Property to be sold. Trustee shall cause this notice to be recorded in each county in which any part of the Property is located. Lender or Trustee shall mail copies of the notice as prescribed by Applicable Law to Borrower and to the other persons prescribed by Applicable Law. Trustee shall give public notice of sale to the persons and in the manner prescribed by Applicable Law. After the time required by Applicable Law, Trustee, without demand on Borrower, shall sell the Property at public auction to the highest bidder at the time and place and under the terms designated in the notice of sale in one or more parcels and in any order Trustee determines. Trustee may postpone sale of all or any parcel of the Property by public announcement at the time and place of any previously scheduled sale. Lender or its designee may purchase the Property at any sale.

Trustee shall deliver to the purchaser Trustee's deed conveying the Property without any covenant or warranty, expressed or implied. The recitals in the Trustee's deed shall be prima facie evidence of the truth of the statements made therein. Trustee shall apply the proceeds of the sale in the following order: (a) to all expenses of the sale, including, but not limited to, reasonable Trustee's and attorneys' fees; (b) to all sums secured by this Security Instrument; and (c) any excess to the person or persons legally entitled to it.

23. **Reconveyance.** Upon payment of all sums secured by this Security Instrument, Lender shall request Trustee to reconvey the Property and shall surrender this Security Instrument and all notes evidencing debt secured by this Security Instrument to Trustee. Trustee shall reconvey the Property without warranty to the person or persons legally entitled to it. Lender may charge such person or persons a reasonable fee for reconveying the Property, but only if the fee is paid to a third party (such as the Trustee) for services rendered and the charging of the fee is permitted under Applicable Law. If the fee charged does not exceed the fee set by Applicable Law, the fee is conclusively presumed to be reasonable.

24. **Substitute Trustee.** Lender, at its option, may from time to time appoint a successor trustee to any Trustee appointed hereunder by an instrument executed and acknowledged by Lender and recorded in the office of the Recorder of the county in which the Property is located. The instrument shall contain the name of the original Lender, Trustee and Borrower, the book and page where this Security Instrument is recorded and the name and address of the successor trustee. Without conveyance of the Property, the successor trustee shall succeed to all the title, powers and duties conferred upon the Trustee herein and by Applicable Law. This procedure for substitution of trustee shall govern to the exclusion of all other provisions for substitution.

25. **Statement of Obligation Fee.** Lender may collect a fee not to exceed the maximum amount permitted by Applicable Law for furnishing the statement of obligation as provided by Section 2943 of the Civil Code of California.

Deed of Trust

BY SIGNING BELOW, Borrower accepts and agrees to the terms and covenants contained in this Security Instrument and in any Rider executed by Borrower and recorded with it.

Witnesses:

_____   _____ (Seal)
                                                              - Borrower

_____   _____ (Seal)
                                                              - Borrower

_____**[Space Below This Line for Acknowledgment]**_____

Before you leave this chapter, **there are** *two main distinctions between a mortgage and a deed of trust* **that are worth highlighting**.

The Two Main Distinctions Between a Mortgage and a Deed of Trust:

☆ Number of Parties Involved

A **mortgage has two parties**: the *mortgagor (borrower)* and the *mortgagee (lender).*

A **deed of trust has three parties**: the *trustor (borrower),* the *beneficiary (lender)* and *the trustee (the third party who retains title to your property while the trustor makes his or her payments).*

☆ Power of Sale Clause

The **deed of trust** contains a "**power of sale clause**" while *a mortgage typically does not.* (However, you will learn in **Chapter 5** that there a few states where lenders sometimes use a mortgage with a **power of sale clause**).

Most of the time, *a lender with a mortgage needs to file a lawsuit to foreclose on the property.* **A deed of trust**, on the other hand, **grants the beneficiary (lender) the right to request the trustee (third party) to sell the property without having to file a lawsuit.** Without judicial intervention, the "**power of sale clause**" *is truly a powerful clause – for the lender, at least.*

Foreclosing on both of these security instruments will be discussed at greater length in the next chapter, which explains **the two types of foreclosure actions**: *judicial* and *non-judicial.*

Chapter 4

Understanding the Foreclosure Process, Part II: Judicial or Non-Judicial?

This Chapter Discusses:

★ **Judicial Foreclosure**
★ **Non-Judicial Foreclosure**

Now that you understand the basic premise behind the promissory note and its applicable security instrument for your state (the mortgage or deed of trust), you need to understand the process by which each of these is foreclosed.

As you know, legal procedures in general are as boring as working a tollbooth. So with that in mind, **we've done our best to describe each type of foreclosure proceeding so you can still enjoy this chapter** along with a cup of coffee, tea, milk, water, grape soda… or anything else that quenches your thirst, because (despite our efforts) some of this legal stuff can still leave you feeling a little parched.

<u>Please note</u>: **Each state has it own variation of laws and procedures,** *that are summarized in Chapter 5.* But don't jump ahead just yet, because **the first two sections in this chapter detail the most common steps and procedures.** And **before you even begin,** *you need to determine which type of foreclosure process is usually followed in your state for a primary residence.* **A chart has been provided on the next two pages for your reference.** (Another way of helping you remember your state's foreclosure process is to be aware that, in general, the *judicial process requires a mortgage that does not have a power of sale clause* and the *non-judicial process requires a deed of trust or mortgage with a power of sale clause*.)

Each State's Most Commonly Used Foreclosure Process

Alabama	Non-Judicial
Alaska	Non-Judicial
Arizona	Non-Judicial
Arkansas	Non-Judicial
California	Non-Judicial
Colorado	Non-Judicial
Connecticut	Judicial (Strict) enforcing Mortgage
Delaware	Judicial
District of Columbia	Non-Judicial
Florida	Judicial
Georgia	Non-Judicial
Hawaii	Non-Judicial
Idaho	Non-Judicial
Illinois	Judicial
Indiana	Judicial
Iowa	Judicial
Kansas	Judicial
Kentucky	Judicial
Louisiana	Judicial (Executory) enforcing Mortgage (with a Confession of Judgment)
Maine	Judicial (Strict) enforcing Mortgage
Maryland	Non-Judicial enforcing Mortgage (with a Power of Sale clause)
Massachusetts	Non-Judicial enforcing Mortgage (with a Power of Sale clause)
Michigan	Non-Judicial
Minnesota	Non-Judicial enforcing Mortgage (with a Power of Sale clause)
Mississippi	Non-Judicial enforcing Mortgage (with a Power of Sale clause)
Missouri	Non-Judicial

Montana	Non-Judicial
Nebraska	Non-Judicial
Nevada	Non-Judicial
New Hampshire	Non-Judicial enforcing Mortgage (with a Power of Sale clause)
New Jersey	Judicial
New Mexico	Judicial
New York	Judicial
North Carolina	Non-Judicial enforcing Mortgage (with a Power of Sale clause)
North Dakota	Judicial
Ohio	Judicial
Oklahoma	Non-Judicial enforcing Mortgage (with a Power of Sale clause)
Oregon	Non-Judicial
Pennsylvania	Judicial
Rhode Island	Non-Judicial enforcing Mortgage (with a Power of Sale clause)
South Carolina	Judicial
South Dakota	Non-Judicial
Tennessee	Non-Judicial
Texas	Non-Judicial
Utah	Non-Judicial
Vermont	Judicial
Virginia	Non-Judicial enforcing Mortgage (with a Power of Sale clause)
Washington	Non-Judicial
West Virginia	Non-Judicial
Wisconsin	Judicial
Wyoming	Non-Judicial

Judicial Foreclosure

This type of process **involves a promissory note and its counterpart, the mortgage**. It's a *long and expensive process* (thanks to the lender's attorney) that **requires the lender filing a lawsuit to begin foreclosing on the property**.

Once again, *each state's laws and procedures will vary*. For clarification purposes, we've chosen to **detail the common steps of the judicial foreclosure process for the state of California**:

Note: *State-specific summaries are outlined in Chapter 5.*

The Common Steps of the Judicial Foreclosure Process:

☆ Step 1: Complaint and Summons

The *complaint* is **usually a several-page document that is filed with the court in the county where the property is located.** This document *initiates a lawsuit against all parties involved (defendants)* – including the owners of the property as well as any tenants and lien holders. **It will allege that the borrower willingly signed a mortgage and a promissory note and is now in default.** This complaint – along with a **court summons** announcing the lawsuit – will then be *served upon all of the defendants*.

A **sample complaint and summons is shown on the next four pages for your review**…

Everything U Need to Know...™

Complaint

IN THE _____ COURT OF THE _____,

IN AND FOR _____ COUNTY, _____.

_____ DIVISION

CASE NO: _____

_____

PLAINTIFF

Vs.

_____

DEFENDANT(S)

COMPLAINT TO FORECLOSE MORTGAGE

Plaintiff, sues the Defendant(s) and alleges:

1. This is an action for the foreclosure of a mortgage upon certain real estate located in _____ County, _____.

2. Plaintiff is a corporation or other legal entity doing business in the State of _____.

3. Plaintiff is the owner and holder of the Note and Mortgage, described hereafter and the subject of this action.

4. Some lien on or interest in the real estate, the subject of this action, may be claimed by the Defendant(s) herein.

5. The Defendant(s) herein described as judgment creditors have by filing said judgments designated their attorney entering the judgment as their agent for service of process under the provisions of Section _____ of the Code of Laws of _____.

6. Heretofore, on or about _____, _____ made, executed and delivered unto _____ a certain Note ("Note") in the principal

SAMPLE

Complaint

sum of $_____, a copy of which is attached hereto as Exhibit "A" and made a part hereof by reference.

7. In order to secure the payment of the Note according to the terms and conditions thereof, _____ made, executed and delivered unto _____ a certain real estate mortgage ("Mortgage") covering the following described property:

_____

This being the identical property conveyed to _____ by deed of _____ dated_____, and recorded _____, in Deed Book _____ at Page ___.

PROPERTY ADDRESS:_____
TMS #:_____

8. The Mortgage was signed, witnessed and probated; thereafter the Mortgage was recorded in the _____ for _____ County on _____, in Mortgage Book _____ at Page _____, a copy of which is attached hereto as Exhibit "B" and made a part hereof by reference.

9. The Mortgage evidences and secures the repayment of money advanced by the mortgagee to, or on behalf of, the mortgagor(s) and constitutes a purchase money first lien on the mortgaged premises.

10. Any notice required by the terms of the mortgage or by state or federal statutes has been given to the applicable defendant(s) prior to the commencement of this action.

11. The monthly payments due on the Note and Mortgage are in default since _____, and the conditions of the Note and Mortgage have been broken and the Plaintiff elects to and does declare the entire balance of said indebtedness due and payable, and that there is due on the Note and Mortgage as of _____, the sum of $_____, with interest at the rate of _____% per thereon, together with any taxes or insurance premiums which may be due, with reasonable attorney's fees, and for the costs of this action.

(3) Order the reimbursement of all costs for inspecting and securing the property incurred by the Plaintiff as a result of the delinquency.

(4) Appoint a Receiver to collect the rents, issues, profits or designated sums from the mortgagor(s), and/or the grantee(s) of the mortgagor(s), and/or tenant(s) occupying or exercising control over the mortgaged premises and hold the same subject to the further order of this Court.

(5) Under the direction of this Court, sell the mortgaged premises, bar any equity of redemption, and apply the proceeds of sale as follows:

First, to the costs and expenses of the within action and sale;

SAMPLE

Complaint

Second, to the payment and discharge of the amount due on Plaintiff's Note and Mortgage, together with attorney's fees as aforesaid.

(6) Issue an order directing the Sheriff of _____ County, _____, to place the successful purchaser at said foreclosure sale in possession of the property should the same become necessary.

(7) Order such other and further relief as may be just and proper.

Attorney for Plaintiff

NOTICE REQUIRED BY THE FAIR DEBT COLLECTION PRACTICES ACT

15 U.S.C. Section 1601, As Amended

1. The amount of the debt is stated in the Complaint attached hereto.

2. The Plaintiff as named in the attached Summons and Complaint is the creditor to whom the debt is owed.

3. If the original creditor is different from the current creditor, the creditor's law firm will provide the debtor with the name and address of the original creditor if requested by the debtor, in writing, within thirty (30) days of the receipt of this notice.

4. The debt described in the Complaint attached hereto and evidenced by the Note and Mortgage described therein will be assumed to be valid by the creditor's law firm unless the debtor, within thirty (30) days after the receipt of this notice, disputes, in writing, the validity of the debt or some portion thereof.

5. If the debtor notifies the creditor's law firm in writing within thirty (30) days of the receipt of this notice that the debt or any portion thereon is disputed, the creditor's law firm will obtain a verification of the debt, and a copy of the verification will be mailed to the debtor by the creditor's law firm.

6. Written requests should be addressed to _____
_____

THIS IS AN ATTEMPT TO COLLECT A DEBT, AND ANY INFORMATION OBTAINED WILL BE USED FOR THAT PURPOSE.

Summons

IN THE _____ COURT OF THE _____,

IN AND FOR _____ COUNTY, _____.

_____DIVISION

CASE NO: _____

_____

PLAINTIFF PERSONAL SERVICE ON A NATURAL PERSON

Vs. CIVIL ACTION SUMMONS

_____

DEFENDANT(S)

YOU ARE HEREBY COMMANDED to serve this summons and a copy of the complaint/amended complaint or petition *in* this action on defendant(s): _____

A LAWSUIT HAS BEEN FILED AGAINST YOU. YOU HAVE 30 CALENDAR DAYS AFTER THIS SUMMONS IS SERVED ON YOU TO FILE A WRITTEN RESPONSE TO THE ATTACHED COMPLAINT WITH THE CLERK OF THIS COURT. A PHONE CALL WILL NOT PROTECT YOU; YOUR WRITTEN RESPONSE, INCLUDING THE CASE NUMBER GIVEN ABOVE AND THE NAMES OF THE PARTIES, MUST BE FILED IF YOU WANT THE COURT TO HEAR YOUR SIDE OF THE CASE. IF YOU DO NOT FILE YOUR RESPONSE ON TIME, YOU MAY LOSE THE CASE, AND YOUR WAGES, MONEY AND PROPERTY MAY THEREAFTER BE TAKEN WITHOUT FURTHER WARNING FROM THE COURT. THERE ARE OTHER LEGAL REQUIREMENTS. YOU MAY WANT TO CALL AN ATTORNEY RIGHT AWAY. IF YOU DO NOT KNOW AN ATTORNEY, YOU MAY CALL AN ATTORNEY REFERRAL SERVICE OR LEGAL AID OFFICE

(LISTED IN THE PHONE BOOK)

IF YOU CHOOSE TO FILE A WRITTEN RESPONSE YOURSELF, AT THE SAME TIME YOU FILE YOUR WRITTEN RESPONSE TO THE COURT, YOU MUST ALSO MAIL OR TAKE A CARBON COPY OR PHOTOCOPY OF YOUR WRITTEN RESPONSE TO THE "PLAINTIFF'S ATTORNEY" LISTED BELOW:

_____

_____

DATED: BY:_____

DEPUTY CLERK OF COURT

ANY PERSONS WITH A DISABILITY REQUIRING REASONABLE ACOMMODATIONS SHOULD CALL (____) ____-_____ (V/TDD), N0 LATER THAN _____ (_____) DAYS PRIOR TO ANY PROCEEDING.

SAMPLE

☆ Step 2: Lis Pendens

"Lis Pendens" is Latin for *"notice of pending action"* and is **usually recorded simultaneously with the complaint** and **a copy is mailed to each defendant**. The *purpose* of the *Lis Pendens* is *to warn anyone interested in buying the property or using it as collateral that there is pending action that must first be resolved*.

☆ Step 3: Response Period

Upon receiving the complaint, **the borrower (defendant) usually has 30 days to respond to the allegations.** *If the defendant fails to respond, then the court will automatically and immediately rule in the lender's favor.*

☆ Step 4: Reinstatement Period

The **borrower has the right to bring the loan current and end the lawsuit at any time before the court decides the case.** This means that if the borrower were to pay the total sum of all payments that were missed plus any legal fees incurred by the lender, the lender would have no choice but to cancel the lawsuit.

The period of time within which to exercise this right *begins at the time the complaint is being filed!* **The longer you wait, the higher the fees accrue – making it more difficult to catch up.**

☆ Step 5: Discovery

Each party of the lawsuit has **the right to request various pieces of evidence from either side.** You may have heard of the terms "**depositions**" and "**interrogatories**" – which are *all a part of any good attorney's representation if you intend on fighting foreclosure.*

If you decide to fight a foreclosure, *we strongly suggest you retain an attorney.* If you don't have the financial resources to hire an expensive attorney, *contact your county or state bar association for referral to a low-cost legal aid panel* or **see the enclosed CD-ROM for a list of foreclosure prevention resources.**

 Step 6: Trial

If you decide to actually take the foreclosure lawsuit all the way to trial, **be prepared** – *because your lender will have a full arsenal of evidence stacked against you!* Once again, **the use of an attorney is strongly advised,** *because you will have to prove the lender to be wrong about most of what they are asserting to be true.*

If you're unable to do so, then the court will rule in the lender's favor and enter a *judgment of foreclosure.*

Step 7: Redemption Period

As soon as the court rules in the lender's favor, **you are given another opportunity to preclude foreclosure –** *but this time it will require paying off the entire loan balance* (not just the missed payments) *plus the lender's attorney fees and court costs!*

Depending on your state, **the period of time given to exercise this option ranges from a few weeks to several months.** *The time frame for each state is provided in* **Chapter 5.** And needless to say, **coming up with this kind of cash would most likely require selling the property to an expeditious buyer**.

Step 8: Writ of Sale

Since most buyers do not have the financial strength or are unable to redeem the property by selling it, **the court will issue a** *"writ of sale"* once the redemption period has expired. A *writ of sale* is an order by the court instructing the sheriff to sell the property in accordance with the court's conditions.

☆ Step 9: Notice of Sale

After the sheriff receives the writ of sale from the court, **the sheriff will issue a *notice of sale* – informing all defendants and the general public when and where the property will be sold *("auctioned," technically).***

☆ Step 10: Foreclosure Sale

Don't worry – *there will undoubtedly be plenty of buyers lined up to place their bid.* After all, this is an auction publicized by the sheriff that will take place in or outside a government building.

Ironically, anyone can bid on the property including the lender and you. *The winning bid must be paid in cash* (e.g., paper currency, certified check, electronic funds transfer) *unless you are the lender.* The lender receives a credit up to the full amount of the judgment awarded by the court.

In the end, **the sheriff will divvy up the proceeds by *first* collecting its share of fees for the cost of the sale, *then* paying the lender up to the full amount of its judgment. If any money is *still* left over, then it is given to any junior lien holders in line behind the lender** (i.e., second mortgages or equity loans and lines of credit).

If you are having a *very* lucky day, and if there are any funds still remaining after all that, you will be paid the rest – *but don't count on it* unless you had a substantial amount of equity in the property at the time this entire process began.

★ Step 11: Deficiency Judgment

If the **lender does not recover the full amount of the foreclosure judgment** awarded by the court, **it can petition the court to award a** *deficiency judgment* **against the borrower for the amount that remains unpaid**.

If the foreclosure judgment entitled the lender to $500,000 and the sale of the property netted only $450,000, the lender may sue you for the remaining $50,000. **However, the lender must have included in its original complaint its option to pursue a deficiency judgment.** After the sale, **the lender will then have a limited amount of time to file a separate application to request the court to award a deficiency judgment.** Otherwise, *if the lender waits too long, it may lose its right to collect the difference.*

EXAMPLE

You have the option of disputing the deficiency judgment if you feel the property was sold below market value. In order to do this, *you need to have had an appraiser determine the property's value at or around the time of the sale.* If you are able to convince the court that your claim is true, then **the court, at its sole discretion, may** *adjust the amount* **of the deficiency judgment originally awarded to the lender**.

TIP

★ Step 12: Notice of Right to Redemption

In many states, **the sheriff will issue a notice to you giving you the right to redeem your property one last time.** However, *this may now involve not only the full amount of your lender's judgment, but also all of the costs incurred* by the sheriff *for the sale of the property* (plus interest).

Add to that any assessments or taxes which may be owed – and let's not forget about the new owner of the property and **whatever fees he or she paid to make to repair, insure, maintain or improve the property.** *Understandably, this may not be* the best time *to exercise your right of redemption.*

And so, **if you don't redeem your property, the sheriff will record a sheriff's deed granting complete and full title to the buyer,** bringing this entire process to a close.

Non-Judicial Foreclosure

This foreclosure process is *not nearly as expensive or as lengthy as the judicial one,* **because non-judicial foreclosures can involve either a** *deed of trust* **or a** *mortgage* **as long as there is a** *power of sale clause.* (As mentioned in **Chapter 3**, this clause **entitles the lender to sell your property without having to file a lawsuit or appear in court**, thereby reducing its attorney fees and court costs.)

However, the borrower is not left empty-handed. **Non-judicial foreclosures do not include the use of a** *deficiency judgment* – **which means that the lender is** *only entitled* **to receive the proceeds from the sale of the property.** The other benefit for the borrower is that **non-judicial foreclosures are** *much easier to prevent* **than judicial ones.** See **Chapter 6** regarding *how to stall or prevent a non-judicial foreclosure.*

Before you jump ahead, **you need to familiarize yourself with the basic steps that are inherent to a** *non-judicial foreclosure.* Once again, **these steps have been based upon California law, which are similar to the rest of the non-judicial states** – *but not identical!*

Note: *State-specific summaries are outlined in Chapter 5.*

The Common Steps of the Non-Judicial Foreclosure Process:

☆ Step 1: Notice of Default

The non-judicial process **begins with the lender requesting the trustee to file a** *notice of default* – which simply means the borrower has not been making the required payments. **This notice is mailed to the borrower, published in a local newspaper and recorded in the public record.**

The interesting part about the commencement of this foreclosure process is that the lender or trustee is not required to confirm delivery to the borrower, as is necessitated in the judicial system with a process server. So… **if you** *don't* **ever receive this notice** – because the neighbor's dog ate your mail or you were out of town for an extended period of time – the foreclosure process gallops ahead (unless you can prove it was mailed to the wrong address when the correct one was known all along – and *only then the trustee might have to start all over again).*

A copy of an *actual notice of default* **has been provided for your review on the next three pages…**

Everything U Need to Know...™

Notice of Default

Requested by and after recording, return to:

_____

_____

_____

NOTICE OF DEFAULT AND ELECTION TO SELL

RE: Trust Deed from:

[BORROWER]

                  Grantor

To

[TRUSTEE]

                  Trustee

SAMPLE

Reference is made to that certain Deed of Trust and Assignment of Leases and Rents (the "Trust Deed") made by [Borrower] as grantor, (the "Grantor") to [Trustee] as trustee (the "Trustee"), in favor of [Lender] as beneficiary, (the "Beneficiary") dated _____, recorded _____, in the Records of ___ _____ County, Oregon, as document No. _____, covering the following described real property situated in the above-mentioned county and state, to-wit:

_____commonly known as _____.

The undersigned hereby certifies that no assignments of the Trust Deed by the Trustee or by the Beneficiary and no appointments of a successor trustee have been made, except as recorded in the Records of the county or counties in which the Property is situated. Further, no action has been instituted to recover the debt, or any part thereof, now remaining secured by the Trust Deed, or, if such action has been instituted, such action has been dismissed except as permitted by ORS 86.735(4).

There is a default by Grantor owing an obligation, performance of which is secured by the Trust Deed, with respect to provisions therein which authorize sale in the event of default of such provisions. The default for which foreclosure is made is Grantor's failure to pay when due the following sums, or as a result of the following action or inaction:

      1.   Failure of the Grantor to

By reason of the default, the Beneficiary has declared all sums owing on the obligation secured by the Trust Deed immediately due and payable, those sums being the following estimated amounts, to-wit:

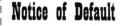
Notice of Default

1. Unpaid Principal: $

2. Accrued and unpaid interest through and including _____ 2007(and continuing at the combined stated and default rate of $_____/day): $

3. Late Charges as of _____, 2007: $

4. Attorney Fees and Costs, as of _____, 2007 (and continuing): $

5. Trustee's Sale Guarantee Report: $

6. Subtotal: $

7. Plus title expenses, trustee's fees, recording fees, and additional attorneys' fees incurred herein by reason of said default and any further sums advanced by the Beneficiary for the protection of the Property and its interest therein.

Notice hereby is given that the Beneficiary and Trustee, by reason of the default, have elected and do hereby elect to foreclose the Trust Deed by advertisement and sale pursuant to ORS 86.705 to 86.795, and to cause to be sold at public auction to the highest bidder for cash the interest in the Property which Grantor had, or had the power to convey, at the time of the execution by Grantor of the Trust Deed, together with any interest Grantor or Grantor's successor in interest acquired after the execution of the Trust Deed, to satisfy the obligations secured by the Trust Deed and the expenses of the sale, including the compensation of the Trustee as provided by law, and the reasonable fees of Trustee's attorneys.

The sale will be held at the hour of **10:00 o'clock, A.M.,** in accord with the standard of time established by ORS 187.110 on **Friday, _____, 2008,** at the following place: the front outside steps to the Multnomah County Courthouse - District No. 4, located at 1021 SW 4th Avenue, Portland, OR 97204.

Other than as shown of record, neither the Beneficiary nor the Trustee has any actual notice of any person having or claiming to have any lien upon or interest in the Property herein-above described subsequent to the interest of the Trustee in the Trust Deed, or of any successor in interest to Grantor or of any lessee or other person in possession of or occupying the Property, except:

Name and Last Known Address   Nature of Right, Lien or Interest

None   None

Notice is further given that any person named in ORS 86.753 has the right, at any time prior to five days before the date last set for the sale, to have this foreclosure proceeding dismissed and the Trust Deed reinstated by payment to the Beneficiary of the entire amount then due (other than such portion of the principal as would not then be due had no default occurred) and by curing any other default complained of herein that is capable of being cured by tendering the performance required under the obligation or Trust Deed, and in addition to paying the sums or tendering the performance necessary to cure the default, by paying all costs and expenses actually incurred in enforcing the obligation and Trust Deed, together with

SAMPLE

Notice of Default

trustee's and attorney fees, subject to the limitations, as applicable, imposed by ORS 86.753.

In construing this notice, the singular includes the plural, the word "Grantor" includes any successor in interest to the Grantor as well as any other person owing an obligation, the performance of which is secured by the Trust Deed, and the words "trustee" and "beneficiary" include their respective successors in interest, if any.

Dated: _____ _____, 2007.

Trustee:

_____

[Trustee]

STATE OF OREGON   )
) ss:
County of Multnomah   )

On _____ _____, 2007, before me, personally appeared [Trustee], personally known to me or proved to me on the basis of satisfactory evidence to be the person whose name is subscribed to the within instrument and acknowledged to me that he executed the same in his authorized capacity and that by his signature on the instrument, the person or entity upon behalf of which the person acted, executed the instrument.

WITNESS my hand and official seal.

_____

Notary Public - State of Oregon
My Commission Expires: _____

CONTACT INFORMATION FOR TRUSTEE:

_____
_____
_____

★ Step 2: Reinstatement Period

As soon as the notice of default is filed, **the borrower has a right to reinstate the loan by bringing it current and reimbursing all outstanding fees incurred by the lender and trustee.** In other words, *you can save your property up until a few days before its sale (auction), so long as you have the cash to settle those missed payments and additional fees*.

Each state will dictate how much time you have; this **information is provided in Chapter 5.**

★ Step 3: Notice of Trustee's Sale

If you don't have the financial resources to reinstate the loan (Step 2), then **the trustee will issue its *notice of sale* to publicize when and where the auction will be conducted.**

Once again, each state will require a certain number of days after the notice of sale is issued before your property can be sold.

The reinstatement deadline will remain in effect until the actual sale. The problem is, however, that *the outstanding fees continue to accrue.* So **the longer you wait to reinstate, the more difficult it becomes** to pull your home out of foreclosure.

CAUTION

Contrary to the notice of default in Step 1, *most states now require the trustee to document the delivery of the notice of sale to the borrower.* **A copy of an *actual notice of trustee's sale* has been provided on the next two pages...**

Notice of Trustee's Sale

Trustee's No. _____
Order No. _____
Escrow No. _____
Loan No. _____

WHEN RECORDED MAIL TO:

_____
_____
_____
_____

SPACE ABOVE THIS LINE FOR RECORDER'S USE

NOTICE OF TRUSTEE'S SALE

On _____ at _____ a.m. _____, Trustee, or Successor Trustee or Substituted Trustee of that certain Deed of Trust executed by _____ and recorded _____ as Instrument No. _____, in Book _____, Page _____, of Official Records of _____ County, California, and pursuant to that certain Notice of Default thereunder recorded _____ as instrument No. _____, in Book _____, Page _____, of Official Records of said County, will under and pursuant to said Deed of Trust sell at public auction for cash, lawful money of the United States of America, a cashier's check payable to said Trustee drawn on a state or national bank, a check drawn by a state or federal credit union, or a check drawn by a state or federal savings and loan association, or savings bank specified in Section 5102 of the Financial Code and authorized to do business in this state, at _____, California,

(INSERT THE STREET ADDRESS AND THE SPECIFIC PLACE AT SUCH ADDRESS WHERE THE SALE WILL BE CONDUCTED)

all that right, title and interest conveyed to and now held by it under said Deed of Trust in the property situated in said County and State described as: _____

Assessor's Parcel Number: _____

(Check one of the following)

(____)   The street address or other common designation of said property: _____

(____)   Name and address of the beneficiary at whose request the sale is being conducted: _____

Directions to the above property may be obtained by requesting same in writing from the beneficiary within 10 days from the first publication of this notice.

Said sale will be made without covenant or warranty, express or implied, as to title, possession or encumbrances to satisfy the unpaid balance due on the note or notes secured by said Deed of Trust, to wit: $_____, plus the following estimated costs, expenses and advances at the time of the initial publication of this Notice of Sale: _____

SAMPLE

Notice of Trustee's Sale

NOTICE TO PROPERTY OWNER

YOU ARE IN DEFAULT UNDER A DEED OF TRUST, DATED _____
UNLESS YOU TAKE ACTION TO PROTECT YOUR PROPERTY, IT MAY BE SOLD AT A
PUBLIC SALE. IF YOU NEED AN EXPLANATION OF THE NATURE OF THE PROCEEDING
AGAINST YOU, YOU SHOULD CONTACT A LAWYER.

DATED:

(TRUSTEE'S NAME OR OTHER PERSON CONDUCTING SALE)

PUBLISH:

(STREEET ADDRESS)

(TELEPHONE NUMBER)

⭐ Step 4: Redemption Period

Depending on the state, **you will have a *limited* number of days immediately following the expiration of the reinstatement period – up until when the first bid is placed – to redeem the property and prevent foreclosure.** This step, however, *requires the borrower to pay the* **entire** *loan balance, in addition to all fees incurred by the lender and trustee*. Good luck with that! **This would most likely require refinancing the mortgage, selling the property, begging friends and family for their gold fillings or perhaps winning the lottery**.

In case you are wondering about **those foreclosure scams that claim to be able save your home prior to being auctioned off to the highest bidder, they will be addressed** later in **Chapter 10**.

⭐ Step 5: Trustee's Sale

This is *the very last step* in the non-judicial foreclosure process. By this point, you've obviously missed your opportunity to reinstate and have not been able to exercise your last-minute rights to redeem your property with a fistful of dollars.

Your property will now be sold at a public auction that is conducted by the trustee on behalf of the beneficiary (the lender). *And – unlike a judicial foreclosure, which allows for a further redemption period after the sale – there is no such opportunity afforded in this instance!* **Your home will be immediately awarded to the highest bidder, along with a trustee's deed to record the sale with the county recorder's office.**

If you're lucky – after the trustee disperses the funds to the lender, itself and any other lenders or lien holders that may have staked a claim against the property – **you *may* receive some leftover money for yourself, but don't count on it!**

On a slight positive note: **If the sale does not cover the outstanding fees owed to the lender,** *you cannot be sued by the lender for the remaining amount.* **However, any junior lien holders that remain unsatisfied may file a separate lawsuit to recover their moneys.**

Another situation worth mentioning is that *junior lien holders* (those who are lower on the totem pole as far as lien position – such as banks who offer home equity loans) *can initiate foreclosure even if the first (primary) lien holder is paid on time.* This doesn't happen as often, but it does happen – and, as odd as it sounds, **the first-position lien holder remains attached to the property through the trustee's auction…** *Which means that it's the new owner's problem, not yours!*

By the way, *property tax liens* – **regardless of when they were attached to your property** – *will supercede any other lien.* As you're probably well aware, the government always gets its share first!

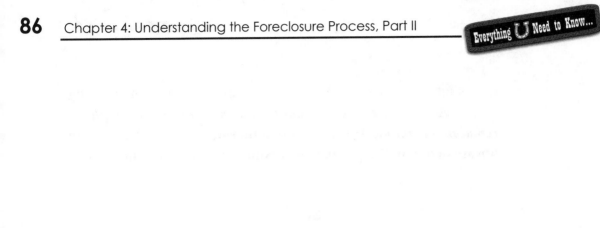

Understanding the Foreclosure Process, Part III: State by State

This Chapter Discusses:

★ **All 50 States - plus D.C. (in alphabetical order)**

I n case you haven't read **Chapters 3** and **4, we would suggest taking the time to review them to understand some of the basic steps and terminology before jumping ahead to the summary of your state's foreclosure procedures.** With that being said, this chapter is in fact *a collection of individual state summaries*.

Each state could easily take up an entire volume, *so we've done our best to assist you with a basic understanding of these intricate procedures...*

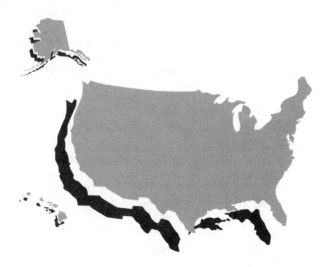

Alabama

Judicial Foreclosure:	Yes
Non-Judicial Foreclosure:	Yes
Security Instrument:	Deed of Trust or Mortgage
Approximate Time Frame:	30 to 60 days
Typical Foreclosure Process:	Non-Judicial enforcing Deed of Trust with a Power of Sale clause
Reinstatement Period:	The total past due amount owed plus additional fees and legal costs can be paid in full up until the day of the foreclosure sale unless the Deed of Trust or mortgage says otherwise.
Notification Requirements:	The property owner is not required to be notified either of the pending foreclosure due to default or of the foreclosure sale unless it is stated in the Deed of Trust or mortgage that they must be. However, notification of the foreclosure sale time, day, and place, as well as a description of the property and the terms of the sale, must be printed in a county newspaper (or an adjoining county's newspaper if the county in which the property is located does not have a newspaper) once a week for 3 consecutive weeks if the mortgage has a Power of Sale clause, or 4 weeks if there is no Power of Sale clause and a foreclosure lawsuit is not filed.
Judicial (No Power of Sale) Process:	The party foreclosing on the property either can file a lawsuit with the court to obtain a judgment of foreclosure, or can simply foreclose on the property by selling it. If they chose to forgo the lawsuit, they would simply have to publish a Notice of Foreclosure in the county newspaper for 4 weeks which must include a description of the property, the time, day, and place of the sale, as well as the terms of the sale. They are then free to sell the property on the date indicated to the highest bidder at the front door of the county courthouse. The property owner would have the right to redeem the property up to a year after the foreclosure sale and the lender would have the right to seek a deficiency judgment.
Non-Judicial (Power-of-Sale) Process:	The party foreclosing on the property must file a Notice of Sale which indicates the property is pending foreclosure. They then have to publish a Notice of Foreclosure in the county newspaper for 3 weeks. The foreclosure sale takes place by the sheriff between the hours of 11:00am and 4:00pm, usually at the front door of the county courthouse. The property owner would have the

	right to redeem the property up to a year after the foreclosure sale and the lender would have the right to seek a deficiency judgment.
Deficiency Judgment Rights:	A judgment can be obtained if the property is sold for less than the loan amount due in either a Judicial or Non-Judicial foreclosure. If a deed is turned over to the lender in lieu of foreclosure on the property, there is no right to a deficiency judgment.
Redemption Rights:	The total loan amount owed plus additional fees and legal costs can be paid in full within 12 months of the property's foreclosure sale in either a Judicial or Non-Judicial foreclosure. If a deed is turned over to the lender in lieu of foreclosure on the property, there is no right to redemption.
Investor Note:	Payment in full required at auction.

Everything U Need to Know...™

Alaska

Judicial Foreclosure:	Yes
Non-Judicial Foreclosure:	Yes
Security Instrument:	Deed of Trust or Mortgage
Approximate Time Frame:	90 days
Typical Foreclosure Process:	Non-Judicial enforcing Deed of Trust with a Power of Sale clause
Reinstatement Period:	The total past due amount owed plus additional fees and legal costs can be paid in full up until the day before the foreclosure sale unless the property owner has twice previously had a foreclosure proceeding initiated for the same property; then the trustee can refuse to allow the loan to be reinstated and may proceed with the foreclosure.
Notification Requirements:	The lender must file a Notice of Default, in the county where the property is located, indicating intent to sell the property. It must contain a number of items including the foreclosure sale date, time, and place as well as a description of the property. This filing can only occur after 30 days has past since the loan went into default and must also be at least 3 months before the date of the intended sale. A copy of this notice must be sent via certified mail, or delivered in person, to the homeowner within 10 days of its filing.
Judicial (No Power of Sale) Process:	The party foreclosing on the property must file a lawsuit with the court to obtain a judgment of foreclosure if there is no Power of Sale clause in the Deed of Trust. Once the court issues the judgment, the property is sold to the highest bidder at the front door of the county courthouse. The property owner would not have the right to redeem the property but the lender would have the right to seek a deficiency judgment.
Non-Judicial (Power of Sale) Process:	The lender must file a Notice of Default indicating intent to sell the property after the loan has been in default for at least 30 days but also 3 months before the intended sale. A copy of this notice must be sent via certified mail, or delivered in person, to the homeowner within 10 days of its filing. The foreclosure sale usually takes place at the county courthouse. The property owner would not have the right to redeem the property unless the Deed of Trust allows for it and the lender would not have the right to seek a deficiency judgment.

Deficiency Judgment Rights: A judgment can be obtained if the property is sold for less than the loan amount due in a Judicial foreclosure only.

Redemption Rights: None, unless the Deed of Trust grants specific rights.

Investor Note: Payment in full required at auction.

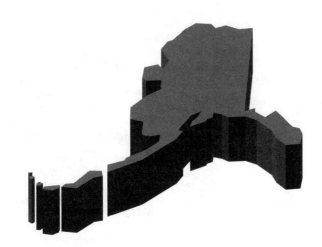

Arizona

Judicial Foreclosure:	Yes
Non-Judicial Foreclosure:	Yes
Security Instrument:	Deed of Trust or Mortgage
Approximate Time Frame:	120 days
Typical Foreclosure Process:	Non-Judicial enforcing Deed of Trust with a Power of Sale clause
Reinstatement Period:	The total past due amount owed plus additional fees and legal costs can be paid in full up until 5:00pm the day before the foreclosure sale.
Notification Requirements:	The trustee must file a Notice of Foreclosure Sale with the county recorder's office. It must contain a number of items including the foreclosure sale date, time, and place as well as a description of the property. A copy of this notice must be sent via certified mail to the homeowner within 5 days of its filing. Notification of the foreclosure sale must be printed in a county newspaper once a week for 4 consecutive weeks. The foreclosure sale cannot take place before 10 days from the date of the last notice publication. Alternatively, the trustee can post the Notice of Foreclosure Sale on the property at least 20 days before the intended foreclosure sale date and at the county courthouse.
Judicial (No Power of Sale) Process:	The party foreclosing on the property must file a lawsuit with the court to obtain a judgment of foreclosure if there is no Power of Sale clause in the Deed of Trust. Once the court issues the judgment, the property is sold to the highest bidder at the front door of the county courthouse. The property owner would not have the right to redeem the property but the lender would have the right to seek a deficiency judgment.
Non-Judicial (Power of Sale) Process:	The party foreclosing on the property must publish a Notice of Foreclosure Sale in the county where the property is located once a week for 4 consecutive weeks. They then have to post notification of the sale on the property and at the county recorder's office within 20 days of the sale date. The foreclosure sale takes place by the trustee between the hours of 9:00am and 5:00pm on any day other than a Saturday or legal holiday at the location specified. The property owner would not have the right to redeem the property and the lender would have limited rights to seek a deficiency judgment.

Deficiency Judgment Rights: A judgment can be obtained if the property is sold for less than the loan amount due in either a Judicial or Non-Judicial foreclosure. The judgment amount is limited to the difference between the amount owed and the fair market value. However, if the property is less than 2 and 1/2 acres and was used as a single one- or two-family home, the lender is not allowed to seek a deficiency judgment.

Redemption Rights: None

Investor Note: $10,000 deposit required prior to auction, payment in full required by 5:00pm the day after the auction unless that day is a Saturday or legal holiday.

Arkansas

Judicial Foreclosure:	Yes
Non-Judicial Foreclosure:	Yes
Security Instrument:	Deed of Trust or Mortgage
Approximate Time Frame:	120 days
Typical Foreclosure Process:	Non-Judicial enforcing Deed of Trust with a Power of Sale clause
Reinstatement Period:	The total past due amount owed plus additional fees and legal costs can be paid in full up until the day of the foreclosure sale in a Non-Judicial foreclosure. In a Judicial foreclosure, the court will determine the amount in default and will provide the homeowner with a short period of time in which to pay that amount to avoid foreclosure.
Notification Requirements:	The lender must file a Notice of Default, in the county where the property is located, indicating intent to sell the property. It must contain a number of items including the foreclosure sale date, time, and place as well as a description of the property. A copy of this notice must be sent via certified mail to the homeowner within 30 days of its filing. There must be 60 days between the filing and further action. Notification of the foreclosure sale must be printed in a county newspaper once a week for 4 consecutive weeks. The foreclosure sale must take place within 10 days from the date of the last notice publication. Notification must also be posted by a third party at the courthouse as well as on the Internet.
Judicial (No Power of Sale) Process:	The party foreclosing on the property must file a lawsuit with the court to obtain a judgment of foreclosure if there is no Power of Sale clause in the Deed of Trust or if a Mortgage is used. Once the court issues the judgment, the property is sold to the highest bidder at the county courthouse. The property must sell for at least 2/3 of its appraised value at auction. If it does not, the property must be put up for auction again within 12 months and the highest bid at the second auction will be the sales price even if it is not 2/3 of the appraised value. The property owner would have the right to redeem the property but the lender would not have the right to seek a deficiency judgment.
Non-Judicial (Power of Sale) Process:	The lender must file a Notice of Default, in the county where the property is located, indicating intent to sell the property. A copy must be sent via certified mail to the homeowner within 30 days of its filing and there must be

60 days between the filing and further action. Notification must then be printed in a county newspaper once a week for 4 consecutive weeks and the foreclosure sale must take place within 10 days from the date of the last notice publication. Notification must also be posted by a third party at the courthouse as well as on the Internet. The foreclosure sale takes place by the trustee between the hours of 10:00am and 4:00pm, either at the county courthouse or the property, and cannot take place on any Saturday, Sunday or legal holiday. The property must sell for at least 2/3 of its appraised value at auction. If it does not, the property must be put up for auction again within 12 months and the highest bid at the second auction will be the sales price even if it is not 2/3 of the appraised value. The property owner would not have the right to redeem the property but the lender would have the right to seek a deficiency judgment.

Deficiency Judgment Rights:
A judgment can be obtained if the property is sold for less than the loan amount due in a Non-Judicial foreclosure only. The judgment can only be for the difference between the amount due and the fair market value or the amount due and the amount of the sale, whichever is less.

Redemption Rights:
The total loan amount owed plus additional fees and legal costs can be paid in full within 12 months of the property's foreclosure sale in a Judicial foreclosure only unless the Deed of Trust or mortgage says otherwise.

Investor Note:
Payment in full required within 10 days of the auction.

California

Judicial Foreclosure:	Yes
Non-Judicial Foreclosure:	Yes
Security Instrument:	Deed of Trust or Mortgage
Approximate Time Frame:	120 days
Typical Foreclosure Process:	Non-Judicial enforcing Deed of Trust with a Power of Sale clause
Reinstatement Period:	The total past due amount owed plus additional fees and legal costs can be paid in full up until 5 days before the day of the foreclosure sale.
Notification Requirements:	The lender must file a Notice of Default, in the county where the property is located, indicating intent to sell the property. There must be 60 days between the filing and further action. A Notice of Foreclosure Sale must then be recorded with the county at least 21 days before the sale. It must contain a number of items including the foreclosure sale date, time, and place as well as a description of the property. A copy of this notice must be sent to the homeowner via certified mail, posted on the property as well as in one public place, and also printed in a county newspaper once a week for 3 consecutive weeks. The foreclosure sale cannot take place before 21 days after the first publication.
Judicial (No Power of Sale) Process:	The party foreclosing on the property must file a lawsuit with the court to obtain a judgment of foreclosure if there is no Power of Sale clause in the Deed of Trust. Once the court issues the judgment, the property is sold to the highest bidder at the county courthouse. The property owner would have a limited right to redeem the property and the lender would have the right to seek a deficiency judgment.
Non-Judicial (Power of Sale) Process:	The lender must file a Notice of Default, in the county where the property is located, indicating intent to sell the property. There must be 60 days between the filing and further action. A Notice of Foreclosure Sale must then be recorded with the county at least 21 days before the sale. A copy of this notice is sent to the homeowner via certified mail, posted on the property as well as in one public place, and also printed in a county newspaper once a week for 3 consecutive weeks. The foreclosure sale takes place by the trustee between the hours of 9:00am and 5:00pm on any business day at the location specified. The homeowner cannot redeem the property and the lender cannot seek a deficiency judgment.

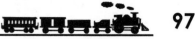
Deficiency Judgment Rights: A judgment can be obtained if the property is sold for less than the loan amount due in a Judicial foreclosure only.

Redemption Rights: The total loan amount owed plus additional fees and legal costs can be paid in full within 12 months of the property's foreclosure sale in a Judicial foreclosure only. However, if the lender is the highest bidder with a full price bid, redemption is limited to 3 months. Also, if a deficiency judgment is waived or otherwise prohibited, there is no right to redemption.

Investor Note: Payment in full required at auction.

Colorado

Judicial Foreclosure:	Yes
Non-Judicial Foreclosure:	Yes
Security Instrument:	Deed of Trust or Mortgage
Approximate Time Frame:	60 to 70 days
Typical Foreclosure Process:	Non-Judicial enforcing Deed of Trust with a Power of Sale clause
Reinstatement Period:	The total past due amount owed plus additional fees and legal costs can be paid in full up until 12:00pm the day before the foreclosure sale as long as the homeowner files an Intent to Cure with the trustee at least 15 days before the scheduled date of foreclosure sale.
Notification Requirements:	The lender must first file a Notice of Election and Demand with the public trustee in the property's county. The trustee must then record the notice with the recorder's office within 10 business days of the filing. It must contain a number of items including the foreclosure sale date, time, and place as well as a description of the property. Notification of the foreclosure sale must be printed in a county newspaper once a week for 5 consecutive weeks. A copy of this notice must be sent to the homeowner within 10 days of its initial publication. The homeowner must also be sent instructions on how to redeem the property at least 21 days before the sale date from the trustee. In addition, a Notice of Sale must be recorded in the property's county.
Judicial (No Power of Sale) Process:	The party foreclosing on the property must file a lawsuit with the court to obtain a judgment of foreclosure if there is no Power of Sale clause in the Deed of Trust. Once the court issues the judgment, the property is sold to the highest bidder at the county courthouse. The property owner would have the right to redeem the property and the lender would have the right to seek a deficiency judgment.
Non-Judicial (Power of Sale) Process:	The lender must first file a Notice of Election and Demand with the public trustee in the property's county. The trustee must then record the notice with the recorder's office within 10 business days of the filing. Notification of the foreclosure sale must be printed in a county newspaper once a week for 5 consecutive weeks. A copy of this notice must be sent to the homeowner within 10 days of its initial publication. The

homeowner must also be sent instructions on how to redeem the property at least 21 days before the sale date from the trustee. In addition, a Notice of Sale must be recorded in the property's county. The foreclosure sale must occur within 45 to 60 days from the date of the filing of the Notice of Election and Demand. However, prior to the sale a hearing must take place so that it can be determined if the foreclosure process is legally sound. This hearing may be foregone if the homeowner does not respond to the notification of this hearing. The property owner would have the right to redeem the property and the lender would have the right to seek a deficiency judgment.

Deficiency Judgment Rights: A judgment can be obtained if the property is sold for less than the loan amount due in both a Judicial and Non-Judicial foreclosure.

Redemption Rights: The total loan amount owed plus additional fees and legal costs can be paid in full within 75 days of the property's foreclosure sale in either a Judicial or Non-Judicial foreclosure if the homeowner files an Intent to Redeem at least 15 days before the end of the redemption period. After filing, the homeowner would receive the payoff amount required to redeem the property within 8 days.

Investor Note: Payment in full required at auction.

Connecticut

Judicial Foreclosure:	Yes
Non-Judicial Foreclosure:	No
Security Instrument:	Mortgage only
Approximate Time Frame:	60 to 75 days
Typical Foreclosure Process:	Judicial (strict) enforcing Mortgage without a Power of Sale clause
Reinstatement Period:	The total past due amount owed plus additional fees and legal costs can be paid in full up until the day before the sale if the foreclosure is processed with a Decree of Sale. Otherwise, if the foreclosure is a strict Judicial foreclosure, the judge will provide a specific time frame during which the homeowner can pay the amount in full to stop the foreclosure.
Notification Requirements:	The lender must file a lis pendens with the court and a complaint for foreclosure is served to the homeowner at least 12 days before they are scheduled to appear in court.
Judicial (No Power of Sale) Process:	The Judicial process can be either a strict foreclosure or by Decree of Sale. In a strict foreclosure the lender has a complaint for foreclosure served on the homeowner at least 12 days before the court date. At the court hearing the lender simply needs to prove there is a default on the mortgage and the court conveys title to the property immediately to the lender. There is no sale or auction involved. The property owner is usually granted a short period of time by the court to redeem the property and the lender would have the right to seek a deficiency judgment. In a foreclosure by Decree of Sale the lender has a complaint for foreclosure served on the homeowner at least 12 days before the court date. At the court hearing, if the lender proves there is a default on the mortgage, the court sets the date of the foreclosure sale, and appoints a committee to handle the sale. The foreclosure sale takes place usually at the property on a Saturday. The property owner is usually granted a short period of time by the court to redeem the property and the lender would have the right to seek a deficiency judgment.
Non-Judicial (Power of Sale) Process:	None
Deficiency Judgment Rights:	A judgment can be obtained if the property is sold at auction for less than the loan amount due.

Redemption Rights:	None, however, the court may grant a short period of time in which the total loan amount owed plus additional fees and legal costs can be paid in full in order to redeem the property.
Investor Note:	10% deposit required from winning bidder, payment in full required within 30 days.

Everything U Need to Know...

Delaware

Judicial Foreclosure:	Yes
Non-Judicial Foreclosure:	No
Security Instrument:	Mortgage only
Approximate Time Frame:	90 to 180 days
Typical Foreclosure Process:	Judicial enforcing Mortgage without a Power of Sale clause
Reinstatement Period:	The total past due amount owed plus additional fees and legal costs can be paid in full up until the court makes a ruling on the foreclosure.
Notification Requirements:	The lender must file a lis pendens with the court and a complaint for foreclosure is served to the homeowner. The homeowner must then appear in court within 20 days to prove they are not in default.
Judicial (No Power of Sale) Process:	The lender must file a lis pendens with the court and a complaint for foreclosure is served to the homeowner. The homeowner must then appear in court within 20 days to prove they are not in default. However, the lender does not have to prove the default. If the court rules that the homeowner is in default, the sheriff will be ordered to sell the property. A Notice of Sale must be posted at the property as well as at other public places throughout the county at least 14 days before the date of the foreclosure sale. The foreclosure sale takes place by the sheriff usually at the county courthouse or the property. The sale would then have to be confirmed by the court. The property owner might have a limited right to redeem the property and the lender would have the right to seek a deficiency judgment.
Non-Judicial (Power of Sale) Process:	None
Deficiency Judgment Rights:	A judgment can be obtained if the property is sold for less than the loan amount due.
Redemption Rights:	None, however, the judge may allow the total loan amount owed plus additional fees and legal costs to be paid in full between the date of the foreclosure sale and the date of the sale's confirmation by the court, which is usually 30 days later.
Investor Note:	Payment in full required at auction.

District of Columbia

Judicial Foreclosure:	Yes
Non-Judicial Foreclosure:	Yes
Security Instrument:	Deed of Trust or Mortgage
Approximate Time Frame:	30 to 60 days
Typical Foreclosure Process:	Non-Judicial enforcing Deed of Trust with a Power of Sale clause
Reinstatement Period:	The total past due amount owed plus additional fees and legal costs can be paid in full up until the day of the foreclosure sale unless the Deed of Trust or mortgage says otherwise.
Notification Requirements:	The property owner is not required to be notified either of the pending foreclosure due to default or of the foreclosure sale unless it is stated in the Deed of Trust or mortgage that they must be. However, notification of the foreclosure sale time, day, and place, as well as a description of the property and the terms of the sale, must be printed in a county newspaper (or an adjoining county's newspaper if the county in which the property is located does not have a newspaper) once a week for 3 consecutive weeks if the mortgage has a Power of Sale clause, or 4 weeks if there is no Power of Sale clause and a foreclosure lawsuit is not filed.
Judicial (No Power of Sale) Process:	The party foreclosing on the property either can file a lawsuit with the court to obtain a judgment of foreclosure, or can simply foreclose on the property by selling it. If they chose to forgo the lawsuit, they would simply have to publish a Notice of Foreclosure in the county newspaper for 4 weeks which must include a description of the property, the time, day, and place of the sale, as well as the terms of the sale. They are then free to sell the property on the date indicated to the highest bidder at the front door of the county courthouse. The property owner would have the right to redeem the property up to a year after the foreclosure sale and the lender would have the right to seek a deficiency judgment.
Non-Judicial (Power of Sale) Process:	The party foreclosing on the property must file a Notice of Sale which indicates the property is pending foreclosure. They then have to publish a Notice of Foreclosure in the county newspaper for 3 weeks. The foreclosure sale takes place by the sheriff between the hours of 11:00am and 4:00pm, usually at the front door of the county courthouse. The property owner would have the

right to redeem the property up to a year after the foreclosure sale and the lender would have the right to seek a deficiency judgment.

Deficiency Judgment Rights:
A judgment can be obtained if the property is sold for less than the loan amount due in either a Judicial or Non-Judicial foreclosure. If a deed is turned over to the lender in lieu of foreclosure on the property, there is no right to a deficiency judgment.

Redemption Rights:
The total loan amount owed plus additional fees and legal costs can be paid in full within 12 months of the property's foreclosure sale in either a Judicial or Non-Judicial foreclosure. If a deed is turned over to the lender in lieu of foreclosure on the property, there is no right to redemption.

Investor Note:
Payment in full required at auction.

Everything U Need to Know...™

Florida

Judicial Foreclosure:	Yes
Non-Judicial Foreclosure:	No
Security Instrument:	Mortgage
Approximate Time Frame:	180 to 200 days
Typical Foreclosure Process:	Judicial enforcing Mortgage without a Power of Sale clause
Reinstatement Period:	The total past due amount owed plus additional fees and legal costs can be paid in full up until the day of the foreclosure sale.
Notification Requirements:	None
Judicial (No Power of Sale) Process:	The lender must file a foreclosure lawsuit with the court. The entire foreclosure process is then controlled by the court. The court sets all the procedures that are to be followed including whether or not notification of the sale is to be published in the newspaper and the specifications for conducting the foreclosure sale.
Non-Judicial (Power of Sale) Process:	None
Deficiency Judgment Rights:	A judgment can be obtained if the property is sold for less than the loan amount due.
Redemption Rights:	The court may allow the total loan amount owed plus additional fees and legal costs to be paid in full up until the court confirms the property's foreclosure sale, which is usually within 10 days of the sale.
Investor Note:	5% deposit required at time of auction, payment in full required by the end of the day.

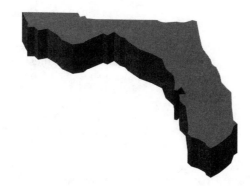

Georgia

Judicial Foreclosure:	Yes
Non-Judicial Foreclosure:	Yes
Security Instrument:	Security Deed or Mortgage
Approximate Time Frame:	60 to 90 days
Typical Foreclosure Process:	Non-Judicial enforcing Security Deed with a Power of Sale clause
Reinstatement Period:	None if a Non-Judicial process is used, unless the Security Deed or Mortgage specifically allows for the homeowner to be able to bring the loan current. However, the foreclosure process can be stopped if the entire loan balance is paid in full prior to the foreclosure sale. If a Judicial process is used, the homeowner is given 30 days to pay in full the amount indicated to be in default in the foreclosure petition filed with the court by the lender.
Notification Requirements:	A demand letter requesting payment in full of the total amount past due must be sent to the homeowner 10 days before official foreclosure proceedings can be started. If the past due amount is not paid, notification of the foreclosure sale must be printed in a county newspaper once a week for 4 consecutive weeks. A copy of this notice must be sent via certified mail to the homeowner at least 15 days before the foreclosure sale date.
Judicial (No Power of Sale) Process:	If the homeowner does not pay in full the amount indicated in the demand letter within 10 days, official foreclosure proceedings can be started. The party foreclosing on the property must file a lawsuit with the court to obtain a judgment of foreclosure if there is no Power of Sale clause in the Security Deed. The court will give the homeowner 30 days to pay the amount in default and, if they do not, then the court issues a foreclosure judgment. The property is then sold to the highest bidder at the county courthouse. The property owner would not have the right to redeem the property and the lender would have the right to seek a deficiency judgment.
Non-Judicial (Power of Sale) Process:	If the homeowner does not pay in full the amount indicated in the demand letter within 10 days, official foreclosure proceedings can be started. The party foreclosing on the property must publish a Notice of Foreclosure Sale in the county where the property is located once a week for 4 consecutive weeks. A copy

of this notice must be sent via certified mail to the homeowner at least 15 days before the foreclosure sale date. The foreclosure sale takes place by the trustee between the hours of 10:00am and 4:00pm on the first Tuesday of any month at the courthouse. The property owner would not have the right to redeem the property and the lender would have the right to seek a deficiency judgment.

Deficiency Judgment Rights: A judgment can be obtained if the property is sold for less than the loan amount due in either a Judicial or Non-Judicial foreclosure.

Redemption Rights: None

Investor Note: Payment in full required at auction.

Everything U Need to Know...

Hawaii

Judicial Foreclosure:	Yes
Non-Judicial Foreclosure:	Yes
Security Instrument:	Deed of Trust or Mortgage
Approximate Time Frame:	60 to 90 days
Typical Foreclosure Process:	Non-Judicial enforcing Deed of Trust with a Power of Sale clause
Reinstatement Period:	The total past due amount owed plus additional fees and legal costs can be paid in full up until 3 days before the foreclosure sale unless the lender and homeowner agree otherwise.
Notification Requirements:	Notification of the foreclosure sale must be printed in a county newspaper once a week for 3 consecutive weeks. The last publication cannot occur less than 14 days prior to the date of the foreclosure sale. A copy of this notice must be sent via certified mail to the homeowner or served on them in person at least 21 days before the foreclosure sale date.
Judicial (No Power of Sale) Process:	The party foreclosing on the property must file a lawsuit with the court to obtain a judgment of foreclosure if there is no Power of Sale clause in the Deed of Trust or Mortgage. A copy of the filing must be served on the homeowner and they have 20 days to respond to the court. If the homeowner does not respond, the court will find them in default. Once the court issues the judgment, the property is scheduled to be sold to the highest bidder at the county courthouse. The property owner would not have the right to redeem the property but the lender would have the right to seek a deficiency judgment.
Non-Judicial (Power of Sale) Process:	Notification of the foreclosure sale must be printed in a county newspaper once a week for 3 consecutive weeks with the last publication not to occur less than 14 days prior to the foreclosure sale. A copy of this notice must be sent via certified mail to the homeowner or served on them in person at least 21 days before the foreclosure sale date. The foreclosure sale takes place as specified in the notice. The property owner would not have the right to redeem the property and the lender would have the right to seek a deficiency judgment.
Deficiency Judgment Rights:	A judgment can be obtained if the property is sold for less than the loan amount due in either a Judicial or Non-Judicial foreclosure.

Redemption Rights:	None
Investor Note:	10% deposit required from winning bidder, payment in full required within 45 days.

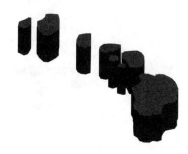

Idaho

Judicial Foreclosure:	Yes
Non-Judicial Foreclosure:	Yes
Security Instrument:	Deed of Trust or Mortgage
Approximate Time Frame:	150 days
Typical Foreclosure Process:	Non-Judicial enforcing Deed of Trust with a Power of Sale clause
Reinstatement Period:	The total past due amount owed plus additional fees and legal costs can be paid in full within 115 days of the filing of the Notice of Default with the court.
Notification Requirements:	The lender must file a Notice of Default indicating intent to sell the property. It must contain a number of items including the foreclosure sale date, time, and place as well as a description of the property. A copy of this notice must be personally served on the homeowner and/or the occupants of the property at least 120 days before the foreclosure sale. Notification of the default must also be printed in a county newspaper for 4 consecutive weeks. The foreclosure sale cannot take place less than 30 days from the date of the last notice publication.
Judicial (No Power of Sale) Process:	The party foreclosing on the property must file a lawsuit with the court to obtain a judgment of foreclosure if there is no Power of Sale clause in the Deed of Trust or if the property is larger than 40 acres. Once the court issues the judgment, the property is sold to the highest bidder at the county courthouse. The property owner would not have the right to redeem the property but the lender would have the right to seek a deficiency judgment.
Non-Judicial (Power of Sale) Process:	The lender must file a Notice of Default indicating intent to sell the property. A copy of this notice must be personally served on the homeowner and/or the occupants of the property at least 120 days before the foreclosure sale. Notification of the default must also be printed in a county newspaper for 4 consecutive weeks. The foreclosure sale cannot take place less than 30 days from the date of the last notice publication and usually takes place by the trustee between the hours of 9:00am and 4:00pm. The property owner would not have the right to redeem the property and the lender would have the right to seek a deficiency judgment.
Deficiency Judgment Rights:	A judgment can be obtained if the property is sold for less than the loan amount due in either a Judicial or Non-Judicial foreclosure.

Redemption Rights:	None
Investor Note:	Payment in full required at auction.

Illinois

Judicial Foreclosure:	Yes
Non-Judicial Foreclosure:	No
Security Instrument:	Mortgage only
Approximate Time Frame:	215 days
Typical Foreclosure Process:	Judicial enforcing Mortgage without a Power of Sale clause
Reinstatement Period:	The total past due amount owed plus additional fees and legal costs can be paid in full within 90 days of the filing of the foreclosure complaint. However, the right to reinstate the loan can only be exercised once in every 5 years. Also, if the foreclosure is consented to, and thus expedited, by the homeowner, there is no right to a reinstatement period.
Notification Requirements:	Notice of the lender's intent to foreclose must be given to the homeowner 30 days before a judgment of foreclosure can be issued.
Judicial (No Power of Sale) Process:	The lender must file a foreclosure lawsuit with the court and the entire foreclosure process is then controlled by the court. The court sets all the procedures that are to be followed including the specifications for conducting the foreclosure sale. Notice of the lender's intent to foreclose must be given to the homeowner 30 days before a judgment of foreclosure can be issued. If the total past due amount owed plus additional fees and legal costs are paid in full within 90 days of the filing of the foreclosure complaint, the loan can be reinstated and the foreclosure process stopped. Once the court issues the judgment of foreclosure, the property is sold by the sheriff to the highest bidder at the county courthouse. The total loan balance owed plus additional fees and legal costs can be paid in full within 7 months of the filing of the foreclosure complaint or 3 months from the issuance of a final foreclosure judgment, which ever is longer, and the sale cannot take place before this time is up. However, if the property is abandoned, the redemption period is shortened to 30 days from the date the foreclosure judgment is entered. Once the sale has occurred, there is no further right to redeem. The lender would have the right to seek a deficiency judgment unless a deed is turned over to the lender in lieu of foreclosure or if the foreclosure is consented to, and thus expedited, by the homeowner. If the homeowner is still occupying the property, they will be allowed to stay for 30 days after the date of the sale.

Non-Judicial (Power of Sale) Process: None

Deficiency Judgment Rights: A judgment can be obtained if the property is sold for less than the loan amount due in the Judicial foreclosure. If a deed is accepted by the lender in lieu of foreclosure on the property, there is no right to a deficiency judgment. Also, if the foreclosure is consented to, and thus expedited, by the homeowner, there is no right to a deficiency judgment.

Redemption Rights: The total loan balance owed plus additional fees and legal costs can be paid in full within 7 months of the filing of the foreclosure complaint or 3 months from the issuance of a final foreclosure judgment, whichever is longer. However, if the lender waives their right to seek a deficiency judgment, the redemption period is shortened to 60 days from the date the foreclosure judgment is entered. In addition, if the property is abandoned, this period is shortened to 30 days from the date the foreclosure judgment is entered. Also, if a deed is turned over to the lender in lieu of foreclosure on the property, there is no right to redemption. Also, if a deed is turned over to the lender in lieu of foreclosure or if the foreclosure is consented to, and thus expedited, by the homeowner, there is no right to redemption.

Investor Note: 10% deposit required at time of auction, payment in full required within 24 hours.

Indiana

Judicial Foreclosure:	Yes
Non-Judicial Foreclosure:	No
Security Instrument:	Mortgage only
Approximate Time Frame:	150 to 200 days
Typical Foreclosure Process:	Judicial enforcing Mortgage without a Power of Sale clause
Reinstatement Period:	The total past due amount owed plus additional fees and legal costs can be paid in full prior to the judgment of foreclosure being issued to stop the foreclosure process. Once the judgment has been entered, the total loan balance owed plus additional fees and legal costs can be paid in full before the day of the sale.
Notification Requirements:	Notice of the lender's foreclosure judgment must be given to the homeowner 3 months before a judgment of sale can be issued unless the property is abandoned; then the judgment of sale may be issued immediately. Once the judgment of sale is issued, notification of the foreclosure sale must be printed in a county newspaper once a week for 3 consecutive weeks. A copy of this notice must be served on the homeowner at the time of the first publication, posted in 3 different public places in the county, and at the door of the county courthouse. The foreclosure sale cannot take place before 30 days from the date of the first notice publication.
Judicial (No Power of Sale) Process:	The lender must first file a foreclosure lawsuit with the court. Notice of the lender's foreclosure judgment must be given to the homeowner 3 months before a judgment of sale can be issued. However, if the property is abandoned, the court can forego this waiting period. Once the court issues the judgment of sale, notification of the foreclosure sale must be printed in a county newspaper once a week for 3 consecutive weeks. A copy of this notice must be served on the homeowner at the time of the first publication, posted in 3 different public places in the county, and at the door of the county courthouse. The foreclosure sale cannot take place before 30 days from the date of the first notice publication. The property is then sold by the sheriff to the highest bidder between the hours of 10:00am and 4:00pm on any day other than a Sunday at the location specified. The total loan balance owed plus additional fees and legal costs can be paid in full before the day of the sale to stop the foreclosure process. Once the sale has occurred, there is no further right to redeem. The

lender would have the right to seek a deficiency judgment unless the foreclosure is consented to, and thus expedited, by the homeowner.

Non-Judicial (Power of Sale) Process: None

Deficiency Judgment Rights: A judgment can be obtained if the property is sold for less than the loan amount due in the Judicial foreclosure. However, if the homeowner consents to the foreclosure by waiving the time limit between the filing of the foreclosure suit and the sale, there is no right to a deficiency judgment.

Redemption Rights: None

Investor Note: Payment in full required at auction.

Iowa

Judicial Foreclosure:	Yes
Non-Judicial Foreclosure:	No
Security Instrument:	Deed of Trust or Mortgage
Approximate Time Frame:	150 to 180 days
Typical Foreclosure Process:	Judicial enforcing Mortgage without a Power of Sale clause
Reinstatement Period:	The total past due amount owed plus additional fees and legal costs can be paid in full during the time period set by the court.
Notification Requirements:	Notification of the foreclosure sale must be printed before the sale date in a county newspaper once a week for 2 weeks, the first of which must be at least 4 weeks before the date of the sale. If the homeowner is occupying the property, they must be personally served a copy of the notice at least 20 days before the scheduled sale date. Notification must also be posted in 2 public places as well as at the county courthouse.
Judicial (No Power of Sale) Process:	The lender must file a foreclosure lawsuit with the court and the entire foreclosure process is then controlled by the court. If the total past due amount owed plus additional fees and legal costs are paid in full within the period of time set by the court, the loan can be reinstated and the foreclosure process stopped. If not, the court issues a notice of sale and the property is scheduled to be sold. Notification of the foreclosure sale must be printed before the sale date in a county newspaper once a week for 2 weeks, the first of which must be at least 4 weeks before the date of the sale. The homeowner must be personally served a copy of the notice at least 20 days before the scheduled sale date if they are occupying the property. A copy of the notification must also be posted in 2 public places as well as at the county courthouse. The foreclosure sale takes place by the sheriff between the hours of 9:00am and 4:00pm, usually at the county courthouse. The total loan balance owed plus additional fees and legal costs can be paid in full within 12 months of the property's foreclosure sale in order to redeem the property. The redemption period is shortened to 6 months if the lender waives their right to seek a deficiency judgment and to only 60 days if the property is abandoned. The lender would have the right to seek a deficiency judgment unless this right is waived in order to shorten the redemption period.

Non-Judicial (Power of Sale) Process: None

Deficiency Judgment Rights: A judgment can be obtained if the property is sold for less than the loan amount due in the Judicial foreclosure. This right may be waived by the lender in order to shorten or eliminate the redemption period.

Redemption Rights: The total loan amount owed plus additional fees and legal costs can be paid in full within 12 months of the property's foreclosure sale in the Judicial foreclosure. If the lender waives their right to seek a deficiency judgment, the redemption period is shortened to 6 months. In addition, if the property is abandoned, the redemption period may be shortened to only 60 days by the court.

Investor Note: Payment in full with sealed bid required at auction.

Kansas

Judicial Foreclosure:	Yes
Non-Judicial Foreclosure:	Yes
Security Instrument:	Mortgage only
Approximate Time Frame:	120 to 140 days
Typical Foreclosure Process:	Judicial enforcing Mortgage without a Power of Sale clause
Reinstatement Period:	The total past due amount owed plus additional fees and legal costs can be paid in full up to 10 days after the court has ruled that the homeowner is in default.
Notification Requirements:	Notification of the foreclosure sale must be printed in a county newspaper once a week for 3 consecutive weeks, the last of which cannot be less than 7 days before the sale date or more than 14 days before the sale date. A copy of this notice must be sent to the homeowner within 5 days of the first publication.
Judicial (No Power of Sale) Process:	The lender must file a foreclosure lawsuit with the court and the entire foreclosure process is then controlled by the court. A copy of the foreclosure filing is either personally served on the homeowner or sent by mail to them. The homeowner will then have at least 20 days to respond to the court. If they do not respond, the court will rule them to be in default and they will be given 10 days to pay the total amount past due plus any additional fees and costs. If this amount is not paid, the court issues a notice of sale and the property is scheduled to be sold. Notification of the foreclosure sale must be printed in a county newspaper once a week for 3 consecutive weeks. The foreclosure sale must take place between 7 and 14 days after the last publication. A copy of this notice must be sent to the homeowner within 5 days of the first publication. The foreclosure sale takes place by the sheriff, usually at the county courthouse. The total loan balance owed plus additional fees and legal costs can be paid in full within 12 months of the property's foreclosure sale if only less than 1/3 of the market value of the property remains unpaid. This period is shortened to 3 months if the homeowner has paid only up to 1/3 of the loan's principal balance. If the property is abandoned, the court may shorten or eliminate the redemption period. The lender would have the right to seek a deficiency judgment.
Non-Judicial (Power of Sale) Process:	None

Deficiency Judgment Rights: A judgment can be obtained if the property is sold for less than the loan amount due in the Judicial foreclosure.

Redemption Rights: The total loan balance owed plus additional fees and legal costs can be paid in full within 12 months of the property's foreclosure sale if only less than 1/3 of the market value of the property remains unpaid. However, if the homeowner has paid only less than 1/3 of the loan's principal balance the redemption period is shortened to 3 months. If the property is abandoned, the redemption period may be shortened or eliminated at the discretion of the court.

Investor Note: Payment in full required at auction.

Kentucky

Judicial Foreclosure:	Yes
Non-Judicial Foreclosure:	Yes
Security Instrument:	Mortgage only
Approximate Time Frame:	150 days
Typical Foreclosure Process:	Judicial enforcing Mortgage without a Power of Sale clause
Reinstatement Period:	The total past due amount owed plus additional fees and legal costs can be paid in full during the time period set by the court, at least 21 days, to stop the foreclosure process.
Notification Requirements:	Notice of the lender's foreclosure complaint must be given to the homeowner 21 days before a judgment of sale can be issued. Once the judgment of sale is issued, notification of the foreclosure sale must be printed in a county newspaper once a week for 3 consecutive weeks.
Judicial (No Power of Sale) Process:	The lender must file a foreclosure lawsuit with the court and the entire foreclosure process is then controlled by the court. A copy of the foreclosure filing is personally served on the homeowner if they can be located. The homeowner will then have 21 days to respond to the court and pay the total amount past due plus any additional fees and costs to stop the foreclosure process. If the court finds them to be in default, the court issues a notice of sale and the property is scheduled to be sold. Notification of the foreclosure sale must be printed in a county newspaper once a week for 3 consecutive weeks. Prior to the foreclosure sale an appraisal of the property must be conducted. The foreclosure sale takes place by a master commissioner, who is a court official, usually at the county courthouse. If the foreclosure sales price is less than 2/3 of the appraised value of the property, the total amount paid by the highest bidder plus additional fees and legal costs can be paid in full by the homeowner within 12 months of the sale to redeem the property. This right to redeem may be sold to a third party. The lender would have the right to seek a deficiency judgment if the homeowner was personally served with the foreclosure complaint and/or did not respond to the complaint within 21 days.
Non-Judicial (Power of Sale) Process:	None

Deficiency Judgment Rights: A judgment can be obtained if the property is sold for less than the loan amount due only if the homeowner was personally served with the foreclosure complaint and/or did not respond to the complaint within 21 days.

Redemption Rights: The total amount paid by the highest bidder plus additional fees and legal costs can be paid in full within 12 months of the property's foreclosure sale only if the foreclosure sales price is less than 2/3 of the appraised value of the property. The right to redeem may be sold to a third party.

Investor Note: Payment in full required at auction or bond may be posted to allow payment in installments.

Louisiana

Judicial Foreclosure:	Yes
Non-Judicial Foreclosure:	No
Security Instrument:	Mortgage only
Approximate Time Frame:	60 to 180 days
Typical Foreclosure Process:	Judicial enforcing Mortgage with a Confession of Judgment clause using the Executory Process
Reinstatement Period:	The total past due amount owed plus additional fees and legal costs can be paid in full within 3 days of the issuing of the Notice of Default to stop the foreclosure process if the lender is using the Executory Process. If the lender is using the Ordinary Process to foreclose, this time period will be set by the court.
Notification Requirements:	If the lender is using the Executory Process to foreclose, notice of the default must be given to the homeowner 3 days before a judgment of sale can be issued. Once the judgment of sale is issued, notification of the foreclosure sale must be printed in a county newspaper once a week for 30 days. Notification will be dictated by the court if the Ordinary Process is used to foreclose.
Judicial (No Power of Sale) Process:	The party foreclosing on the property either can file a traditional lawsuit with the court in an Ordinary Process to obtain a judgment of foreclosure, or can use the Executory Process, which expedites the foreclosure by a number of months, if a Confession of Judgment is included in the mortgage. If the lender is using the Executory Process to foreclose, a notice of default is given to the homeowner 3 days before a judgment of sale can be issued. The total past due amount owed plus additional fees and legal costs can be paid in full within these 3 days to stop the foreclosure process. Once the judgment of sale is issued, notification of the foreclosure sale is printed in a county newspaper once a week for 30 days. The property will then be sold on the date indicated to the highest bidder. Reinstatement rights as well as notification will be dictated by the court if the Ordinary Process is used. The property owner would have no right to redeem the property and the lender would have the right to seek a deficiency judgment in either judicial process.
Non-Judicial (Power of Sale) Process:	None
Deficiency Judgment Rights:	A judgment can be obtained if the property is sold for less than the loan amount due in the Judicial foreclosure.

Redemption Rights:	None
Investor Note:	Payment in full required at auction. In some cases a 10% deposit may be accepted with payment in full required within 30 days.

Maine

Judicial Foreclosure:	Yes
Non-Judicial Foreclosure:	No
Security Instrument:	Mortgage only
Approximate Time Frame:	425 days
Typical Foreclosure Process:	Strict judicial process enforcing Mortgage without a Power of Sale clause
Reinstatement Period:	None
Notification Requirements:	Notification of the foreclosure sale must be printed in a county newspaper once a week for 3 consecutive weeks, the first of which must be published not more than 90 days from the expiration of the redemption period. A copy of the notice must also be mailed to the homeowner within 30 days of the sale date. The foreclosure sale must take place within 30 to 45 days from the date of the first publication of the notice.
Judicial (No Power of Sale) Process:	The party foreclosing on the property either can file a lawsuit with the court to obtain a judgment of foreclosure, or can use the Strict Foreclosure process to expedite the foreclosure. A Strict Foreclosure allows the lender to either simply take possession of the property or file for an immediate order of sale once the homeowner has not met a condition of the mortgage. In either case, the total loan amount owed plus additional fees and legal costs can be paid in full to redeem the property within 12 months of the initial filing or repossession. This redemption period must be over in order for the actual foreclosure sale to take place. If the lender chooses to forgo the lawsuit, they would simply have to publish a Notice of Foreclosure Sale in a county newspaper once a week for 3 consecutive weeks, the first of which must be published not more than 90 days from the expiration of the redemption period. A copy of the notice must also be mailed to the homeowner within 30 days of the sale date. The foreclosure sale must take place within 30 to 45 days from the date of the first publication of the notice. They are then free to sell the property on the date indicated to the highest bidder at either the county courthouse or the property. The homeowner would not have any further right to redeem the property and the lender would have the right to seek a deficiency judgment.
Non-Judicial (Power of Sale) Process:	None

Deficiency Judgment Rights:
A judgment can be obtained if the property is sold for less than the loan amount due in the Judicial foreclosure. The judgment amount is limited to the difference between the amount owed and the fair market value of the property as determined by an appraisal.

Redemption Rights:
The total loan amount owed plus additional fees and legal costs can be paid in full within 12 months of either the initial filing of the foreclosure lawsuit or the repossession of the property by the lender in a Judicial foreclosure. The redemption period must be over in order for the foreclosure sale to take place and after the sale there is no further right to redemption.

Investor Note:
A deposit, the amount of which is indicated in the notice of sale, may be accepted with payment in full required within 30 days.

Everything U Need to Know...

Maryland

Judicial Foreclosure:	Yes
Non-Judicial Foreclosure:	Yes
Security Instrument:	Deed of Trust or Mortgage
Approximate Time Frame:	90 to 100 days
Typical Foreclosure Process:	Non-Judicial enforcing Mortgage with a Power of Sale clause
Reinstatement Period:	If the lender uses a judicial process for foreclosure and files a lawsuit to obtain a decree of sale, the court will rule on the amount in default and will provide the homeowner with a short period of time to pay that amount in full. Otherwise, no reinstatement period is required.
Notification Requirements:	The homeowner is not required to be notified of the pending foreclosure due to default. Notification of the foreclosure sale must be printed in a county newspaper once a week for 3 consecutive weeks. The foreclosure sale cannot take place within 15 days of the first publication, and must be within 1 week of the last notice publication. A copy of this notice must be sent to the homeowner via certified registered mail not less than 10 or more than 30 days before the sale date.
Judicial (No Power of Sale) Process:	The Judicial process can be either a strict foreclosure or by an Assent to Decree. In a strict foreclosure the lender files a complaint for foreclosure on the homeowner. At the court hearing the lender simply needs to prove there is a default on the mortgage and the court then rules on the amount that is in default. The court will give the homeowner a short period of time to pay the full amount in default and, if they do not, then the court issues a foreclosure judgment and the sale date will be set. When the loan documents include an Assent to Decree clause, the lender files a complaint for foreclosure with the court, however, a court hearing is not required. The lender can simply move forward with the foreclosure sale. In either process, notification of the foreclosure sale must be printed in a county newspaper once a week for 3 consecutive weeks. The foreclosure sale cannot take place within 15 days of the first publication, and must be within 1 week of the last notice publication. A copy of this notice must also be sent to the homeowner via certified registered mail between 10 and 30 days before the sale date. The foreclosure sale takes place by a licensed auctioneer, usually at the county courthouse.

Non-Judicial (Power of Sale) Process:	The party foreclosing on the property must file a foreclosure order with the court but no hearing is required to proceed with foreclosure. They then have to publish a notification of the foreclosure sale in a county newspaper once a week for 3 consecutive weeks. The foreclosure sale cannot take place within 15 days of the first publication, and must occur within 1 week of the last notice publication. A copy of this notice must also be sent to the homeowner via certified registered mail between 10 and 30 days before the sale date. The foreclosure sale takes place by a licensed auctioneer, usually at the county courthouse. The homeowner would not have the right to redeem the property and the lender would have the right to seek a deficiency judgment.
Deficiency Judgment Rights:	A judgment can be obtained if the property is sold for less than the loan amount due in either a Judicial or Non-Judicial foreclosure.
Redemption Rights:	None
Investor Note:	Payment in full required at auction.

Massachusetts

Judicial Foreclosure:	Yes
Non-Judicial Foreclosure:	Yes
Security Instrument:	Mortgage only
Approximate Time Frame:	75 to 90 days
Typical Foreclosure Process:	Non-Judicial enforcing Mortgage with a Power of Sale clause
Reinstatement Period:	None. If a Judicial process is used, however, the homeowner can stop the foreclosure process if the entire loan balance plus additional fees and legal costs are paid in full within 2 months of the foreclosure judgment.
Notification Requirements:	The lender must file a Notice of Foreclosure Sale with the county recorder's office. It must contain a number of items including the foreclosure sale date, time, and place as well as a description of the property. A copy of this notice must be sent via certified mail to the homeowner at least 14 days before the scheduled date of sale. Notification of the foreclosure sale must be printed in a county newspaper once a week for 3 consecutive weeks. The first date of publication must be at least 21 days before the foreclosure sale date.
Judicial (No Power of Sale) Process:	The party foreclosing on the property must file a lawsuit with the court to obtain a judgment of foreclosure if there is no Power of Sale clause in the Mortgage. Once the court issues the judgment, the property can be sold to the highest bidder at the property. The homeowner would have the right to redeem the property and the lender would have the right to seek a deficiency judgment. Otherwise the lender may maintain possession of the property for 3 years, at which point the homeowner would no longer have the right to redeem it, and the lender would still have the right to seek a deficiency judgment.
Non-Judicial (Power of Sale) Process:	The party foreclosing on the property must file a Notice of Foreclosure Sale in the county where the property is located. It must contain a number of items including the foreclosure sale date, time, and place as well as a description of the property. Notification of the sale must be printed in a county newspaper once a week for 3 consecutive weeks. The sale date must be at least 21 days after the first date of publication. Also, a copy of this notice must be sent via certified mail to the homeowner at least 14 days before the foreclosure sale.

The sale then takes place by an auctioneer at the date and location specified. The property owner would not have the right to redeem the property and the lender would have the right to seek a deficiency judgment. However, if the lender seeks a deficiency judgment and later recovers the judgment, the homeowner could file a redemption suit within one year.

Deficiency Judgment Rights: A judgment can be obtained if the property is sold for less than the loan amount due in either a Judicial or Non-Judicial foreclosure. However, if the lender obtains a deficiency judgment against the homeowner, and later recovers the judgment, the homeowner would have 1 year from that recovery to file a suit for redemption even if the 3-year limit is expired.

Redemption Rights: None if the foreclosure is done through the Power of Sale process. If the foreclosure is done through the Judicial process, the homeowner will have 3 years, from the date of notification of the lender's intent to seek possession of the property for foreclosure, to redeem the property if the lender maintains possession of the property for those 3 years. Also, if the lender obtains a deficiency judgment against the homeowner, and later recovers the judgment, the homeowner would have 1 year from that recovery to file a suit for redemption even if the 3-year limit is expired.

Investor Note: Deposit, as indicated in foreclosure sale notice, required from winning bidder, and payment in full required within 30 days.

Michigan

Judicial Foreclosure:	Yes
Non-Judicial Foreclosure:	Yes
Security Instrument:	Deed of Trust or Mortgage
Approximate Time Frame:	60 days
Typical Foreclosure Process:	Non-Judicial enforcing Deed of Trust with a Power of Sale clause
Reinstatement Period:	The right to reinstate the loan is dictated in the loan documents for a Non-Judicial foreclosure. In a Judicial foreclosure, the court will determine the amount in default and will provide the homeowner with a short period of time in which to pay that amount to avoid foreclosure.
Notification Requirements:	The property owner is not required to be notified of the pending foreclosure due to default unless it is stated in the Deed of Trust or Mortgage that they must be. However, notification of the foreclosure sale time, day, and place, as well as a description of the property, the terms of the sale, and the length of the redemption period, must be printed in a county newspaper once a week for 4 consecutive weeks. A copy of this notice must also be posted on the property within 15 days of the first publication date.
Judicial (No Power of Sale) Process:	The lender must file a foreclosure lawsuit with the court and the entire foreclosure process is then controlled by the court. If the total past due amount owed plus additional fees and legal costs are paid in full within the period of time set by the court, the loan can be reinstated and the foreclosure process stopped. If not, the court issues a notice of sale and the property is scheduled to be sold. Notification of the foreclosure sale time, day, and place, as well as a description of the property, the terms of the sale, and the length of the redemption period, must be printed in a county newspaper once a week for 4 consecutive weeks. A copy of this notice must also be posted on the property within 15 days of the first publication date. The foreclosure sale takes place by the sheriff between the hours of 9:00am and 4:00pm at the county courthouse. The total loan balance owed plus additional fees and legal costs can be paid in full after the property's foreclosure sale in order to redeem the property; however, the time frame in which this can take place varies from 30 days to 1 year based on certain property and loan characteristics.

Non-Judicial (Power of Sale) Process: The party foreclosing on the property must publish a notification of the foreclosure sale time, day, and place, as well as a description of the property, the terms of the sale, and the length of the redemption period, in a county newspaper once a week for 4 consecutive weeks. A copy of this notice must also be posted on the property within 15 days of the first publication date. The foreclosure sale takes place by the trustee or the sheriff between the hours of 9:00am and 4:00pm at the county courthouse. The total loan balance owed plus additional fees and legal costs can be paid in full after the property's foreclosure sale in order to redeem the property; however, the time frame in which this can take place varies from 30 days to 1 year based on certain property and loan characteristics. The lender would have the right to seek a deficiency judgment.

Deficiency Judgment Rights: A judgment can be obtained if the property is sold for less than the loan amount due in either a Judicial or Non-Judicial foreclosure.

Redemption Rights: The total loan balance owed plus additional fees and legal costs can be paid in full within 6 months of the property's foreclosure sale if the property is residential with no more than 4 units, 3 acres or less, and if the homeowner had paid only less than 1/3 of the loan's principal balance at the time of foreclosure. If the property is residential with no more than 4 units and abandoned, the redemption period is shortened to 3 months. However, if the property is residential with no more than 4 units, and if the homeowner had paid only less than 1/3 of the loan's principal balance at the time of foreclosure, the redemption period is shortened to 1 month. Otherwise, the redemption period is 1 year from the date of the foreclosure sale unless the property is abandoned, in which case the redemption period is only 30 days or until all notification requirements are met, whichever is later.

Investor Note: Payment in full required at auction.

Minnesota

Judicial Foreclosure:	Yes
Non-Judicial Foreclosure:	Yes
Security Instrument:	Mortgage only
Approximate Time Frame:	60 to 90 days
Typical Foreclosure Process:	Non-Judicial enforcing Mortgage with a Power of Sale clause
Reinstatement Period:	None
Notification Requirements:	The lender must have their attorney file a Power of Attorney with the county recorder's office which indicates a foreclosure sale is pending. The attorney then publishes a Notice of Foreclosure Sale in a county newspaper once a week for 6 consecutive weeks. A copy of this notice must also be served on the homeowner at least 4 weeks before the scheduled date of sale, 8 weeks if a homestead property.
Judicial (No Power of Sale) Process:	The lender must file a foreclosure lawsuit with the court and the entire foreclosure process is then controlled by the court. Once the court rules there is a default, a notice of foreclosure is issued and the property is scheduled to be sold. The foreclosure sale takes place by the sheriff between the hours of 8:00am and sundown, usually at the sheriff's office. The total loan balance owed plus additional fees and legal costs can be paid in full after the property's foreclosure sale in order to redeem the property; however, the time frame in which this can take place varies from 5 weeks to 1 year based on certain property and loan characteristics. The lender would have the right to seek a deficiency judgment.
Non-Judicial (Power of Sale) Process:	The lender's attorney files a Power of Attorney with the county recorder's office which indicates a foreclosure sale is pending. The attorney then publishes a Notice of Foreclosure Sale in a county newspaper once a week for 6 consecutive weeks. A copy of this notice must also be served on the homeowner at least 4 weeks before the scheduled date of sale, 8 weeks if a homestead property. The foreclosure sale takes place by the sheriff between the hours of 8:00am and sundown, usually at the sheriff's office. The total loan balance owed plus additional fees and legal costs can be paid in full after the property's foreclosure sale in order to redeem the property; however, the time frame in which this can take place varies from 5 weeks to 1

year based on certain property and loan characteristics. The lender would have the right to seek a deficiency judgment.

Deficiency Judgment Rights: A judgment can be obtained if the property is sold for less than the loan amount due in either a Judicial or Non-Judicial foreclosure. The judgment amount is limited to the difference between the amount owed and the fair market value.

Redemption Rights: The total loan balance owed plus additional fees and legal costs can be paid in full within 6 months of the property's foreclosure sale. However, the redemption period is extended to 12 months if any of the following apply: the property exceeds 40 acres, or less than 2/3 of the loan's principal balance remains unpaid, or the property is more than 10 acres and the mortgage was executed before July 1, 1987, or the property is more than 10 but less than 40 acres and was in agricultural use. If the property is abandoned, the redemption period may be shortened to 5 weeks by the court.

Investor Note: Payment in full required at auction.

Mississippi

Judicial Foreclosure:	Yes
Non-Judicial Foreclosure:	Yes
Security Instrument:	Deed of Trust or Mortgage
Approximate Time Frame:	60 to 90 days
Typical Foreclosure Process:	Non-Judicial enforcing Mortgage with a Power of Sale clause
Reinstatement Period:	The total past due amount owed plus additional fees and legal costs can be paid in full at any time prior to the foreclosure sale.
Notification Requirements:	The trustee must file a Notice of Sale with the county clerk. It must contain a number of items including the foreclosure sale date, time, and place as well as a description of the property. A copy of this notification must be posted at the door of the courthouse as well as printed in a county newspaper once a week for 3 consecutive weeks.
Judicial (No Power of Sale) Process:	The party foreclosing on the property must file a lawsuit with the court to obtain a judgment of foreclosure if there is no Power of Sale clause in the loan documents. Once the court issues the judgment, the property is scheduled to be sold. The foreclosure sale takes place by the sheriff between the hours of 11:00am and 4:00pm, usually at the county courthouse. The property owner would not have the right to redeem the property and the lender would have the right to seek a deficiency judgment.
Non-Judicial (Power of Sale) Process:	The party foreclosing on the property must file a Notice of Sale which indicates the property is pending foreclosure. A copy of this notification must be posted at the door of the courthouse as well as printed in a county newspaper once a week for 3 consecutive weeks. The foreclosure sale takes place by the sheriff between the hours of 11:00am and 4:00pm, usually at the county courthouse. The property owner would not have the right to redeem the property and the lender would have the right to seek a deficiency judgment.
Deficiency Judgment Rights:	A judgment can be obtained if the property is sold for less than the loan amount due in either a Judicial or Non-Judicial foreclosure.
Redemption Rights:	None
Investor Note:	Payment in full required at auction.

Missouri

Judicial Foreclosure:	Yes
Non-Judicial Foreclosure:	Yes
Security Instrument:	Deed of Trust or Mortgage
Approximate Time Frame:	60 to 90 days
Typical Foreclosure Process:	Non-Judicial enforcing Deed of Trust with a Power of Sale clause
Reinstatement Period:	The total past due amount owed plus additional fees and legal costs can be paid in full before the foreclosure sale.
Notification Requirements:	The trustee must publish a Notice of Foreclosure Sale in a county newspaper once a week, on the same day every week, for 4 consecutive weeks if the property is located in a city with a population less than 50,000. The foreclosure sale cannot take place more than a week from the date of the last notice publication. However, if the property is located in a city with a population of 50,000 or more, the notice must be published at least 20 times in a daily newspaper including on the day of the sale. In either case, a copy of this notice must also be sent via certified or registered mail to the homeowner within 20 days of the date of the foreclosure sale.
Judicial (No Power of Sale) Process:	The party foreclosing on the property must file a lawsuit with the court to obtain a judgment of foreclosure if there is no Power of Sale clause in the loan documents. Once the court issues the judgment, the property is scheduled to be sold. The foreclosure sale takes place by the trustee between the hours of 9:00am and 5:00pm, usually at the county courthouse. The property owner would have a limited right to redeem the property and the lender would not have the right to seek a deficiency judgment.
Non-Judicial (Power-of-Sale) Process:	The party foreclosing on the property must publish a Notice of Foreclosure Sale in a county newspaper once a week, on the same day every week, for 4 consecutive weeks if the property is located in a city with a population less than 50,000. The last publication must be no more than a week before the sale date. However, if the property is located in a city with a population of 50,000 or more, the notice must be published at least 20 times in a daily newspaper including on the day of the sale. Within 20 days of the date of the foreclosure sale, a copy of this notice must also be sent via certified or registered mail to the homeowner. The property owner

would have a limited right to redeem the property and the lender would not have the right to seek a deficiency judgment.

Deficiency Judgment Rights: None

Redemption Rights: If the highest bidder at the auction is the lender and the homeowner gives notice at the foreclosure sale, or 10 days prior to the sale, and then posts a bond within 20 days of the sale, the property may be redeemed. The total loan amount owed plus additional fees and legal costs can then be paid in full within 12 months of the property's foreclosure sale in either a Judicial or Non-Judicial foreclosure.

Investor Note: Payment in full required at auction.

Montana

Judicial Foreclosure:	Yes
Non-Judicial Foreclosure:	Yes
Security Instrument:	Trust Indenture or Mortgage
Approximate Time Frame:	140 to 150 days
Typical Foreclosure Process:	Non-Judicial enforcing Deed of Trust with a Power of Sale clause
Reinstatement Period:	The total past due amount owed plus additional fees and legal costs can be paid in full any time up until the foreclosure sale.
Notification Requirements:	The lender must file a Notice of Sale with the county clerk at least 120 days before the foreclosure sale. It must contain a number of items including the foreclosure sale date, time, and place as well as a description of the property. A copy of this notice must be sent via certified or registered mail to the homeowner also at least 120 days before the sale date. Notification of the foreclosure sale must be printed in a county newspaper once a week for 3 consecutive weeks. Alternatively, if there is no county newspaper, the notice may be posted in at least 3 public places. The foreclosure sale cannot take place before 20 days from the date of the last notice publication or posting. Also, the Notice of Sale must be posted on the property at least 20 days before the intended foreclosure sale date.
Judicial (No Power of Sale) Process:	The party foreclosing on the property must file a lawsuit with the court to obtain a judgment of foreclosure if there is no Power of Sale clause in the Security Deed. The court may give the homeowner a limited period of time to pay the amount in default and, if they do not, then the court issues a foreclosure judgment. The property is then sold to the highest bidder at the county courthouse between the hours of 9:00am and 4:00pm. The property owner may be given the right to redeem the property by the court and the lender would have the right to seek a deficiency judgment.
Non-Judicial (Power-of-Sale) Process:	The party foreclosing on the property must file a Notice of Sale with the county clerk at least 120 days before the foreclosure sale. Also, a copy of this notice must be sent via certified or registered mail to the homeowner at least 120 days before the sale. Notification of the foreclosure sale must be printed in a county newspaper once a week for 3 consecutive weeks, the last of which must be at least 20 days before the sale date. A copy of

the Notice of Sale must be posted on the property at least 20 days before the intended foreclosure sale date. The foreclosure sale takes place by the trustee between the hours of 9:00am and 4:00pm, usually at the county courthouse. The property owner would not have the right to redeem the property and the lender would not have the right to seek a deficiency judgment.

Deficiency Judgment Rights: A judgment can be obtained if the property is sold for less than the loan amount due in a Judicial foreclosure only.

Redemption Rights: None, unless the court allows for a redemption period in a Judicial foreclosure.

Investor Note: Payment in full required at auction.

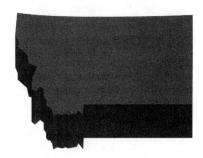

Nebraska

Judicial Foreclosure:	Yes
Non-Judicial Foreclosure:	Yes
Security Instrument:	Deed of Trust or Mortgage
Approximate Time Frame:	90 to 120 days
Typical Foreclosure Process:	Non-Judicial enforcing Deed of Trust with a Power of Sale clause
Reinstatement Period:	The total past due amount owed plus additional fees and legal costs can be paid in full up until the foreclosure sale in a Non-Judicial foreclosure. In a Judicial foreclosure, the court will determine the amount in default and will provide the homeowner with a short period of time, usually 20 days, in which to pay that amount to avoid foreclosure.
Notification Requirements:	In a Non-Judicial foreclosure, the lender must file a Notice of Default, in the county where the property is located, indicating intent to sell the property. A copy of this notice must be sent via certified mail to the homeowner within 10 days of its filing. Notification of Foreclosure Sale, which may or may not be included with the Notice of Default, must be sent to the homeowner 20 days before the scheduled date of sale. Also, notification of the foreclosure sale must be printed in a county newspaper once a week for 5 consecutive weeks. The foreclosure sale must take place between 10 and 30 days from the date of the last notice publication. In a Judicial foreclosure, the Notice of Sale must be printed in a county newspaper once a week for 4 consecutive weeks. The foreclosure sale must take place between 10 and 30 days from the date of the last notice publication. A copy of the notice must also be posted at the courthouse as well as in 5 other public places.
Judicial (No Power of Sale) Process:	The party foreclosing on the property must file a lawsuit with the court to obtain a judgment of foreclosure if there is no Power of Sale clause in the loan documents. Once the court issues the judgment, the property is scheduled to be sold to the highest bidder at the county courthouse. The homeowner may request a delay of up to 9 months before the court issues the Order of Sale once the ruling of judgment has been entered. If a delay is not requested, the Order of Sale is issued 20 days after the judgment. At any time before the Order of Sale, the homeowner may pay the amount in default plus any additional fees and legal costs to stop the

foreclosure process. However, the legal rulings would remain in effect in the event that the homeowner goes into default again. A Notice of Sale must be printed in a county newspaper once a week for 4 consecutive weeks and the sale must take place between 10 and 30 days from the date of the last notice publication. A copy of the notice must also be posted at the courthouse as well as in 5 other public places. The property owner might be granted a very limited right to redeem the property and the lender would have the right to seek a deficiency judgment.

Non-Judicial (Power of Sale) Process: The party foreclosing on the property must file a Notice of Default, in the county where the property is located, indicating intent to sell the property. Within 10 days of this filing, a copy of this notice must be sent via certified mail to the homeowner. Notification of Foreclosure Sale must be sent to the homeowner 20 days before the scheduled date of sale. Also, notification of the foreclosure sale must be printed in a county newspaper once a week for 5 consecutive weeks. The foreclosure sale must take place between 10 and 30 days from the date of the last notice publication. The foreclosure sale takes place by the trustee at the time and place indicated in the sale notice. The property owner would not have the right to redeem the property and the lender would have the right to seek a deficiency judgment.

Deficiency Judgment Rights: A judgment can be obtained if the property is sold for less than the loan amount due in either a Judicial or Non-Judicial foreclosure. The judgment amount is limited to the difference between the amount owed and the fair market value.

Redemption Rights: None. However, the judge may allow the total loan amount owed plus additional fees and legal costs to be paid in full between the date of the foreclosure sale and the date of the sale's confirmation by the court, which is usually 2 - 3 weeks later, in a Judicial foreclosure.

Investor Note: Payment in full required at auction.

Nevada

Judicial Foreclosure:	Yes
Non-Judicial Foreclosure:	Yes
Security Instrument:	Deed of Trust or Mortgage
Approximate Time Frame:	120 days
Typical Foreclosure Process:	Non-Judicial enforcing Deed of Trust with a Power of Sale clause
Reinstatement Period:	The total past due amount owed plus additional fees and legal costs can be paid in full within 35 days of the Notice of Default if the homeowner files an Intend to Cure at least 15 days before the foreclosure sale date and pays the amount due by 12:00pm the day before the foreclosure sale.
Notification Requirements:	The lender must file a Notice of Default and Election to Sell with the county recorder's office and send a copy via certified mail to the homeowner. The homeowner would then have 35 days to cure the default by paying the past due amount. Then, no more than 3 months after the Notice of Default is filed, a Notice of Foreclosure Sale must be printed in a county newspaper once a week for 3 consecutive weeks. This notice must also be posted in 3 public places for 20 consecutive days as well as sent via certified mail, or personally served, to the homeowner.
Judicial (No Power of Sale) Process:	The party foreclosing on the property must file a lawsuit with the court to obtain a judgment of foreclosure if there is no Power of Sale clause in the loan documents. Once the court issues the judgment, the property is sold to the highest bidder between the hours of 9:00am and 5:00pm at the county courthouse. The property owner would have the right to redeem the property up to 12 months after the foreclosure sale and the lender would have the right to seek a deficiency judgment.
Non-Judicial (Power of Sale) Process:	The party foreclosing on the property must file a Notice of Default and Election to Sell with the county recorder's office and send a copy via certified mail to the homeowner. No earlier than 3 months after the Notice of Default is filed, a Notice of Foreclosure Sale must be printed in a county newspaper once a week for 3 consecutive weeks. This notice must also be posted in 3 public places for 20 consecutive days and sent via certified mail, or personally served, to the homeowner. The foreclosure sale takes place by the trustee between the hours of 9:00am and 5:00pm, usually at the

	courthouse. The homeowner would not have the right to redeem the property but the lender would have the right to seek a deficiency judgment.
Deficiency Judgment Rights:	A judgment can be obtained if the property is sold for less than the loan amount due in either a Judicial or Non-Judicial foreclosure.
Redemption Rights:	The total loan amount owed plus additional fees and legal costs can be paid in full up to 12 months from the property's foreclosure sale in a Judicial foreclosure only.
Investor Note:	Payment in full required at auction.

New Hampshire

Judicial Foreclosure:	Yes
Non-Judicial Foreclosure:	Yes
Security Instrument:	Mortgage only
Approximate Time Frame:	60 to 70 days
Typical Foreclosure Process:	Non-Judicial enforcing Mortgage with a Power of Sale clause
Reinstatement Period:	The total past due amount owed plus additional fees and legal costs can be paid in full up until the foreclosure sale in a Non-Judicial foreclosure. In a Judicial foreclosure, the court will determine the amount in default and will provide the homeowner with a short period of time in which to pay that amount to avoid foreclosure.
Notification Requirements:	The lender must file a Notice of Sale with the county recorder's office. It must contain a number of items including the foreclosure sale date, time, and place as well as a description of the property. A copy of this notice must be sent via certified or registered mail to the homeowner at least 25 days before the foreclosure sale date. Notification of the foreclosure sale must also be printed in a county newspaper once a week for 3 consecutive weeks. The foreclosure sale cannot take place less than 20 days from the date of the initial publication.
Judicial (No Power of Sale) Process:	The party foreclosing on the property must file a lawsuit with the court to obtain a judgment of foreclosure if there is no Power of Sale clause in the Mortgage. The court will give the homeowner a short period of time in which to pay the amount in default and, if they do not, then the court issues a foreclosure judgment. Once the court issues the judgment, the property is sold to the highest bidder, usually at the property. The property owner would not have the right to redeem the property but the lender would have the right to seek a deficiency judgment.
Non-Judicial (Power of Sale) Process:	The party foreclosing on the property must file a Notice of Sale with the county recorder's office. A copy of this notice must be sent via certified or registered mail to the homeowner at least 25 days before the foreclosure sale date. Notification of the foreclosure sale must also be printed in a county newspaper once a week for 3 consecutive weeks. The date of initial publication cannot be less than 20 days from the date of the

	foreclosure sale. The foreclosure sale takes place by the trustee or an auctioneer at the property. The property owner would not have the right to redeem the property but the lender would have the right to seek a deficiency judgment.
Deficiency Judgment Rights:	A judgment can be obtained if the property is sold for less than the loan amount due in either a Judicial or Non-Judicial foreclosure.
Redemption Rights:	None
Investor Note:	Payment in full required within 60 days of the auction.

New Jersey

Judicial Foreclosure:	Yes
Non-Judicial Foreclosure:	Yes
Security Instrument:	Mortgage only
Approximate Time Frame:	250 days
Typical Foreclosure Process:	Judicial enforcing Mortgage without a Power of Sale clause
Reinstatement Period:	The total past due amount owed plus additional fees and legal costs can be paid in full during the time period set by the court, usually 35 days.
Notification Requirements:	The lender must file a lis pendens with the court and a complaint for foreclosure is served to the homeowner. The homeowner is then given 35 days to answer the complaint. If there is no response, the default will be entered and in 45 days a final judgment of foreclosure will be ruled on and the sale date can be scheduled. The homeowner must be notified of the foreclosure sale date at least 10 days before it is to occur. A copy of the foreclosure notice must also be posted in the county offices, on the property, and in 2 county newspapers.
Judicial (No Power of Sale) Process:	The party foreclosing on the property must file a lis pendens with the court and a complaint for foreclosure is served to the homeowner. The homeowner then has 35 days to file an answer to the complaint. If there is no response from the homeowner, the court will enter the default and in 45 days a final judgment of foreclosure will be ruled on. Once the court issues the judgment, the property can be scheduled to be sold. The home-owner must be notified of the foreclosure sale date at least 10 days beforehand. A copy of the foreclosure notice must also be posted in the county offices, on the property, and in 2 county newspapers. The foreclosure sale takes place by the sheriff usually at the county courthouse or the property. The property owner has a limited right to redeem the property and the lender would have the right to seek a deficiency judgment.
Non-Judicial (Power of Sale) Process:	None
Deficiency Judgment Rights:	A judgment can be obtained if the property is sold for less than the loan amount due in the Judicial foreclosure. The judgment amount is limited to the difference between the amount owed and the fair market value. However, if the lender obtains a deficiency judgment against the homeowner, and later

recovers the judgment, the homeowner would have 6 months from that recovery to file a suit for redemption.

Redemption Rights: The total loan amount owed plus additional fees and legal costs can then be paid in full within 10 days of the property's foreclosure sale in the Judicial foreclosure.

Investor Note: 20% deposit required at auction, payment in full required within 30 days of auction.

New Mexico

Judicial Foreclosure:	Yes
Non-Judicial Foreclosure:	Yes
Security Instrument:	Either Deed of Trust or Mortgage; however a Deed of Trust is rare and must be specifically consented to by the homeowner
Approximate Time Frame:	120 to 180 days
Typical Foreclosure Process:	Judicial enforcing Mortgage without a Power of Sale clause
Reinstatement Period:	The total past due amount owed plus additional fees and legal costs can be paid in full within 30 days of the initial filing of the foreclosure complaint.
Notification Requirements:	In a Judicial foreclosure, the lender initially files a foreclosure complaint and the homeowner has 30 days to respond. Once the court issues a Notice of Sale, a copy of the notice must be printed in a county newspaper once a week for at least 4 consecutive weeks, and the foreclosure sale date must be at least 30 days for the Notice of Sale.
Judicial (No Power of Sale) Process:	The lender must file a foreclosure complaint with the court and the homeowner will then have 30 days to respond to the court and/or pay the amount in default. If they do not respond, the court will rule them to be in default and issue a Notice of Sale. A copy of the notice must be printed in a county newspaper once a week for at least 4 consecutive weeks. The foreclosure sale date cannot be less than 30 days from the date of the court's issuance of the Notice of Sale. The foreclosure sale takes place by the sheriff between the hours of 9:00am and sundown at a public place. The property owner would have the right to redeem the property and the lender would have the right to seek a deficiency judgment.
Non-Judicial (Power of Sale) Process:	Foreclosing on a residential property in a Non-Judicial process is extremely rare as both the lender and the homeowner would have to initially consent to having a Deed of Trust, which limits deficiency rights.
Deficiency Judgment Rights:	A judgment can be obtained if the property is sold for less than the loan amount due in a Judicial foreclosure only.
Redemption Rights:	The total loan amount owed plus additional fees and legal costs can then be paid in full within 9 months of the property's foreclosure sale in a Judicial foreclosure.

Investor Note:

Payment in full required at auction and winning bid must be at least 2/3 of the appraised value of the property.

New York

Judicial Foreclosure:	Yes
Non-Judicial Foreclosure:	Yes
Security Instrument:	Mortgage only
Approximate Time Frame:	120 to 180 days
Typical Foreclosure Process:	Judicial enforcing Mortgage without a Power of Sale clause
Reinstatement Period:	At any time before the court issues a judgment for sale, the homeowner may pay the amount in default plus any additional fees and legal costs to stop the foreclosure process. This amount may be paid any time after the judgment but before the actual sale; however, the legal rulings would remain in effect in the event that the homeowner goes into default again.
Notification Requirements:	In a Judicial foreclosure, the lender initially files a foreclosure complaint and the homeowner has 20 days to respond. Once the court rules to allow the property to be sold, the Notice of Sale must be printed in a county newspaper once a week for at least 4 consecutive weeks.
Judicial (No Power of Sale) Process:	The lender must file a foreclosure complaint with the court and the homeowner will then have 20 days to respond to the court. If they do not respond, the court will rule them to be in default and issue a judgment of foreclosure. The court will then determine the amount in default or appoint a referee to issue a report to the court determining the amount. The Order of Sale is issued after the judgment and determination of the amount in default which can take many months. Once the court issues the order, the property is scheduled to be sold by the sheriff or referee to the highest bidder, usually at the courthouse. A Notice of Sale must be printed in a county newspaper once a week for at least 4 consecutive weeks. At any time before the actual sale, the homeowner may pay the amount in default plus any additional fees and legal costs to stop the foreclosure process. Finally, the court must confirm the sale. The property owner would not have the right to redeem the property but the lender would have the right to seek a deficiency judgment.
Non-Judicial (Power of Sale) Process:	The Non-Judicial process is very rarely used and the statutes governing the process have been repealed effective July 1, 2009.

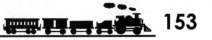

Deficiency Judgment Rights: A judgment can be obtained if the property is sold for less than the loan amount due in both Judicial and Non-Judicial foreclosures.

Redemption Rights: None

Investor Note: 10% deposit required at auction, and payment in full required within 30 days of auction.

North Carolina

Judicial Foreclosure:	Yes
Non-Judicial Foreclosure:	Yes
Security Instrument:	Deed of Trust or Mortgage
Approximate Time Frame:	90 to 120 days
Typical Foreclosure Process:	Non-Judicial enforcing Mortgage with a Power of Sale clause
Reinstatement Period:	None
Notification Requirements:	Before a Power of Sale foreclosure can occur, a preliminary hearing must occur. Notification of the hearing, as well as the total amount in default, must be sent to the homeowner via certified registered mail, or personally served on them, at least 10 days before the hearing. The county clerk determines at the hearing if the foreclosure sale can take place. Notification of the foreclosure sale must be printed in a county newspaper once a week for at least 2 consecutive weeks, and at least 7 days apart. The foreclosure sale must take place within 10 days of the last publication. A copy of this notice must be posted at the courthouse and sent to the homeowner via regular mail not less than 20 days before the sale date.
Judicial (No Power of Sale) Process:	The party foreclosing on the property must file a lawsuit with the court to obtain a judgment of foreclosure if there is no Power of Sale clause in the loan documents. Once the court issues the judgment, the property is scheduled to be sold. The foreclosure sale takes place, usually at the courthouse, between the hours of 10:00am and 4:00pm, on any day other than a Sunday, legal holiday, or when the courthouse is closed. The property owner would have a limited right to redeem the property and the lender would have the right to seek a deficiency judgment.
Non-Judicial (Power of Sale) Process:	The party foreclosing on the property must file a Notice of Hearing in the county where the property is located before a Power of Sale foreclosure can take place. Notification of the hearing, as well as the total amount in default, must be sent to the homeowner via certified registered mail, or personally served on them, at least 10 days before the hearing. At the preliminary hearing, the county clerk determines if the foreclosure sale can occur. Notification of the foreclosure sale must be printed in a county newspaper once a week for at least 2 consecutive weeks, at least 7 days apart. The last

publication must be within 10 days of the foreclosure sale date. A copy of this notice must also be posted at the courthouse and sent to the homeowner via regular mail, not less than 20 days before the sale date. The foreclosure sale takes place by the trustee, usually at the courthouse, between the hours of 10:00am and 4:00pm, on any day other than a Sunday, legal holiday, or when the courthouse is closed. The property owner would have a limited right to redeem the property and the lender would have the right to seek a deficiency judgment.

Deficiency Judgment Rights:

A judgment can be obtained if the property is sold for less than the loan amount due in either a Judicial or Non-Judicial foreclosure. However, the homeowner can seek to have the deficiency limited to the difference between the amount owed and the fair market value.

Redemption Rights:

The total loan balance owed plus additional fees and legal costs can be paid in full within 10 days of the property's foreclosure sale, or until the upset bid process is completed.

Investor Note:

Deposit, amount as stated in loan documents, or no more than 5% or at least $750 if loan documents do not stipulate amount, required from winning bidder, payment in full required within 30 days. North Carolina has a unique upset bid process in which a person other than the winning bidder can submit a bid, up to 10 days after the foreclosure sale, that is 5%, or at least $750, more than the winning bid and become the winning bidder. Anyone else, including the original winning bidder, then has another 10 days to submit a bid that is at least 5% or $750 higher than the upset bid to become the winning bidder, and this continues until there are no additional upset bids.

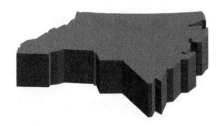

North Dakota

Judicial Foreclosure:	Yes
Non-Judicial Foreclosure:	No
Security Instrument:	Mortgage only
Approximate Time Frame:	90 days
Typical Foreclosure Process:	Judicial enforcing Mortgage without a Power of Sale clause
Reinstatement Period:	The total past due amount owed plus additional fees and legal costs can be paid in full within 30 days of the Notice of Foreclosure being served.
Notification Requirements:	The lender must send a Notice of Foreclosure via certified registered mail, or have it personally served, to the homeowner at least 30 days, and not more than 90, before the foreclosure suit is filed. It must contain a number of items including the amount in default as well as a description of the property.
Judicial (No Power of Sale) Process:	The party foreclosing on the property must send a Notice of Foreclosure via certified registered mail to the homeowner, or have it personally served on them, at least 30 days, but not more than 90 days, before a foreclosure suit can be filed. The homeowner then has 30 days from the date of the Notice of Foreclosure being served to pay the amount in default and stop the foreclosure process. Once the reinstatement period is over, the foreclosure lawsuit is filed with the court to obtain a Decree of Foreclosure. Once the court issues the judgment, the property is scheduled to be sold. The foreclosure sale takes place, usually at the courthouse, by the sheriff. The property owner would have the right to redeem the property and the lender would have limited rights to seek a deficiency judgment.
Non-Judicial (Power of Sale) Process:	None
Deficiency Judgment Rights:	A judgment cannot be obtained if the property is residential with 4 or less units and 40 or less acres. A judgment can be obtained for all other residential property types if sold for less than the loan amount due in the Judicial foreclosure. In that case, the judgment is limited to the difference between the property's appraised value and the loan amount due.
Redemption Rights:	The total loan balance owed plus additional fees and legal costs can be paid in full within 60 days of a residential property's foreclosure sale. This time period

is extended to 1 year from the filing of the court summons for agricultural property.

Investor Note: Payment in full required at auction.

Ohio

Judicial Foreclosure:	Yes
Non-Judicial Foreclosure:	No
Security Instrument:	Mortgage only
Approximate Time Frame:	150 to 180 days
Typical Foreclosure Process:	Judicial enforcing Mortgage without a Power of Sale clause
Reinstatement Period:	None; however, the court may allow a short period of time to pay the total past due amount owed plus additional fees and legal costs.
Notification Requirements:	The lender must file a foreclosure lawsuit with the court and the homeowner then has 28 days to respond to the court. Once the foreclosure judgment has been issued, notification of the foreclosure sale must be printed in a county newspaper once a week, on the same day, for 3 consecutive weeks. The first printing must be at least 30 days before the sale.
Judicial (No Power of Sale) Process:	The lender must file a foreclosure lawsuit with the court and the entire foreclosure process is then controlled by the court. The homeowner will then have 28 days to respond to the court. If they do not respond, the court will rule them to be in default and they will be given a short period of time to pay the total amount past due plus any additional fees and costs. If this amount is not paid, the court issues a Foreclosure Decree and the property is scheduled to be sold. Additionally, the court then orders 3 appraisals to be performed by separate parties to determine the value of the property. Notification of the foreclosure sale must be printed in a county newspaper once a week, on the same day, for 3 consecutive weeks, with the first printing being at least 30 days prior to the sale date. The homeowner is not required to receive a copy of the foreclosure sale notice. The foreclosure sale takes place by the sheriff, usually at the county courthouse, and the starting bid must not be less than 2/3 of the appraised value of the property. Finally, the sale then has to be confirmed by the court. The homeowner would have the right to redeem the property only up until the court confirms the sale and the lender would have the right to seek a deficiency judgment.
Non-Judicial (Power of Sale) Process:	None

Deficiency Judgment Rights: A judgment can be obtained if the property is sold for less than the loan amount due in the Judicial foreclosure.

Redemption Rights: The total loan amount owed plus additional fees and legal costs can be paid in full until the property's foreclosure sale is confirmed by the court in the Judicial foreclosure.

Investor Note: Payment in full required at auction.

Oklahoma

Judicial Foreclosure:	Yes
Non-Judicial Foreclosure:	Yes
Security Instrument:	Mortgage only
Approximate Time Frame:	90 days
Typical Foreclosure Process:	Non-Judicial enforcing Mortgage with a Power of Sale clause
Reinstatement Period:	The total past due amount owed plus additional fees and legal costs can be paid in full within 35 days of the lender sending the homeowner notification of their intent to foreclose. However, if the property is homestead property and in the last 24 months foreclosure proceedings have been initiated 4 other times, then this preliminary notice of intent is not required. For all other property, this notice is not required if foreclosure has been started 3 times in the past 24 months.
Notification Requirements:	The lender must send via certified mail to the homeowner notification of their intent to foreclose 35 days before proceeding with the sale. Within 10 days of the expiration of this reinstatement period, Notice of Sale must then be recorded with the county. A copy of this notice must be personally served to the homeowner no less than 30 days before the sale date. Notification of the foreclosure sale must also be printed in a county newspaper once a week for 4 consecutive weeks. The first printing must be at least 30 days before the sale.
Judicial (No Power of Sale) Process:	The party foreclosing on the property must file a lawsuit with the court to obtain a judgment of foreclosure if there is no Power of Sale clause in the Mortgage. Once the court issues the judgment, the property is scheduled to be sold to the highest bidder. The foreclosure sale takes place between the hours of 9:00am and 5:00pm, usually at the county courthouse or the property, on any day but a Sunday or legal holiday. The property owner would not have the right to redeem the property but the lender would have limited rights to seek a deficiency judgment.
Non-Judicial (Power of Sale) Process:	The party foreclosing on the property must send notification to the homeowner, via certified mail, of their intent to foreclose 35 days before proceeding with the sale. Notice of Sale must then be recorded with the county within 10 days of the expiration of this reinstatement period. A copy of the notice must be personally served to the homeowner at least 30 days

before the sale. Notification of the foreclosure sale must also be printed in a county newspaper once a week for 4 consecutive weeks with the first printing being at least 30 days before the sale date. If the property is homestead, the homeowner can send notice via certified mail to the lender at least 10 days before the foreclosure sale electing to have a judicial foreclosure. Otherwise, the foreclosure sale takes place between the hours of 9:00am and 5:00pm, usually at the county courthouse or the property, on any day but Sunday or legal holidays. The property owner would not have the right to redeem the property but the lender would have limited rights to seek a deficiency judgment. If the property is homestead, the lender can be prevented from seeking a judgment if the homeowner sends notice to them, via certified mail, that the property is homestead and they elect against a deficiency judgment.

Deficiency Judgment Rights:

A judgment can be obtained in both Judicial and Non-Judicial foreclosures if the property is sold for less than the loan amount due if the property is not homestead. If the property is homestead, the homeowner can send via certified mail a notice to the lender electing against a deficiency judgment because the property is homestead. Otherwise, the judgment can be limited to the difference between the property's fair market value and the loan amount due if the homeowner requests and proves the value is higher than the sale price at the judgment hearing.

Redemption Rights:

None

Investor Note:

10% deposit required within 24 hours of the auction, payment in full required within 10 days of auction, unless otherwise agreed to by lender.

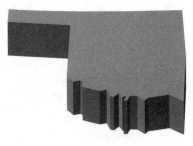

Oregon

Judicial Foreclosure:	Yes
Non-Judicial Foreclosure:	Yes
Security Instrument:	Deed of Trust or Mortgage
Approximate Time Frame:	180 days
Typical Foreclosure Process:	Non-Judicial enforcing Deed of Trust with a Power of Sale clause
Reinstatement Period:	The total past due amount owed plus additional fees and legal costs can be paid in full up until 5 days before the day of the foreclosure sale.
Notification Requirements:	The lender must file a Notice of Default, in the county where the property is located, indicating intent to sell the property, at least 120 days before the foreclosure sale. A copy must be sent via regular and certified mail, or personally served, to the homeowner also at least 120 days before the sale. The notice must be printed in a county newspaper once a week for 4 consecutive weeks with the last publication being at least 20 days before the sale date.
Judicial (No Power of Sale) Process:	The party foreclosing on the property must file a lawsuit with the court to obtain a judgment of foreclosure if there is no Power of Sale clause in the Deed of Trust or Mortgage. Once the court issues the judgment, the property is sold to the highest bidder at the county courthouse. The foreclosure sale takes place by the sheriff between the hours of 9:00am and 4:00pm. The property owner would have the right to redeem the property but the lender would not have the right to seek a deficiency judgment.
Non-Judicial (Power of Sale) Process:	The lender must file a Notice of Default, in the county where the property is located, indicating intent to sell the property. A copy must be sent via regular and certified mail, or personally served, to the homeowner and filed with the county court at least 120 days before the foreclosure sale date. The notice must then be printed in a county newspaper once a week for 4 consecutive weeks with the last publication being at least 20 days before the sale. The foreclosure sale takes place by the trustee between the hours of 9:00am and 4:00pm. The property owner would have the right to redeem the property but the lender would not have the right to seek a deficiency judgment.
Deficiency Judgment Rights:	None

Redemption Rights: The total loan amount owed plus additional fees and legal costs can be paid in full within 180 days of the property's foreclosure sale in either a Judicial or Non-Judicial foreclosure. The homeowner must file notice of intent to redeem with the sheriff at least 2 days, but not more than 30 days, before the redemption.

Investor Note: Payment in full required at auction.

Pennsylvania

Judicial Foreclosure:	Yes
Non-Judicial Foreclosure:	Yes
Security Instrument:	Mortgage only
Approximate Time Frame:	120 days
Typical Foreclosure Process:	Judicial enforcing Mortgage without a Power of Sale clause
Reinstatement Period:	The total past due amount owed plus additional fees and legal costs can be paid in full up until 1 hour before the foreclosure sale.
Notification Requirements:	Notice of Default must be sent to the homeowner at least 10 days before the lender can seek judicial action. If the loan is an FHA loan with less than $50,000 in default, the notice must be sent to the homeowner via certified mail within 60 days of the default. This notice allows for 30 days to arrange a payment plan or pay the amount in default. If the loan is a conventional or VA loan with less than $60,000 in default, an Act 91 notice must also be sent to the homeowner via regular mail. This notice informs the homeowner that they may be able to get assistance with stopping the foreclosure through a loan from the state-sponsored Homeowners Emergency Mortgage Assistance Program. Once the lender files a foreclosure complaint with the court, the homeowner has 20 days to respond to the court. Notification of the foreclosure sale must be posted on the property and sent via registered mail to the homeowner at least 30 days before the sale date. The notice must also be printed in a county newspaper once a week for 3 consecutive weeks.
Judicial (No Power of Sale) Process:	At least 10 days before seeking judicial action, the lender must give notice to the homeowner that they are in default. The lender must then file a foreclosure complaint with the court and the homeowner will then have 20 days to respond to the court. If they do not respond, the court will rule them to be in default. The court issues an Order to Foreclose and the property is scheduled to be sold. Notification of the foreclosure sale must be posted on the property and sent via registered mail to the homeowner at least 30 days before the sale date, as well as printed in a county newspaper once a week for 3 consecutive weeks. The homeowner has until 1 hour before the sale to pay the amount in default to stop the foreclosure. The foreclosure sale takes place by the sheriff at either the

county courthouse or the property. The property owner would not have the right to redeem the property but the lender would have the right to seek a deficiency judgment.

Non-Judicial (Power of Sale) Process: None

Deficiency Judgment Rights: A judgment can be obtained if the property is sold for less than the loan amount due in the Judicial foreclosure.

Redemption Rights: None

Investor Note: Payment in full required at auction.

Rhode Island

Judicial Foreclosure:	Yes
Non-Judicial Foreclosure:	Yes
Security Instrument:	Deed of Trust or Mortgage
Approximate Time Frame:	60 to 80 days
Typical Foreclosure Process:	Non-Judicial enforcing Mortgage with a Power of Sale clause
Reinstatement Period:	None
Notification Requirements:	Notice of Sale must be sent via certified mail to the homeowner no less than 30 days (20 days if not an individual consumer mortgagor) before the first publication of the notice. Notification of the foreclosure sale must also be printed in a county newspaper once a week for 3 consecutive weeks before the sale. The first printing must be at least 21 days before the sale.
Judicial (No Power of Sale) Process:	The party foreclosing on the property either can file a lawsuit with the court to obtain a judgment of foreclosure, or can simply foreclose on the property by taking possession of it. If they chose to forgo the lawsuit, they would simply have to peaceably take possession of the property in front of 2 witnesses who give the lender a notarized certificate of possession. Otherwise, they must file a lawsuit with the court to obtain a judgment of foreclosure if there is no Power of Sale clause in the Deed of Trust or Mortgage. Once the court issues the judgment, the property is scheduled to be sold to the highest bidder. The foreclosure sale takes place by the sheriff between the hours of 9:00am and 5:00pm, usually at the county courthouse. The property owner would have a limited right to redeem the property only if the foreclosure was by possession and the lender would have the right to seek a deficiency judgment.
Non-Judicial (Power of Sale) Process:	Before initiating the foreclosure, the lender's attorney must conduct a title search on the property. Then, a Notice of Sale must be sent via certified mail to the homeowner no less than 30 days (20 days if not an individual consumer mortgagor) before the notice is first printed in the newspaper. Notification of the foreclosure sale must be printed in a county newspaper once a week for 3 consecutive weeks and the first printing must be at least 21 days before the sale. The foreclosure sale takes place by the sheriff between the hours of 9:00am and 5:00pm, usually at the county courthouse.

	The property owner would not have the right to redeem the property but the lender would have the right to seek a deficiency judgment.
Deficiency Judgment Rights:	A judgment can be obtained if the property is sold for less than the loan amount due in both Judicial and Non-Judicial foreclosures.
Redemption Rights:	The total loan amount owed plus additional fees and legal costs can be paid in full within 3 years of the property's foreclosure in a Judicial foreclosure only if the lender has maintained possession of the property.
Investor Note:	Payment in full required at auction.

South Carolina

Judicial Foreclosure:	Yes
Non-Judicial Foreclosure:	No
Security Instrument:	Mortgage only
Approximate Time Frame:	150 to 180 days
Typical Foreclosure Process:	Judicial enforcing Mortgage without a Power of Sale clause
Reinstatement Period:	The total past due amount owed plus additional fees and legal costs can be paid in full during the 30-day time period allowed for the homeowner to answer the foreclosure complaint.
Notification Requirements:	The homeowner is given 30 days to answer the foreclosure complaint. A copy of the Notice of Sale must be posted in the county courthouse and in 2 public places for 3 weeks before the foreclosure sale date. Notification of the foreclosure sale must also be printed in a county newspaper once a week for 3 consecutive weeks.
Judicial (No Power of Sale) Process:	The lender must file a lis pendens with the court and a complaint for foreclosure is served to the homeowner. The homeowner is then given 30 days to answer the complaint. If there is no response, the default will be entered and a final judgment of foreclosure will be ruled on and the sale date can be scheduled. A copy of the Notice of Sale must be posted in the county courthouse and in 2 public places for 3 weeks before the foreclosure sale date. Notification of the foreclosure sale must also be printed in a county newspaper once a week for 3 consecutive weeks. The foreclosure sale takes place by the sheriff on the first Monday of the month, or Tuesday if Monday is a holiday, between the hours of 11:00am and 5:00pm at the courthouse. The property owner would not have the right to redeem the property but the lender would have the right to seek a deficiency judgment.
Non-Judicial (Power of Sale) Process:	None
Deficiency Judgment Rights:	A judgment can be obtained if the property is sold for less than the loan amount due in the Judicial foreclosure. The homeowner can petition the court within 30 days of the foreclosure sale for an Order of Appraisal to seek to have the judgment amount lessened to the difference between the outstanding loan amount and the appraised value instead of the auction sale price.

Redemption Rights:	None
Investor Note:	5% deposit required from winning bidder, payment in full required within 30 days. Upset bidding is allowed for 30 days after the auction.

South Dakota

Judicial Foreclosure:	Yes
Non-Judicial Foreclosure:	Yes
Security Instrument:	Deed of Trust or Mortgage
Approximate Time Frame:	90 to 150 days
Typical Foreclosure Process:	Non-Judicial enforcing Deed of Trust with a Power of Sale clause
Reinstatement Period:	None
Notification Requirements:	The lender must publish a Notice of Foreclosure Sale in a county newspaper once a week for 4 consecutive weeks. It must contain a number of items including the foreclosure sale date, time, and place as well as a description of the property. A copy of this notice must be personally served on the homeowner at least 21 days before the sale date; this notice period is extended to 8 weeks if the property is homestead.
Judicial (No Power of Sale) Process:	The lender must file a foreclosure complaint with the court and the homeowner will then have 30 days to respond to the court. If they do not respond, the court will rule them to be in default, issue a Notice of Sale and schedule the property to be sold at auction. The foreclosure sale takes place by the sheriff between the hours of 9:00am and 5:00pm. The property owner would have the right to redeem the property and the lender would have the right to seek a deficiency judgment.
Non-Judicial (Power of Sale) Process:	The lender is not required to send a Notice of Default to the homeowner prior to initiating the foreclosure unless the loan documents specifically state they must. The lender must simply publish a Notice of Foreclosure Sale in a county newspaper once a week for 4 consecutive weeks. At least 21 days before the sale, a copy of this notice must be personally served on the homeowner unless the property is homestead; then notice must be served 8 weeks prior to the sale. The foreclosure sale takes place by the sheriff between the hours of 9:00am and 5:00pm as indicated in the foreclosure sale notice. The property owner would have the right to redeem the property and the lender would have the right to seek a deficiency judgment.
Deficiency Judgment Rights:	A judgment can be obtained if the property is sold at auction for less than the loan amount due in either a Judicial or Non-Judicial foreclosure. The judgment is

limited to the difference between the amount due and the fair market value of the property.

Redemption Rights:

The total loan amount owed plus additional fees and legal costs can be paid in full within 12 months of the property's foreclosure sale in either a Judicial or Non-Judicial foreclosure. However, if the property is 40 acres or less and there is a Power of Sale clause, this period is shortened to 180 days. In addition, if the property is abandoned, the redemption period may be shortened to only 60 days.

Investor Note:

Payment in full required at auction.

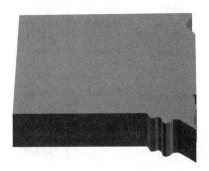

Tennessee

Judicial Foreclosure:	Yes
Non-Judicial Foreclosure:	Yes
Security Instrument:	Deed of Trust or Mortgage
Approximate Time Frame:	90 to 120 days
Typical Foreclosure Process:	Non-Judicial enforcing Deed of Trust with a Power of Sale clause
Reinstatement Period:	None, unless the court allows for one in a Judicial foreclosure.
Notification Requirements:	The lender must publish a Notice of Sale in a county newspaper once a week for 3 consecutive weeks and the first printing must be at least 20 days before the foreclosure sale. If there is no newspaper, the notice must be posted in 3 public places, as well as at the courthouse and the property, at least 30 days before the sale date. Also, a copy of the notice must be personally served on the homeowner at least 20 days before the sale.
Judicial (No Power of Sale) Process:	The lender must file a foreclosure complaint with the court and the homeowner may be given a short period of time to pay the default amount in full. If the default is not paid, the court will issue a Decree of Foreclosure and schedule the property to be sold at auction. The foreclosure sale takes place by the sheriff between the hours of 10:00am and 4:00pm. The property owner may have the right to redeem the property and the lender would have the right to seek a deficiency judgment.
Non-Judicial (Power of Sale) Process:	The lender must publish a Notice of Sale in a county newspaper once a week for 3 consecutive weeks with the first printing being at least 20 days before the sale date. If there is no newspaper, the notice must be posted at the courthouse, on the property, and at 3 other public places at least 30 days before the sale. A copy of this notice must be personally served on the homeowner at least 20 days before the foreclosure sale date. The foreclosure sale takes place by the sheriff between the hours of 10:00am and 4:00pm. The property owner may have the right to redeem the property and the lender would have the right to seek a deficiency judgment.
Deficiency Judgment Rights:	A judgment can be obtained if the property is sold at auction for less than the loan amount due in either a Judicial or Non-Judicial foreclosure.

Redemption Rights:	The total loan amount owed plus additional fees and legal costs can be paid in full within 2 years of the property's foreclosure sale in either a Judicial or Non-Judicial foreclosure. The right to redeem can be, and usually is, waived in the loan documents.
Investor Note:	Payment in full required at auction. A minimum bid may be set if it is at least 50% of the property's fair market value.

Texas

Judicial Foreclosure:	Yes
Non-Judicial Foreclosure:	Yes
Security Instrument:	Deed of Trust or Mortgage
Approximate Time Frame:	60 days
Typical Foreclosure Process:	Non-Judicial enforcing Deed of Trust with a Power of Sale clause
Reinstatement Period:	The total past due amount owed plus additional fees and legal costs can be paid in full up to 20 days after the lender sends a demand letter for the default amount in a Non-Judicial foreclosure.
Notification Requirements:	Before starting the foreclosure process, the lender must send a demand letter to the homeowner indicating the amount in default. The homeowner will then have 20 days to pay the default amount in full. The lender must then file a Notice of Sale in the county where the property is located at least 21 days before the foreclosure sale. A copy of this notice must also be sent to the homeowner as well as posted at the courthouse at least 21 days before the sale date.
Judicial (No Power of Sale) Process:	The party foreclosing on the property must file a lawsuit with the court to obtain a judgment of foreclosure if there is no Power of Sale clause in the Deed of Trust or Mortgage. Once the court rules them to be in default and issues the judgment, the property is scheduled to be sold at auction. The foreclosure sale takes place at the county courthouse on the first Tuesday of the month, even if it is a legal holiday, between the hours of 10:00am and 4:00pm. The property owner would not have the right to redeem the property but the lender would have the right to seek a deficiency judgment.
Non-Judicial (Power of Sale) Process:	The lender must send a demand letter to the homeowner indicating the amount in default and giving them 20 days to pay it in full. If the default is not paid, the lender must then file a Notice of Sale in the county where the property is located at least 21 days before the foreclosure sale. Within the same time frame, a copy of this notice must also be sent to the homeowner as well as posted at the courthouse. The foreclosure sale takes place by the trustee on the first Tuesday of the month, even if it is a legal holiday, between the hours of 10:00am and 4:00pm at the county courthouse. The property owner would not have the right to redeem the

	property but the lender would have the right to seek a deficiency judgment.
Deficiency Judgment Rights:	A judgment can be obtained if the property is sold at auction for less than the loan amount due in either a Judicial or Non-Judicial foreclosure. The judgment is limited to the difference between the amount due and the fair market value of the property.
Redemption Rights:	None
Investor Note:	Payment in full required at auction.

Utah

Judicial Foreclosure:	Yes
Non-Judicial Foreclosure:	Yes
Security Instrument:	Deed of Trust or Mortgage
Approximate Time Frame:	120 days
Typical Foreclosure Process:	Non-Judicial enforcing Deed of Trust with a Power of Sale clause
Reinstatement Period:	The total past due amount owed plus additional fees and legal costs can be paid in full up to 3 months after the lender sends a demand letter for the default amount in a Non-Judicial foreclosure. In a Judicial foreclosure, the court will allow for a short period of time in which the default amount can be paid.
Notification Requirements:	Before starting the foreclosure process, the lender must send a demand letter to the homeowner indicating the amount in default. The homeowner will then have 3 months to pay the default amount in full. The lender must then file a Notice of Sale at the county recorder's office, as well as at the property, at least 20 days before the foreclosure sale. Notification must also be printed in a county newspaper once a week for 3 consecutive weeks and the foreclosure sale must take place at least 10 days, but no more than 30 days, from the date of the last publication.
Judicial (No Power of Sale) Process:	The party foreclosing on the property must file a lawsuit with the court to obtain a judgment of foreclosure if there is no Power of Sale clause in the Deed of Trust or Mortgage. The homeowner may be given a short period of time to pay the default amount in full and, if it is not paid, the court will rule them to be in default and issue a judgment of foreclosure. The property is then scheduled to be sold at auction. The sale takes place at the courthouse or the property between the hours of 8:00am and 5:00pm. The property owner would not have the right to redeem the property after the foreclosure sale unless the court allows and the lender would have the right to seek a deficiency judgment.
Non-Judicial (Power of Sale) Process:	The lender must send a demand letter to the homeowner indicating the amount in default and giving them 3 months to pay it in full. If the default is not paid, the lender must file a Notice of Sale in the county where the property is located, as well as at the property, at least 20 days before the foreclosure sale. The notice must also be printed in a county newspaper once a

	week for 3 consecutive weeks. The foreclosure sale must take place at least 10 days, but no more than 30 days, from the date of the last publication. The sale takes place at the courthouse or the property between the hours of 8:00am and 5:00pm. The property owner would not have the right to redeem the property after the foreclosure sale unless the court allows and the lender would have the right to seek a deficiency judgment.
Deficiency Judgment Rights:	A judgment can be obtained if the property is sold at auction for less than the loan amount due in either a Judicial or Non-Judicial foreclosure.
Redemption Rights:	None. However, the court may set any period of time for the total loan amount owed plus additional fees and legal costs to be able to be paid in full after the property's foreclosure sale in either a Judicial or Non-Judicial foreclosure.
Investor Note:	Payment in full required at auction.

Vermont

Judicial Foreclosure:	Yes
Non-Judicial Foreclosure:	Yes
Security Instrument:	Mortgage only
Approximate Time Frame:	210 to 230 days
Typical Foreclosure Process:	Judicial enforcing Mortgage without a Power of Sale clause
Reinstatement Period:	The total past due amount owed plus additional fees and legal costs can be paid in full within 30 days of the Notice of Intent to Foreclose being served to the homeowner if the foreclosure is Non-Judicial.
Notification Requirements:	In a Judicial foreclosure, a complaint for foreclosure is served to the homeowner at least 5 days before they are scheduled to appear in court. In a Non-Judicial foreclosure, the homeowner must be notified via certified mail of the lender's intent to foreclose at least 30 days before the foreclosure is started. A Notice of Sale must be sent to the homeowner at least 60 days before the sale as well as printed in the county newspaper at least 30 days before the sale date.
Judicial (No Power of Sale) Process:	The Judicial process can be either a strict foreclosure or by Decree of Sale. In a strict foreclosure the lender has a complaint for foreclosure served on the homeowner at least 5 days before the court date. At the court hearing the lender simply needs to prove there is a default on the mortgage and the court issues a Decree of Foreclosure and the lender can either take possession of the property immediately or schedule its sale. However, if the property has 2 units or less and is owner occupied, a foreclosure by Decree of Sale must be sought by the lender. The lender must serve a complaint for foreclosure on the homeowner at least 5 days before the court date. At the court hearing, if the lender proves there is a default on the mortgage, the court sets the date of the foreclosure sale which must be at least 7 months from the issuance of the decree. In either case, the homeowner would have the right to redeem the property and the lender would have the right to seek a deficiency judgment.
Non-Judicial (Power of Sale) Process:	The lender must first send, via certified mail, to the homeowner a Notice of Intent to Foreclose at least 30 days before any further action can be taken. The homeowner can pay the default amount in full during this time to stop the foreclosure process. If the default

is not paid, the lender then sends a Notice of Sale to the homeowner at least 60 days before the sale date. A copy is also published in a county newspaper at least 30 days before the foreclosure sale date. The sale takes place at the property according to the terms outlined in the notice. The homeowner would have the right to redeem the property and the lender would have the right to seek a deficiency judgment.

Deficiency Judgment Rights:

A judgment can be obtained if the property is sold at auction for less than the loan amount due in either a Judicial or Non-Judicial foreclosure.

Redemption Rights:

The total loan amount owed plus additional fees and legal costs can be paid in full within 6 months of the property's foreclosure sale in either a Judicial or Non-Judicial foreclosure.

Investor Note:

Payment in full required at auction.

Virginia

Judicial Foreclosure:	Yes
Non-Judicial Foreclosure:	Yes
Security Instrument:	Deed of Trust or Mortgage
Approximate Time Frame:	60 to 90 days
Typical Foreclosure Process:	Non-Judicial enforcing Mortgage with a Power of Sale clause
Reinstatement Period:	The total past due amount owed plus additional fees and legal costs can be paid in full any time before the foreclosure sale.
Notification Requirements:	The loan documents usually dictate the publication notification requirements. If not, then the lender must publish a Notice of Foreclosure in a county newspaper once a week for 4 consecutive weeks or once a day for 5 consecutive days. The first printing must be at least 8 days before the foreclosure sale and the last printing must be no more than 30 days before the sale date. Also, a copy of the notice must be personally served on the homeowner at least 14 days before the sale.
Judicial (No Power of Sale) Process:	The lender must file a foreclosure complaint with the court and the homeowner may be given a short period of time to pay the default amount in full. If the default is not paid, the court will issue an Order of Foreclosure and schedule the property to be sold at auction. The foreclosure sale takes place at the courthouse between the hours of 9:00am and 5:00pm. The property owner may have the right to redeem the property if the court allows and the lender would have the right to seek a deficiency judgment.
Non-Judicial (Power of Sale) Process:	The lender must publish a Notice of Foreclosure before foreclosure proceedings can be started. Usually, the loan documents dictate the publication notification requirements. If not, the lender must publish a Notice of Foreclosure in a county newspaper once a week for 4 consecutive weeks or once a day for 5 consecutive days. The first printing of the notice must be at least 8 days before the foreclosure sale with the last printing being no more than 30 days before the sale. A copy of the notice must also be personally served on the homeowner at least 14 days before the sale date. The foreclosure sale takes place by the trustee at the courthouse between the hours of 9:00am and 5:00pm. The property owner would not have redemption rights but the lender could seek a deficiency judgment.

Deficiency Judgment Rights: A judgment can be obtained if the property is sold at auction for less than the loan amount due in either a Judicial or Non-Judicial foreclosure.

Redemption Rights: None. However, the court may allow for one in a Judicial foreclosure.

Investor Note: Payment in full required at auction. The auction is done by written bid, usually requiring a 10% deposit with the bid.

Washington

Judicial Foreclosure:	Yes
Non-Judicial Foreclosure:	Yes
Security Instrument:	Deed of Trust or Mortgage
Approximate Time Frame:	120 days
Typical Foreclosure Process:	Non-Judicial enforcing Deed of Trust with a Power of Sale clause
Reinstatement Period:	The total past due amount owed plus additional fees and legal costs can be paid in full up until 11 days before the foreclosure sale in a Non-Judicial foreclosure. The total loan amount owed plus additional fees and legal costs can be paid in full at any time before the sale.
Notification Requirements:	The lender must send a demand letter via certified mail to the homeowner indicating the amount in default at least 30 days before the sale date. A copy must also be posted on the property or personally served on the homeowner. The homeowner will then have this 30 days to pay the default amount in full. If the default is not paid, the lender must then file a Notice of Sale with the county auditor, as well as mail a copy to the homeowner and either personally serve it on the homeowner or post it at the property, at least 90 days before the foreclosure sale. Notification must also be printed in a county newspaper between 32 and 28 days before the foreclosure sale and again between 11 and 7 days before the sale.
Judicial (No Power of Sale) Process:	The lender must file a foreclosure complaint with the court and the homeowner may be given a short period of time to pay the default amount in full. If the default is not paid, the court will issue an Order of Foreclosure and schedule the property to be sold at auction. The foreclosure sale takes place between the hours of 9:00am and 4:00pm on a Friday, unless the Friday is a holiday, then the following Monday, usually at the county courthouse. The property owner would have the right to redeem the property after the foreclosure sale for 1 year, as well as maintain possession if it is their primary residence, and the lender would have the right to seek a deficiency judgment unless the property has been abandoned for the prior 6 months.
Non-Judicial (Power of Sale) Process:	Before starting the foreclosure process, the lender must send a demand letter to the homeowner, via certified mail, indicating the amount in default at least 30 days

before the sale. A copy must also be posted on the property or personally served on the homeowner. The homeowner then has this 30 days to pay the default amount in full to stop the foreclosure. The lender must then file a Notice of Sale with the county auditor if the default is not paid, as well as mail a copy to the homeowner at least 90 days before the foreclosure sale. A copy must also be personally served on the homeowner or posted at the property. Notification must also be printed in a county newspaper between 32 and 28 days before the foreclosure sale and again between 11 and 7 days before the sale. The foreclosure sale takes place by the trustee between the hours of 9:00am and 4:00pm on a Friday, unless Friday is a holiday, then the following Monday, and must occur within 190 days of the first default unless otherwise extended by the trustee. The property owner would not have the right to redeem the property after the foreclosure sale and the lender would not have the right to seek a deficiency judgment.

Deficiency Judgment Rights: A judgment can be obtained if the property is sold at auction for less than the loan amount due in a Judicial foreclosure only. However, if the property has been abandoned for the 6 months prior to the foreclosure judgment, a deficiency judgment cannot be obtained.

Redemption Rights: The total loan amount owed plus additional fees and legal costs can be paid in full within 1 year of the property's foreclosure sale in a Judicial foreclosure only. The homeowner may keep possession of the property during the redemption period if it is their primary residence.

Investor Note: Payment in full required at auction.

West Virginia

Judicial Foreclosure:	Yes
Non-Judicial Foreclosure:	Yes
Security Instrument:	Deed of Trust or Mortgage
Approximate Time Frame:	60 to 90 days
Typical Foreclosure Process:	Non-Judicial enforcing Deed of Trust with a Power of Sale clause
Reinstatement Period:	The total past due amount owed plus additional fees and legal costs can be paid in full within 10 days of receiving the required notice of default in a Non-Judicial foreclosure. However, if the homeowner has previously been in default 3 or more times, they do not have to be afforded this reinstatement period. The total loan amount owed plus additional fees and legal costs can be paid in full at any time before the sale.
Notification Requirements:	The lender must send a demand letter to the homeowner indicating the amount in default at least 10 days before the foreclosure process can start. The homeowner will then have this 10-day period to pay the default amount in full. If the default is not paid, the lender must then publish a Notice of Sale in a county newspaper once a week for 2 consecutive weeks. A copy of the notice must also be posted at the courthouse and 3 other public places, as well as personally served on the homeowner at least 20 days before the foreclosure sale.
Judicial (No Power of Sale) Process:	The lender must file a foreclosure complaint with the court and the homeowner may be given a short period of time to pay the default amount in full. If the default is not paid, the court will issue an Order of Foreclosure and schedule the property to be sold at auction. The foreclosure sale takes place at the date and location instructed by the court. The property owner would not have the right to redeem the property after the foreclosure sale and the lender would not have the right to seek a deficiency judgment.
Non-Judicial (Power of Sale) Process:	Before the foreclosure process can start, the lender must send a demand letter to the homeowner indicating the amount in default at least 10 days before. The homeowner has these 10 days to pay the default amount in full to stop the foreclosure process. If the default is not paid, the lender then publishes a Notice of Sale in a county newspaper once a week for 2 consecutive weeks. At least 20 days before the sale,

a copy of the notice must also be posted at the courthouse and 3 other public places, as well as personally served on the homeowner. The foreclosure sale then takes place at the date and location indicated in the notice. The property owner would not have the right to redeem the property after the foreclosure sale and the lender would not have the right to seek a deficiency judgment.

Deficiency Judgment Rights: None

Redemption Rights: None

Investor Note: Deposit equal to 1/3 of sale price required from winning bidder, payment in full required within 30 days.

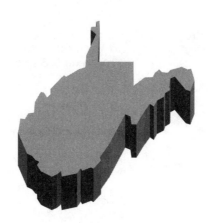

Wisconsin

Judicial Foreclosure:	Yes
Non-Judicial Foreclosure:	Yes
Security Instrument:	Deed of Trust or Mortgage
Approximate Time Frame:	90 days to 1 year
Typical Foreclosure Process:	Judicial enforcing Mortgage without a Power of Sale clause
Reinstatement Period:	None
Notification Requirements:	In a Non-Judicial foreclosure, notification of the foreclosure sale must be served on the homeowner as well as printed in a county newspaper once a week for 6 consecutive weeks. A copy of the notice must also be posted on the property or at 3 public places for at least 3 weeks before the foreclosure sale. In a Judicial foreclosure, the first publication must be not less than 4 months from the foreclosure judgment if the lender has requested an expedited 6-month sale process, or, otherwise, not less than 10 months from the foreclosure judgment.
Judicial (No Power of Sale) Process:	The party foreclosing on the property must file a lawsuit with the court to obtain a judgment of foreclosure if there is no Power of Sale clause in the loan documents. Once the court issues the judgment, the property is scheduled to be sold to the highest bidder by the sheriff. The foreclosure sale date must be at least 1 year from the issuance of the foreclosure judgment unless the lender waives their right to a deficiency judgment. In that case, the sale can take place after 6 months, or, if the property is abandoned, 2 months. The property owner would have a limited right to redeem the property and the lender would have a limited right to seek a deficiency judgment.
Non-Judicial (Power of Sale) Process:	The lender must file a Notice of Sale, in the county where the property is located, indicating intent to sell the property. It must contain a number of items including the foreclosure sale date, time, and place as well as a description of the property. Then the notice must be served on the homeowner and printed in a county newspaper once a week for 6 consecutive weeks prior to the sale date. A copy of the notice must also be posted on the property or at 3 public places for at least 3 weeks before the foreclosure sale. The property is then sold according to the terms in the notice. The property owner would have a limited right to redeem the property

	and the lender would have a limited right to seek a deficiency judgment.
Deficiency Judgment Rights:	A judgment can be obtained if the property is sold at auction for less than the loan amount due in either a Judicial or Non-Judicial foreclosure only if the lender seeks to have the court confirm the sale. The judgment is limited to the difference between the amount due and the fair market value of the property.
Redemption Rights:	The total loan amount owed plus additional fees and legal costs can be paid in full within 12 months of the property's foreclosure sale in either a Judicial or Non-Judicial foreclosure. However, if the lender waives their right to seek a deficiency judgment to expedite the sale of the property, or if the court confirms the sale, the right to redemption is lost. In addition, if the property is abandoned, the redemption period may be shortened to only 2 months.
Investor Note:	10% deposit required from winning bidder, payment in full required within 10 days.

Wyoming

Judicial Foreclosure:	Yes
Non-Judicial Foreclosure:	Yes
Security Instrument:	Deed of Trust or Mortgage
Approximate Time Frame:	90 days
Typical Foreclosure Process:	Non-Judicial enforcing Deed of Trust with a Power of Sale clause
Reinstatement Period:	The total past due amount owed plus additional fees and legal costs can be paid in full within 10 days of receiving the Notice of Intent to Foreclose.
Notification Requirements:	At least 10 days before the foreclosure process can be started, the lender must first send, via certified mail, to the homeowner a Notice of Intent to Foreclose. The lender then must publish a Notice of Default in a county newspaper once a week for 4 consecutive weeks.
Judicial (No Power of Sale) Process:	The party foreclosing on the property must file a lawsuit with the court to obtain a judgment of foreclosure if there is no Power of Sale clause in the loan documents. Once the court issues the judgment, the property is scheduled to be sold. The foreclosure sale then takes place by the sheriff between the hours of 9:00am and 5:00pm, at the county courthouse. The homeowner would have the right to redeem the property and the lender would have the right to seek a deficiency judgment.
Non-Judicial (Power of Sale) Process:	The lender must first send, via certified mail, to the homeowner a Notice of Intent to Foreclose at least 10 days before any further action can be taken. The homeowner can pay the default amount in full during this time to stop the foreclosure process. If the default is not paid, the lender then publishes a Notice of Default in a county newspaper once a week for 4 consecutive weeks. The foreclosure sale takes place by the trustee or sheriff between the hours of 9:00am and 5:00pm, at the county courthouse. The homeowner would have the right to redeem the property and the lender would have the right to seek a deficiency judgment.
Deficiency Judgment Rights:	A judgment can be obtained if the property is sold at auction for less than the loan amount due in either a Judicial or Non-Judicial foreclosure.
Redemption Rights:	The total loan amount owed plus additional fees and legal costs can be paid in full within 3 months of the

property's foreclosure sale in either a Judicial or
Non-Judicial foreclosure.

Investor Note: Payment in full required at auction.

Foreclosure Prevention, Part I: Lender Communication

This Chapter Discusses:

★ Don't Assume Your Problems Will Go Away

★ Why Your Lender Doesn't Want to Foreclose

★ Office of the Comptroller of the Currency Insights Report

★ Don't Discard Your Mail Without Reading It

★ Don't Be Embarrassed to Contact Your Lender

★ Negotiating With Your Lender

This chapter is intended for those that have already fallen *at least one month behind* on their home loan payments. At this point, you need to do your best to work things out, because *most lenders will not give you another home loan if your delinquency persists*. In fact, **as soon as a** *"foreclosure in process"* **remark is added to your credit file** (usually when you are *3 or 4 months behind*), **you may have to wait a couple of years or more before another lender will approve you**.

The exception to this would be either to have a **substantial down payment** (e.g., anywhere from **20% to 35%**) or to know someone with good credit who is willing to co-sign for you. Otherwise, *you'll need to focus on the next several chapters regarding foreclosure prevention – beginning with this one!*

Don't Assume Your Problems Will Go Away

As discussed in the opening chapters, *you need to acknowledge you are suffering a personal financial crisis that will not alleviate itself*.

This is important, because as you've already read, **most states allow a lender to take your home** *within a matter of a few months* **– so you must recognize the problem and act quickly**. And unfortunately, there are a significant number of people out there who *turn a blind eye to dire issues such as a pending foreclosure*, which is *the worst thing you can possibly do!*

As long as you have a source of income, the basic premise behind prevention tactics should work. Although – if at all possible – in the future, *try to recognize the problem in advance*, because this whole situation is much easier to approach.

Don't get us wrong – we do acknowledge those horrible life crises that can bring on a foreclosure at a moment's notice. We just want to emphasize that **being prepared ahead of time gives you a better chance at saving your home, while also saving you a lot of grief**. So if you can detect the problem early on and find a reasonable remedy, *get on it right away* – because that lottery ticket you just picked up at the gas station probably won't solve your problems this weekend.

And for those of you who lost a loved one or suffered an extraordinary hardship, *we will do our best* – as you continue to read through subsequent chapters – *to share all possible strategic maneuvers and stall tactics to help save your home* .

Why Your Lender Doesn't Want to Foreclose

Contrary to what you believe or what's portrayed in movies such as *It's a Wonderful Life*, most banks and lenders don't want to foreclose on their borrowers. As discussed in **Chapters 3** and **4**, the **foreclosure process can be long, involved and expensive**. Lenders – even though they make a lot of money –

also take on a good amount of risk as defined by their own protocol for lending. *Unfortunately, it was greed that ultimately caused many lenders to close their doors in 2007 – and now 2008 – as the current mortgage crisis continues*.

As you now know, **the only chance a lender has for recouping their money is to foreclose and auction off the property to the highest bidder**. *Unfortunately for the lender, the auction price usually falls short of the total amount owed.* If they're lucky, **the state's laws allow the lender to sue for deficiency balances**. But, unfortunately again for the lender, *most judgments go uncollected, because the borrower either has no assets or was clever enough to hide (or protect) anything they did own*. So the lender is definitely motivated to work out a deal – **but the longer you wait, the more difficult and limited your prevention options become.**

Office of the Comptroller of the Currency Insights Report

The **Office of the Comptroller of the Currency** is a bureau of the U.S. Department of the Treasury which charters, regulates and supervises all national banks. In June 2007, they published *"Foreclosure Prevention: Improving Contact with Borrowers,"* an Insights report **to provide banks with strategies and recommendations for preserving homeownership by preventing foreclosures.**

This thirteen-page newsletter is provided on the following pages to demonstrate that even **the federal government is encouraging banks (and lenders) to keep a line of communication open with homeowners.** This document is definitely worth reading for your education as to how banks are being advised by our own government.

Office of the Comptroller of the Currency Insights Report

Comptroller of the Currency
Administrator of National Banks
US Department of the Treasury

Community Developments

June 2007

Insights

Community Affairs
Department

Foreclosure Prevention:
Improving Contact with Borrowers

Abstract

The rapid growth in the subprime and nontraditional mortgage market, combined with a slowdown in the appreciation of home values, may lead to increased foreclosures over the next few years. Nearly $1.5 trillion of adjustable rate mortgages (ARMs) will be eligible to reset during 2007, and between $500 billion to $800 billion will actually reset with new interest rates.[1] Some analysts estimate that defaults from mortgage loans originated over the past few years using adjustable rates, introductory teaser rates, and payment options may lead to as many as 1.1 million foreclosures with losses approximating $112 billion, spread over the next six years or more.[2]

This Insights report reviews strategies that banks are using to prevent foreclosures to mitigate credit losses. The strategies presented in the report involve partnerships developed by banks, nonprofit organizations, state and local governments, and others who have a stake in keeping homeowners in their properties and maintaining the economic health of local communities. The information presented here was obtained from a variety of sources including financial institutions and nonprofit agencies.

I. What Is Foreclosure Prevention?

Over the past two decades, technological innovations in credit scoring, processing, and underwriting of mortgage loans helped fuel the growth of the prime and subprime mortgage markets. Additionally, the growth of the secondary mortgage market, the increased appetite of investors for mortgage backed securities (MBS), and the more recent period of low interest rates, all came together to create a housing boom that increased the nation's homeownership rate from 65 percent in 1995 to 69 percent in 2006.

However, as lenders tried to keep pace with the demand for MBSs, some originators, primarily in the subprime mortgage market, began to combine the underwriting of borrowers with weaker credit scores with other higher risk elements, such as higher loan-to-value ratios or incomplete

---

[1] *See* Doug Duncan, "A Return to Normal," Mortgage Banking, Vol. 67, Issue 4, January 2007.

[2] *See* Christopher L. Cagan, "Mortgage Payment Reset: The Issue and the Impact," First American Core Logic report, p. 2, March 19, 2007.

Office of the Comptroller of the Currency Insights Report

income documentation. The unintended consequence of the mortgage industry's ongoing effort to extend homeownership opportunities to less creditworthy consumers has been an increase in foreclosure rates.[3]

The rise in mortgage foreclosures, and especially the dramatic rise in subprime mortgage foreclosures, has the potential to undermine the significant homeownership gains made by lower-income and minority consumers during the 1990s. Additionally, foreclosed properties can become an eyesore and a location for criminal activity, which can depress area property values and contribute to negative perceptions of a neighborhood, increasing costs and reducing revenues for local communities.

Aside from the devastating impact of foreclosures on borrowers and communities, their increase also costs all participants in the mortgage industry. For investors and insurers of securities issues, foreclosures entail a reduction in cash flow and can lessen the market value of securities. Servicers incur significant expenses attempting to resolve problem loans. Further, income to servicers decreases as loans are removed from the pools backing securities issues.

To address the problems caused by a rising foreclosure rate, banks and others have developed programs to reduce the number of foreclosures. Many of these programs were developed as partnerships between banks acting as loan servicers and nonprofit organizations that provide financial counseling to homeowners.

II. Why Is Foreclosure Prevention of Interest to Banks?

Banks recognize that keeping homeowners in their homes is often the best way to mitigate credit losses, preserve customer relationships, maintain stable neighborhoods, and minimize the detrimental effects vacant properties can have on crime and property values.

Banks that originate and service mortgage loans are aware that prudent attempts to workout loans of homeowners who have defaulted on their contractual obligations are often in the best interests of both the lender and the borrower. Moreover, the federal financial institutions regulatory agencies have encouraged lenders to work proactively with these borrowers.[4] And in the case of servicemembers on active duty, servicers must adhere to the special considerations for the sale, foreclosure, or seizure of their property.[5]

When borrowers default on their home loans, some specific and measurable reasons exist for why banks should be interested in preventing foreclosure. These reasons include:

Reputation Risk

Banks face negative publicity over rising foreclosure rates in general and over individual cases when the bank may have made the loan or is currently servicing the loan. In addition, when a significant number of loans in an investment pool go into default, the secondary market can develop concerns about all loans originated by that institution. These defaults can negatively affect the institution's ability to sell new loans on the secondary market. In addition, investors rely on the Nationally Recognized Statistical Rating Organizations (NRSROs) to gauge the effectiveness of a servicing operation and the quality of loans.[6] A large number of foreclosures can affect negatively a bank's servicing rating assigned by a rating agency.

---

[3] Remarks by Chairman Ben S. Bernanke at the Federal Reserve Bank of Chicago's 43rd Annual Conference on Bank Structure and Competition, Chicago, Illinois, May 17, 2007.

[4] OCC Bulletin 2007-14, Interagency Statement on Working with Mortgage Borrowers.

[5] *See* 50 USC App. 501-596.

[6] *See* 17 CFR 240.3b-10 for the definition of Nationally Recognized Statistical Rating Organizations.

2

Office of the Comptroller of the Currency Insights Report

Costs to Bank-Owned Portfolio

For loans that are held in a bank's portfolio, direct losses can result from foreclosures. These losses are affected by the property's condition, local market conditions, fees, and advances related to the length of time it took to foreclose on the property. General estimates of the losses to lenders on a foreclosure range from 20 to 60 cents on the dollar.

Costs of Servicing

Most mortgage loans are sold to secondary market investors, shifting much of the risk of foreclosure to the servicers and investors and costing banks that service loans. As a delinquency progresses, servicers often make advances for taxes, insurance, property preservation, inspections, and legal costs. Servicers must also make advances on principal and interest to investors, regardless of whether the servicer has received a payment from the borrower. Many, but not all, of these advances are reimbursed once the property is liquidated, but the servicer still faces the cost of funds for advancing fees, expenses, and debt service payments.

In addition, servicing a foreclosure requires the servicer to use additional staff resources. One bank reported that servicing a loan in foreclosure is at least three times as costly as servicing a current loan.

Major Investors Paying Incentives for Workouts

The income from these workout incentive payments can be substantial and offset some of the costs associated with servicing operations. The availability of such incentives is determined by the performance of an investor's loans and the relationships among the various parties involved (servicer, investor, etc.).

Property Values

Vacant and abandoned properties are vulnerable to vandalism, deterioration, and criminal activities. A large number of foreclosures can increase the supply of homes on the market, negatively affect neighborhood values, and drive down sale prices.

Community Reinvestment Act (CRA) Credit

Two primary activities are useful in preventing foreclosures and each may receive positive CRA consideration. First, banks can provide financial counseling to low- or moderate-income homeowners, either directly or through a nonprofit agency, to help keep them in their homes.[7] Second, banks may provide refinancing of higher variable rate mortgages into lower fixed-rate mortgages for low- or moderate-income borrowers.[8] Examiners will consider such a program as responsive in helping to meet the credit needs of its community.

III. How Does Foreclosure Prevention Work?

Effective foreclosure prevention relies on increasing the amount of contact between servicers and delinquent borrowers. All of the banks interviewed for this report described increasing

---

[7] *See* Questions and Answers Regarding Community Reinvestment, 71 Fed. Reg. 12424, 12432 (Mar. 10, 2006) (Q&A § __.12 (i)-3).

[8] *See* Questions and Answers Regarding Community Reinvestment, 66 Fed. Reg. 36620, 36631 (Jul. 12, 2001) (Q&A § __.22 (a)-1).

3

Office of the Comptroller of the Currency Insights Report

the contact rate as the key to success of their foreclosure prevention initiatives. As a result, the strategies banks have developed all focus on methods of increasing their ability to make contact with borrowers who are either behind on payments or alerting them earlier of impending loan rate resets.

Mortgage servicers have found that traditional collection methods are no longer producing satisfactory results. The old method was to flood borrowers with letters and telephone calls, hoping that the borrower would contact the servicer, but knowing that only a small percentage would do so.[9] All of the banks interviewed have found that delinquent borrowers often do not respond to mail notifications from the servicer, and those that have answering machines and caller ID on their telephones screen calls from lenders. Furthermore, cell phones have replaced landline telephones in popularity. In fact, servicers are finding it difficult to obtain a telephone number for borrowers who use cell phones exclusively.

Borrower's Reasons for Avoiding Lender Contact

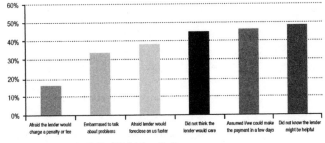

Chart provided by J. Michael Collins, PolicyLab Consulting.[10]

Servicers still use the letter and the telephone as the main means of contacting borrowers whose payments are late, but have adapted these measures by training their loss mitigation staff to convey a number of positive messages early in the call. Many servicers use software that can propose a workout solution with a payment schedule based on such factors as the borrower's income and other expenses. The software also incorporates any investors' requirements into the servicing agreement. These software packages also script the call for the servicing staff.

Default Intermediation

There are three main models for reaching borrowers who are late on payments:

- Direct servicer contact.

- Direct contact by counseling agencies.

- National toll-free number for borrowers to call.

---

[9] *See* http://www.freddiemac.com/service/msp/pdf/foreclosure_avoidance_dec2005.pdf.

[10] Home Ownership Preservation Initiative, Partnership Lessons & Results, Neighborhood Housing Services of Chicago, July 17, 2006, p. 25. www.nhschicago.org/downloads/82HOPI3YearReport_Jul17-06.pdf

4

Office of the Comptroller of the Currency Insights Report

Direct Servicer Contact

Banks are trying a number of direct contact strategies to improve their contact rate. Five of the most common options are:

Behavior scoring

Banks are using scoring models to help them determine which late paying borrowers are priority contacts. These models provide a score that identifies the risk of a borrower going further into delinquency. The models incorporate borrower-specific factors, such as payment patterns and credit scores, combined with economic data, such as local unemployment rate and trends in real estate values. The main purposes of these scoring models are: (1) to streamline collection calls by risk-ranking delinquent accounts to identify loans most likely to benefit from early intervention to avoid foreclosure and (2) to identify loans most likely to create a loss without an intervention.[11]

Non-standard call times

After reviewing behavior scores to determine which borrowers should receive more phone calls, banks are calling on weekends and on weekday evenings to contact borrowers when they are home.[12]

Customer friendly contact

Following are three general messages that servicers use to help engage the borrower on the phone and in letters:

- The loan servicer does not want to take your house.

- The loan servicer on the phone is not judgmental.

- The loan servicer would like to help you stay in your home.

Options that do not require conversations

Banks have developed additional resources for borrowers who do not want to talk to the servicer on the phone. One bank provides a Web site with information about payment and other options. The Web site also outlines information borrowers must provide to the bank to take advantage of one of the workout options. Another bank servicer incorporates a payment plan option in a letter to the borrower. A third bank has developed a DVD, which identifies foreclosure prevention methods, and is mailed to delinquent borrowers who have not contacted the servicer.

Door knockers

Some servicers hire staff to go door-to-door to contact late-paying borrowers. These individuals are trained to explain repayment options to borrowers and provide a brochure explaining these options. The "door knockers" carry cell phones so they can contact the loss mitigation and collections departments at the bank when they have reached a delinquent borrower. This method can result in the door knocker putting the borrower in direct contact with the servicer's loss mitigation staff. They generally attempt to make contact with the borrower well before the loan is 90 days delinquent.

---

[11] Amy Crews Cutts and Richard K. Green, *Innovative Servicing Technology*, Freddie Mac Working Paper 04-03, July 2004, p. 14.

[12] *See* 15 USC 1692a *et seq.* Servicers making direct contact with delinquent borrowers and any counseling agencies acting on behalf of servicers should consider the applicability of the requirements of the Fair Debt Collection Practices Act.

SAMPLE

Office of the Comptroller of the Currency Insights Report

Direct Contact by Counseling Agencies

In addition to the servicers' requirements to notify eligible borrowers of the availability of homeownership counseling by the servicer or a HUD-approved nonprofit counseling agency, many servicers have begun to partner with these counseling agencies.[13] Some servicers have realized that counseling agencies are more trusted by borrowers and that borrowers may be more likely to respond to a call or letter from a counseling agency. These servicers have found that by partnering with a counseling agency, their contact rates with delinquent borrowers have increased. These partnerships capitalize on the desire of both banks and counseling agencies to have borrowers stay in their homes if they can afford their mortgage payments.

Some servicers have contracted with nonprofit housing counseling agencies to make an initial contact with borrowers who are late on payments.[14] Under this scenario, a servicer provides a pre-selected counseling agency with a list of borrowers to contact. The counselor is trained to make a friendly call to the borrower, emphasizing his or her ability to work with the borrower and help the borrower work out a solution with the lender. The borrower has the option of sharing financial information with the counselor.

This strategy begins with a letter from the counseling agency to the borrower, providing a toll-free number and a Web site. The letter states that if the counseling agency does not hear from the borrower, the agency will contact the borrower by telephone. When contact is made, the counselor can collect documentation and information needed to evaluate loss mitigation options, with permission from the borrower. If no feasible plan can be developed, the counselor helps develop a detailed plan for selling the property. Overall, some servicers have concluded that the fees paid to counseling agencies are considerably lower in comparison with the costs of foreclosure.

National Toll-Free Number for Borrowers

Several reputable national nonprofit organizations have partnered with mortgage servicers to provide no cost telephone counseling to delinquent borrowers. NeighborWorks America has partnered with the Homeownership Preservation Foundation to establish a 24 hours a day, seven days a week, toll-free hotline for homeowners to discuss their delinquency problems with a housing counselor.[15] Calls flow into a national call center staffed by English- and Spanish-speaking counselors. Callers are prioritized immediately. Depending on the nature of the problem, counseling can be provided as part of the initial call or through a series of follow-up calls or in-person visits to a local housing counseling service to which the borrower is referred. If a workout can be arranged with the lender, counselors can also provide budgeting assistance and other financial education to help ensure that these borrowers can meet the terms of their workout agreements. In about 25 percent of the counseling sessions, the homeowner is recommended for loan workout, and the counselor helps the homeowner work with the servicer on a loan modification.[16] A further discussion of these partnerships can be found in Section V of this report.

Nationwide lenders who also service loans for others have established their own toll-free numbers to encourage borrowers to contact them. Borrowers who have defaulted on their home loans are advised of these phone numbers by letter or phone call from the servicer or the nonprofit partner.

---

[13] *See* 12 USC 1701x, which was recently augmented with special disclosures for servicemembers.

[14] *See* 15 USC 1692a *et seq.*

[15] *See* "Innovative Partnership to Prevent Foreclosures," Office of the Comptroller of the Currency, *Community Developments*, Spring 2006, at http://www.occ.gov/CDD/spring06b/cd/innovativepartnerships.htm.

[16] In approximately 17 percent of cases, homeowners cannot be helped through a workout. In these cases, the goal is for the homeowner to preserve the equity by selling the home. *See* Testimony of John H. Dalton on behalf of the Housing Policy Council of the Financial Services Roundtable before the U.S. House Financial Services Committee, April 17, 2007.

6

Everything U Need to Know... ™

Office of the Comptroller of the Currency Insights Report

Options for Borrowers and Servicers

Once the servicer has made contact with the delinquent borrower, either directly or through a counseling agency, there are a variety of options to be discussed. These options are divided into two major groups: retention workout options and non-retention options. Retention workout options allow a borrower to retain possession of the home. Alternatively, non-retention options result in the borrower relinquishing the home, but avoiding the expense and stigma of foreclosure process.

Retention Workout Options

Retention options allow a borrower to retain possession of the home. There are several workout options that loan servicers, borrowers, and nonprofits can utilize in their best efforts to keep the borrower in the home.[17] The earlier these conversations occur, the greater is the likelihood of a successful outcome.

Early Contact Discussion of Alternatives. For loans with upward adjusting payments (such as hybrid ARMs and payment-option ARMs), some servicers have begun contacting borrowers prior to the scheduled payment increase to advise them of the new payment amount. If the borrower cannot afford the new payment and is reasonably likely to default, the servicer may be able to modify the loan to create longer-term affordability. In some cases, servicers acting on behalf of lenders are offering to refinance ARMs into lower cost, fixed rate loans.

Repayment Plan. The servicer increases the regular monthly payment until the delinquency is repaid. Typically, the payment period extends over a two- to six-month period.

Loan Modification. A loan is modified in a written agreement between a borrower and servicer that permanently changes one or more of its original terms. The loan modification may include an interest rate concession, reducing the principal balance outstanding, extending the term of the loan, establishing escrows for taxes and insurance, or adding the delinquent interest amount to the unpaid principal balance.

Forebearance. Forebearance is an agreement to allow a reduced or suspended payment for a specific period of time, usually not to exceed three months. The borrower still owes the unpaid amount, which may be worked out later with a loan modification.

Non-retention Options

There are some situations in which the borrower will be unable to retain the home, and foreclosure is inevitable. In these cases, quick action is needed to reduce the financial hardship on the borrower and to limit any losses to the lender. All parties involved must look seriously at the borrower's financial profile and be willing to admit when leaving the home is the best alternative.

Sale of the House: Borrowers are encouraged to sell their house and pay off the mortgage in full. Servicers can assist in the marketing and sale of the home.

Short Sale: A servicer agrees on behalf of an investor to accept the proceeds of a pre-foreclosure sale in satisfaction of the loan, even though the proceeds may be less than the amount owed on the mortgage.

---

[17] Certain accounting and tax issues may limit a servicer's ability to offer these options (see page 11).

7

Office of the Comptroller of the Currency Insights Report

Deed in Lieu of Foreclosure: A workout in which a borrower voluntarily conveys clear property title to the servicer in exchange for a discharge of the debt. This is generally used when the home has been listed for sale for a period of time with no activity.

Developing Options

Some banks that hold mortgage loans in their portfolios have determined that offering fixed-rate loans to refinance a higher rate ARM may save some borrowers from foreclosure. Recent announcements from the government-sponsored enterprises (GSEs), specifically Fannie Mae and Freddie Mac, have indicated a willingness to purchase some of these refinanced loans once program guidelines have been established. This is a significant option for loan servicers to monitor in the near future.[18]

Separately, at least two states are considering a bond sale to establish a pool of funds to refinance higher rate and ARM loans in danger of foreclosure into new fixed rate loans. And certain states have rescue funds that will refinance loans from areas hit by job losses from industrial dislocations. Loan servicers should be aware of options available in various states.

Differences Between Prime and Subprime Servicing

Servicers have found significant differences between servicing prime and subprime loans. Overall, servicing subprime loans is more expensive because it requires frequent calls to borrowers who may also be receiving calls from other collectors. Servicers report that subprime borrowers also are more likely to send in partial payments that require additional resources to process. Since more contact is needed, the number of cases that one employee can handle is lower.

Prime loan servicers will generally call a borrower who has missed a payment 15 to 20 days after the payment was due, if that borrower typically makes payments on time. Subprime loan servicers will call as soon as one to two days after a payment was due, and may sometimes call before a payment is due. In addition, servicers have found that approximately 80 percent of 90-day past due subprime loans roll into foreclosure, so they have to be proactive and aggressive about reaching borrowers. This additional contact creates a higher cost and requires more staff to make the additional calls.

IV. What Are the Key Risks and Regulatory Considerations Presented by Alternatives to Foreclosure?

Banks must consider a number of risks and regulatory issues as part of their foreclosure prevention programs. Most often mentioned issues relate to privacy and the need to obtain third-party authorizations from borrowers.[19] These third-party authorizations would permit the servicer to engage a local nonprofit counseling agency to reach out directly to delinquent borrowers, as the borrowers are more likely to open mail and answer telephone calls from a nonprofit counseling agency. The suggestion has been made that a disclosure explicitly authorizing the servicer to provide information on a borrower to a nonprofit counseling agency if the borrower is in danger of default should be made part of standard mortgage closing documentation.

Foreclosure procedures vary by state. Some states mandate judicial foreclosures, which are processed through the courts, and others allow non-judicial foreclosures, which are processed

---

[18] *See* testimony by Daniel H. Mudd, President and CEO, Fannie Mae, and Richard F. Syron, Chairman and CEO, Freddie Mac, before the U.S. House Committee on Financial Services, Washington, DC, April 17, 2007.

[19] *See* 15 USC 1692a *et seq.* Servicers working with counseling agencies to contact delinquent borrowers should consider the applicability of the requirements of the Fair Debt Collection Practices Act. Lenders should also be aware of their responsibilities regarding agents working on their behalf (see OCC Bulletin 2001-47, Third-party Relationships).

Office of the Comptroller of the Currency Insights Report

without court intervention. Judicial foreclosures take much longer to process, allowing more time for the development of a workout plan, yet providing an incentive for borrowers to remain in their homes without making payments for a significant period of time.

Declining housing prices in some areas create additional risks to lenders, servicers, and investors. Declining values present a scenario in which the servicer has little or no built-in equity margin to serve as a cushion while negotiating a workout with a delinquent borrower. Also, the borrower has no real incentive to agree to the workout plan if the property is worth less now than when it was originally purchased.

There are safety and soundness issues that banks also address as part of offering foreclosure prevention programs. For example, if the lender is capitalizing principal and interest payments, it could cause a need for expanded loan loss coverage.

The federal bank, thrift, and credit union regulatory agencies are encouraging financial institutions to work with homeowners who are unable to make mortgage payments. Prudent workout arrangements that are consistent with safe and sound lending practices are generally in the long-term best interest of both the financial institution and the borrower. Institutions will not face regulatory penalties if they pursue reasonable workout arrangements with borrowers.[20]

V. Who Is in the Foreclosure Prevention Business Today?

Foreclosure prevention in the mortgage servicing business has become a major focus of the loss mitigation function.[21] And while loss mitigation is still the bottom line for all parties involved, much of the mortgage servicing industry has come to recognize that a more customer-friendly approach to the problem of contacting delinquent borrowers will most likely generate better results.

Loan Servicers

In many mortgage operations, loan servicers remain in their historic roles as those primarily responsible to contact delinquent borrowers. Alternatively, foreclosure prevention programs today at many large/national loan servicers are beginning to rely more on partnerships with interested third parties.

Nonprofit Counseling Agencies

A number of nonprofit housing counseling agencies are now working with servicers to develop foreclosure prevention programs.[22] They are: the National Training and Information Center (NTIC), the Association of Community Organizations for Reform Now (ACORN), the National Community Reinvestment Coalition (NCRC), the Neighborhood Assistance Corporation of America (NACA), and NeighborWorks America.

NeighborWorks America has more than 240 affiliated community-based organizations that provide counseling services to at-risk homeowners. NeighborWorks operates the National Center for Foreclosure Solutions, which, in partnership with the Homeownership Preservation Foundation, has established a national toll-free number to channel borrowers to community-based nonprofits to facilitate workouts with lenders.

---

[20] *See* OCC Bulletin 2007-14, Interagency Statement on Working with Mortgage Borrowers.

[21] National banks and their operating subsidiaries originated less than 10 percent of all subprime loans originated (or produced) in 2006.

[22] *See* "National Community Organizations' Foreclosure Prevention Initiatives," *Community Developments*, Office of the Comptroller of the Currency, Spring 2006, p. 9. Available at http://www.occ.gov/CDD/spring06b/cd/nationalcommunityorg.htm.

9

Office of the Comptroller of the Currency Insights Report

The National Foundation for Credit Counseling has a network of local affiliated credit counseling agencies that are available to partner with loan servicers. Other community-based organizations are involved in these initiatives and are listed on HUD's Website (http://www.hud.gov/offices/hsg/sfh/hcc/hcs.cfm).

Government

The detrimental effects of numerous foreclosures in any residential neighborhood are well documented. As a result, some local governments have combined forces with nonprofits and loan servicers to develop outreach programs to delinquent borrowers. For example, Chicago's Homeownership Preservation Initiative (HOPI) links delinquent borrowers with nonprofit credit counseling agencies through a 3-1-1 non-emergency hotline.[23]

Government Sponsored Enterprises (GSEs)

The major secondary market investors, who are the largest purchasers of mortgages in the United States, recognize the benefits of foreclosure prevention programs and are directing their delegated servicers to incorporate them into their operations.

Federal Housing Administration (FHA)

The Federal Housing Administration, a major insurer of mortgages made to subprime borrowers, requires that all delinquent borrowers of FHA-insured loans be referred to nonprofit credit counseling agencies.

VI. How Does the Cost/Pricing Structure Operate?

The business rationale underlying foreclosure prevention is that restoring a delinquent borrower to a current status on his or her loan is preferable to the potential losses inherent to foreclosure.[24] Although none of the banks interviewed could provide a cost on a per-loan basis for their foreclosure prevention programs, one study estimated that lenders lose $58,759 per loan.[25]

Despite the general lack of precise data on the costs of foreclosure prevention, the banks interviewed for this report provided some metrics by which they measure the success of these programs. Some of the standard measures being used by servicers include the number of completed workout cases, the approval ratio by individual staff members, and whether the loans are performing 12 months after their workout.[26] Servicers are beginning to analyze the data they collect from their loss mitigation activities, including analysis performed on each bucket of delinquencies (60-day, 90-day, and 120-day).

---

[23] For best practices from local programs, see *Preserving Homeownership: Analyzing the Elements of Leading Foreclosure Prevention Programs*, NeighborWorks America, Center for Foreclosure Solutions, May 30, 2007.

[24] One study using data on loans owned by Freddie Mac that entered into 60-, 90-, or 120-day delinquency found that 90 percent of loans that start repay plans will cure within 18 months compared with 73 percent for loans that are 90-days delinquent or just 61 percent of loans that are 120-days or more delinquent. The study also found that of loans that get to 120-days delinquent status, 28 percent will fail, but just 4 percent of loans in repay plans will end in home loss for the borrower. *See* footnote 11.

[25] Craig Focardi, "Servicing Default Management: An Overview of the Process and Underlying Technology," *TowerGroup Research Note*, No. 033-13C, November 15, 2002.

[26] *See* Joseph R. Mason, and Joshua Rosner, "How Resilient Are Mortgage Backed Securities to Collateralized Debt Obligation Market Disruptions?" Hudson Institute, February 2007.

10

Office of the Comptroller of the Currency Insights Report

The success rates among servicers varied according to the workout options they reported. Some found that "promise to pay" and repayment plans had a higher success rate than loan modifications, while others found the reverse to be true.

VII. What Barriers Have Constrained the Growth of Foreclosure Prevention?

Many roadblocks have hampered efforts by banks to increase the effect of their foreclosure prevention programs. The greatest obstacle is the inability to contact delinquent borrowers. When these borrowers do not open their mail or answer phone calls from their servicer, they remain unaware of the workout options available to them. Further, some borrowers erroneously assume that it is "too late" to contact the lender after foreclosure proceedings have begun. The Housing Policy Council of the Financial Services Roundtable reported that an estimated 50 percent of borrowers whose homes go into foreclosure never talk to their servicer.[27]

A second obstacle occurs when borrowers who are having problems making payments do not seek help from reputable credit counseling agencies. Not only can these agencies provide objective financial counseling about whether it makes sense to try to retain the home, they can also act as an intermediary with the mortgage lender.

A third obstacle is that some mortgage backed securities' pooling and servicing agreements (PSAs) contain restrictions on actions a servicer may take in conjunction with loan workouts, for example, placing limitations on the percentage of loans in a securitized pool that may be modified.[28] Similarly, modifications of loans in these pools may present certain accounting and tax issues.[29]

A fourth and final barrier may be the disclosures that a servicer who is a debt collector under the Fair Debt Collections Practices Act, must use in all correspondence to delinquent borrowers, both written and verbal. The language used in this disclosure may have the unintended consequence of creating a situation in which delinquent borrowers may not be forthright in revealing their current financial condition. Under the Fair Debt Collections Practices Act, servicers acting as debt collectors must use the following language, *"This is an attempt to collect a debt and any information obtained will be used for that purpose."* Borrowers already fearful that speaking with loan servicers may hasten an unwanted event can be further intimidated by this language, which was intended to protect the consumer.[30]

---

[27] *See* Testimony of John H. Dalton on behalf of the Housing Policy Council of the Financial Services Roundtable before the U.S. House Financial Services Committee, April 17, 2007. p. 8.

[28] *See* "The Day After Tomorrow: Payment Shock and Loan Modifications," Credit Suisse Fixed Income Research, April 5, 2007.

[29] *See* "Servicing Seriously Delinquent Subprime RMBS," Deutsche Bank Global Markets Research, March 26, 2007 for a discussion of tax treatment for Real Estate Mortgage Investment Conduits. *See* written testimony of Larry B. Litton, Jr. of Litton Loan Serving, for example, before the U.S. House Financial Services Committee accessible at: http://www.house.gov/apps/list/hearing/financialsvcs_dem/litton_testimony.pdf.

[30] *See* 15 USC 1692c (11) (Fair Debt Collection Practices Act).

Office of the Comptroller of the Currency Insights Report

VIII. Conclusion

Banks recognize that keeping homeowners in their homes is the best way to mitigate credit losses, preserve customer relationships, and maintain stable neighborhoods. Unfortunately, not all borrowers can avoid the loss of their property. In many instances, however, foreclosure prevention works best when borrowers and loan servicers communicate to determine their options and the best course of action.

For a variety of reasons, borrowers often avoid having this communication with their loan servicers. Because the number of delinquent mortgages is rising, loan servicers are looking at new techniques to improve their contacts with delinquent borrowers to enhance the chances for homeowners to remain in their homes and to reduce losses.

Best practices include: training servicing personnel in customer friendly outreach and on how nonprofit counseling agencies can assist them in this activity; providing servicer training for counseling agencies on acceptable options and outcomes related to delinquent borrowers; and, paying incentives to staff members based on the number of successful workouts they complete.

12

Everything U Need to Know...

Office of the Comptroller of the Currency Insights Report

Resource Guide

OCC Community Developments Newsletter on Foreclosure Prevention
http://www.occ.gov/cdd/spring06b/cd/index.html

Interagency Statement on Working With Mortgage Borrowers
http://www.occ.gov/ftp/bulletin/2007-14.html

NeighborWorks America Center for Foreclosure Solutions
http://www.nw.org/network/neighborworksProgs/foreclosuresolutions/default.asp

HUD Certified Counseling Agencies
http://www.hud.gov/offices/hsg/sfh/hcc/hcs.cfm

Homeownership Preservation Foundation
http://www.hpfonline.org/

Servicemembers Civil Relief Act
http://www.occ.treas.gov/Consumer/servicemember.htm

Samuel Frumkin was the primary author of this report. Also contributing were William Reeves, E. Matthew Quigley, Barry Wides, and Julie Williams. *Community Developments Insights* reports differ from OCC advisory letters, bulletins, and regulations in that they do not reflect agency policy and should not be considered as definitive regulatory or supervisory guidance. Some of the information used in the preparation of this paper was obtained from publicly available sources that are considered reliable. However, the use of this information does not constitute an endorsement of its accuracy by the Office of the Comptroller of the Currency.

13

Don't Discard Your Mail Without Reading It

About a month after you miss your first mortgage payment, you will start to receive mail... A little at first and then bins of it not only from your lender, but eventually from other lenders, scam artists, attorneys and possibly local government authorities. *Needless to say, it is important to pay attention!*

For some, **it may be easier just to ignore the issue,** *but it is better to be informed every step of the way.* Undoubtedly, the bulk of your mail will ultimately be useless junk – *some of which will try to deceive you into thinking it's from an official government entity when it really is just a scam.* The crooked tactics used by these dirty little rascals are exposed in **Chapter 10.**

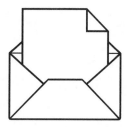

The first letter you will receive will undoubtedly be from your lender informing you of what you should already know: your home loan is in default. **A copy of an actual lender notice appears on the next page.** Once again, **the style or manner in which these are presented will vary,** but nonetheless, it is important to review.

In fact, *every letter sent to you by your lender must be opened and read carefully,* **because it may be an attempt to open a line of communication with** *an offer of assistance that you may not want to pass up.*

Lender Default Notice

SAMPLE

Mortgage Company

Send Correspondence Only

DEFAULT NOTICE

COLLECTION DEPARTMENT
1-800-

2 Regular Monthly Payments	Outstanding Late Charges	TOTAL Amount Due	DUE DATE Mo.	Day	Yr.
12918.58	224.25	13142.83	07	01	07

Loan Number

9000

YOUR MORTGAGE IS IN DEFAULT.

The TOTAL AMOUNT DUE shown above must be paid now to reinstate your account. Additional fees, including property inspections, may be charged to your account. If you are experiencing financial difficulty, free home ownership counseling is available. For additional information, please call the U.S. Department of HUD at **1-800-569-4287.**

Protect your credit. Mail the total amount due today.

PLEASE BE ADVISED THAT [____] MORTGAGE COMPANY IS ACTING AS DEBT COLLECTORS ATTEMPTING TO COLLECT A DEBT. ANY INFORMATION OBTAINED WILL BE USED FOR THAT PURPOSE.

We may report information about your account to credit bureaus. Late payments, missed payments, or other defaults on your account may be reflected in your credit report.

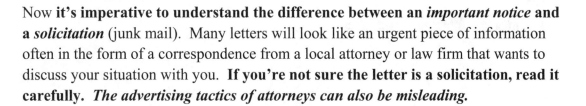
Now **it's imperative to understand the difference between an *important notice* and a *solicitation*** (junk mail). Many letters will look like an urgent piece of information often in the form of a correspondence from a local attorney or law firm that wants to discuss your situation with you. **If you're not sure the letter is a solicitation, read it carefully.** *The advertising tactics of attorneys can also be misleading.*

See for yourself... Attorney letters have gotten so out of hand in certain parts of the country that judiciary committees were formed to address their inappropriate tactics. One such example of this is the opinion written by the **Committee on Attorney Advertising (appointed by the New Jersey Supreme Court) that reviewed attorney advertisements that promoted bankruptcy as a means to prevent foreclosure.** A copy of the entire opinion has been provided on the next eight pages. You should take the time to read it to be aware of the inappropriate language and tactics used by some attorneys to lure in the business of consumers facing foreclosure.

Attorney solicitations can lead you to believe they have the solution for your needs (e.g., bankruptcy). This is when the **"ambulance chaser"** reputation rings true, regardless of the attorney's specialty. Unfortunately, *you can't ignore your mail so you need to at least open each envelope* to determine if it's that one out of a hundred that may actually represent your lender or another lien holder attached to your property (e.g., second mortgage or equity line).

Committee on Attorney Advertising

COMMITTEE ON ATTORNEY ADVERTISING

APPOINTED BY THE NEW JERSEY SUPREME COURT

OPINION 30

Written Solicitation to Represent Clients in Bankruptcy

Introduction

Complaints about sales pitches which solicit potential clients to file petitions in bankruptcy have come to the Committee's attention with increasing frequency. The Committee is publishing this Opinion to describe illustrative abuses in certain client solicitations and to set forth future bankruptcy solicitation requirements within the Rules of Professional Conduct that govern written solicitation for professional employment.

Some attorneys have been aggressively marketing their availability as bankruptcy counsel by reciting a litany of possible disastrous consequences where the only information available to the soliciting attorney is that the prospective client has been sued. The attorney has no information as to the validity of the suit or the likelihood that either party will prevail, the nature or magnitude of the action, the financial condition of the individual, whether he or she is solvent or insolvent, what income the prospective client has, whether the reason for non-payment of the alleged debt is financial inability or a legal defense, what the person's budgetary needs are, or any information as to the prospective client's finances. Often, attorneys make these solicitations knowing only that a public record indicates a suit to be in progress.

Committee on Attorney Advertising

The names of prospective clients are obtained by these attorneys from public record, directly or through the services of an outside agency which specializes in obtaining names of defendants in civil actions, as permitted by Rule 1:38. Many of the letters and attached advertising pieces reviewed by the Committee contain blanket statements purporting to set forth the advantages of bankruptcy, particularly the benefits of Chapter 13 of the Bankruptcy Act. None of the letters reviewed by the Committee, however, set forth the pitfalls or personal obligations inherent in a bankruptcy filing.

These solicitations are invariably formulaic and many of the solicitations, and enclosed information pieces, seem to be virtual copies of each other. The solicitations show a complete lack of knowledge as to the unique problems of the individual debtor and the appropriateness of bankruptcy for the person solicited. Many of the attorney statements have the effect, obviously intended, of creating concern, and even fear, in the civil action defendants that they will lose their homes if they fail to avail themselves of the talents of the soliciting attorney.

Representative Abuses

Overreaching and improper statements which have come to the Committee's attention include:

- "Court records indicate that you are being sued. If you do not act quickly, you could very likely lose your property or home."

- "Whether you know it or not, Court records indicate that a FORECLOSURE action has been filed against YOU. If you do nothing you may

2

Everything U Need to Know...™

Committee on Attorney Advertising

lose your home ... **YOUR HOME IS AN IMPORTANT INVESTMENT AND YOU HAVE A RIGHT TO LEGAL REPRESENTATION."**

• "Court records indicate that a **FORECLOSURE** action has been filed against YOU ultimately seeking to sell your home at a **FORECLOSURE SALE.** You do not have to lose your home, there are legal remedies available to you to **STOP THE FORECLOSURE** and keep your house ... **YOU NEED NOT LOSE YOUR SINGLE MOST IMPORTANT INVESTMENT, BUT YOU MUST ACT SOON."**

• **"YOUR MORTGAGE COMPANY HAS FILED A FORECLOSURE ACTION AGAINST YOU.** In order to save your home you must act quickly and you must do so having been given the right advice... Time is limited."

• "Court records show that a **FORECLOSURE ACTION** was filed in the Superior Court of New Jersey naming you as a party defendant. You must take **immediate action** – if you don't, you may lose your property."

• "State Court records reveal that your property may be in the process of a mortgage or tax foreclosure, which may eventually be sold at a **SHERIFF'S SALE."**

These unsolicited letters, sent to individuals unknown to the attorney, often exert pressure to seek immediate representation by: (a) portraying the defendants' assets, invariably their home, as being in immediate jeopardy of loss, which may not be the circumstance, or (b) indicating that the attorney has a particular expertise and is better equipped than other attorneys in the legal community to successfully represent the unknown individual defendant.

3

Committee on Attorney Advertising

Illustrations of approaches in category (b) are:

- "In order to save your home you must act quickly and you must do so having been given the right advice. I have been helping people just like you save their homes and improve their overall financial condition for the past XX years.... Others may want to charge you a consultation fee while making promises they can't keep."

- **"My law practice is exclusively devoted to debtor relief and I have developed an expertise in assisting homeowners in saving their property."**

- "The **Law Firm of XXX** has been in business since XXX helping people just like you. Only an attorney can properly assist you in this situation and **stop SHERIFF SALES, TAX LIENS."**

- "If you wish to meet with an experienced attorney to discuss your options with regard to the above information, contact me to schedule a **free, no obligation** appointment. I urge you to **compare my experience, reasonable fees, and personal attention**."

- "One print advertisement proudly heralds in bold print **YOUR BANKRUPTCY SPECIALIST**."

Virtually all of the letters, including brochures and enclosures, include a highlighted list of the supposed benefits of Chapter 13 and Chapter 7 of the Bankruptcy Act. These aggressively emphasized benefits are displayed in such a way as to leap from the page, giving the reader the impression that

4

Committee on Attorney Advertising

bankruptcy benefits are universally available and applicable to all debtors. Qualifying words such as "may" or "can," when present, are often de-emphasized to influence the prospective client that bankruptcy is the only prudent course of action. When the solicitation is made to people in the vulnerable position of many who are faced with the possibility of a judgment for money damages, these solicitation letters appear to promise guaranteed legal relief through the bankruptcy process.

Examples of this type of undue influence have included:

"STOP THE FORECLOSURE ACTION AGAINST YOU"

"STOP THE REPOSSESSION OF YOUR CAR"

"STOP UTILITY SHUT OFF"

"STOP CREDITOR HARASSMENT"

"WIPE OUT, OR REDUCE CREDIT CARD DEBT"

"HOW CHAPTER 13 PROTECTS YOU

1. Sheriff's Sales are stopped.

2. Mortgage foreclosure is stopped.

3. Auto repossession is stopped.

4. Utility shut offs are stopped.

5. Levy's, attachments are stopped.

6. Creditor harassment is stopped."

"IMMEDIATELY STOP THE FORECLOSURE AND REQUIRE THE MORTGAGE COMPANY TO ACCEPT YOUR MONTHLY PAYMENTS AGAIN"

5

Committee on Attorney Advertising

"STOP CREDITOR'S HARASSING PHONE CALLS AND LETTERS"

DEMANDING PAYMENTS AND THREATENING SUITS."

"STOP LAWSUITS AND LEVIES AGAINST YOU AND YOUR

PROPERTY"

"STOP UTILITY SHUTOFFS"

"REINSTATE your driver's license"

"STOP ALL CREDITORS' TELEPHONE CALLS"

"STOP PROPERTY AND WAGE ATTACHMENTS"

"STOP UTILITY SHUTOFF"

"EASE SUPPORT ARREARS' PAYMENTS"

"REINSTATE DRIVERS' LICENSES"

STOP AUTOMOBILE REPOSSESSIONS"

STOP LAW SUITS"

STOP THE FORECLOSURE AND GAIN PEACE OF MIND. CALL

ME TODAY.

Conclusions

The overall tone, design and content of these letters soliciting clients to seek legal representation and file a bankruptcy petition have the capacity to cause alarm, great concern and even fear. These attorneys boldly assert the potential benefits of their representation in bankruptcy without hinting at any of the concerns or pitfalls of these complex and far-reaching legal proceedings. Attorneys who send these letters have invariably attempted to exert pressure by reciting potential consequences and benefits when they are no more than

6

Committee on Attorney Advertising

guessing as to whether their "solutions" are applicable to the recipient of the solicitation. The civil action defendant may have a valid defense, the complaint may be in error, the defendant may make payment and cure the claimed default, or use alternative options available under the Fair Foreclosure Act, or the amount in controversy may be modest and capable of satisfaction. These solicitation letters many times violate *R.P.C.* 7.3(c)(2) by use of coercion, duress or overreaching; *R.P.C.* 7.1(a)(2) by raising unjustified expectations; or *R.P.C.* 7.1(a) by making false or misleading communications or by omitting necessary facts. The disclosures required by *R.P.C.* 7.3(a)(5) in many of these solicitation letters appear in an inconspicuous manner.

Future Requirements

In the future, attorneys who seek clients by written solicitation from defendants in civil actions, including foreclosure actions, for which a bankruptcy proceeding is a possible resolution, must:

1)   personally verify the accuracy of all statements contained in the solicitation letter, including the name and address of the addressee, and the specific nature of the litigation which must be recited in the body of the letter;

2)   advise the prospective client that his or her name and the nature of the litigation was obtained by an appropriate inquiry under Rule 1:38;

3)   provide the salutation to the individual to whom the letter is being sent;

4)   include information sufficient to inform an unsophisticated individual, as required in the Fair Debt Collection Practices Act, of the potential

7

Committee on Attorney Advertising

pitfalls and disadvantages of a bankruptcy proceeding. An illustration of an acceptable disclosure, if made in a sufficiently conspicuous manner, is as follows:

NOTICE

The decision to file bankruptcy is a serious choice. Bankruptcy is not for everyone. It is a drastic remedy that can affect your credit for many years and will affect your ability to use the bankruptcy code at a future time when you may need it more. The majority of chapter 13 plans are never successfully completed and the funds paid do not cure the mortgage arrears or allow redemption of property. Upon filing a bankruptcy you may lose control of your property and you may not dismiss a bankruptcy proceeding without court approval once it is filed. The decision of when to file a bankruptcy is also crucial and dependent on your individual circumstances. Be sure to discuss the potential pitfalls of bankruptcy as well as its advantages with any professional you are considering.

5) not attempt to indicate a special relationship, expertise, experience or knowledge which will or may provide a more favorable result than other licensed New Jersey attorneys;

6) not raise unjustified expectations or use language or format susceptible of unduly enticing a person because of possible economic or personal consequences of a judgment; and

7) not raise false hope for relief inapplicable to the individual person's circumstances.

The most important pieces of mail you need to pay attention to are the *official notices* that are issued in accordance with your state's laws. These may include correspondence from local **government authorities** – such as the Clerk of the Court or Sheriff, informing you of a court order, lawsuit, Notice of Sale, Writ of Possession or whatever. **You may even receive important notices from an individual or law firm** *acting as the trustee*. Therefore, *read your mail – all of it! – so that you are informed every step of the way.*

This goes to the heart of this entire volume, which is the focus of almost every chapter pertaining to foreclosure prevention: *Being prepared is the key to having a reasonable chance of saving your home.*

Don't Be Embarrassed to Contact Your Lender

Granted, most of you are probably not embarrassed to contact your lender… but for those of you who haven't picked up the phone yet, *you need to find your lender's phone number on your loan statement or coupon book and call them today*.

The last thing any lender wants to do is transfer your file from their **collections department** to their *loss mitigation department*, where they process foreclosures. With all that has been mentioned previously, you can feel quite confident they would love to hear from you.

Just be sure to have the following information available (listed on the next page) **so you are prepared to handle as much as possible over the phone.**

After all, the clock is ticking…

Information to Have in Front of You When Calling Your Lender:

☆ Loan Number (Account Number)

Just in case you didn't know, **your home loan will have a *number* assigned to it that will be *referenced on your statement or coupon book*.** If you are unable to retrieve it, **any lender should be able to access your account using your social security number**.

☆ A Brief Explanation of Why You Defaulted on Your Loan

You should give *a brief, but compelling, reason for your default*. An excuse or flippant answer is not appropriate here; rehearse what you're going to say, so you are taken seriously. You'd be surprised, but **those within the hierarchy of the lender's operation may respond better than you expect** *if your plead is a gripping one*.

☆ Income Documents

The lender will certainly ask about the specifics of your financial situation, so *have your income documents ready*. These include your **most recent pay stubs, social security benefits,** etc.

☆ List of Liabilities

In addition to your income, the lender will also need to take into account *your monthly bills and obligations* – such as **groceries, utilities, child support, credit cards and car payments.** You should grab your statements and *prepare a list to itemize each bill on a monthly basis.*

By the way, under normal circumstances you should *not* release any personal information, but at this point, you must give a little to get a little. Try to be as honest as possible about your situation without spilling all of the beans and be sure to *listen carefully to how your lender replies* – because they will have already dealt with hundreds (if not thousands) of borrowers in a similar situation. Therefore, you should expect them to have developed a standard procedure by now.

In fact, **your lender will probably fax or mail you an income, debt and asset form to complete and return** (often referred to as a *modification form* or *loan workout form*). **A sample questionnaire appears on the next three pages,** *but each lender's form will vary,* since they usually create these themselves. This, however, will give you the basic idea.

Mortgage Modification Questionnaire

MORTGAGE MODIFICATION QUESTIONNAIRE

LOAN NUMBER _____

PART A - BORROWER INFORMATION

Borrower Name	Social Security No.	Co-Borrower Name	Social Security No.
Borrower Phone No: Day ( ) Evening ( ) Cell ( ) Best Time to Call		Co-Borrower Phone No: Day ( ) Evening ( ) Cell ( ) Best Time to call	
Property Address: Street City, State, Zip Code		Mailing Address: (If Applicable) Street City, State, Zip Code	
Email Address		Email Address	
Employer (Current)	Position	Employer (Current)	Position
Years on Job	Employer Phone	Years on Job	Employer Phone

*If in current job for less than 5 years enter your previous employer information below.

Employer (Previous)	Position	Employer (Previous)	Position
Years on Job	Employer Phone	Years on Job	Employer Phone

*Second job (If Applicable)

Employer (Second)	Position	Employer (Second)	Position
Years on Job	Employer Phone	Years on Job	Employer Phone

PART B – PROPERTY INFORMATION

Property for SALE? List Date / Price	Property for RENT? Monthly Rent	Month Last Paid	Date Lease Expires
Realtor Name			
Realtor Phone			

PART C - MONTHLY INCOME

DESCRIPTION (MONTHLY)	BORROWER	CO-BORROWER	TOTAL
1. Gross Salary/Wages	$	$	$
2. Other Income	$	$	$
3. Other Additional Income (SSI, Rental, Second Job, Child Support)	$	$	$
4. Total Net Income	$	$	$

Mortgage Modification Questionnaire

PART D - ASSETS

DESCRIPTION (MONTHLY)	BORROWER	CO-BORROWER	TOTAL
1. Cash on Hand	$	$	$
2. 401K	$	$	$
3. Savings	$	$	$
4. Checking	$	$	$

PART E - MONTHLY EXPENSES

DESCRIPTION (MONTHLY)	MONTHLY PAYMENT	BALANCE DUE	# MONTHS DELINQUENT
1. Primary Home Mortgage	$	$	
2. Rent Payment (if owner not occupying subject property)	$	$	
3. Maintenance/Homeowners Association Fees	$	$	
4. Property Taxes	$	$	
5. Home Owners Insurance / Flood Insurance	$	$	
6. Other Mortgages	$	$	
7. Automobile Loans	$	$	
8. Other Loans	$	$	
9. Credit Cards (minimum payment)	$	$	
10. Alimony/Child Support	$	$	
11. Child/Dependent Care	$	$	
12. Utilities (water, electricity, gas, cable, etc.)	$	$	
13. Telephone (Land line and Cell phone)	$	$	
14. Insurance (automobile, health, life)	$	$	
15. Medical Expenses (uninsured)	$	$	
16. Car expenses (gas, maintenance, parking)	$	$	
17. Groceries and Toiletries	$	$	
18. Other Monthly Expenses (Explain)	$	$	
19. Other Monthly Expenses (Explain)	$	$	
20. Other Monthly Expenses (Explain)	$	$	
Total	$	$	

SAMPLE

PART F – General Questions

Question:	YES	NO
1. Do you occupy this mortgaged property as a Primary Residence?		
* If you answered, "Yes" to question 1, how long at this residence?	Years:	Months:
2. How many people in the household?		
3. Any dependents under the age of 18? If "Yes", how many?		
4. Do you have any other debts or obligations secured by this property? (Example: Second Mortgage, Home Equity loan, Judgments, or Liens)		
* If you answered, "Yes" to question 2, please itemize.	Amount	
	$	
	$	
	Amount	
3. What is the amount of funds you immediately have available to apply towards your mortgage delinquency?		
4. In addition to the amount stated above, what amount will you have available in 30 days?		

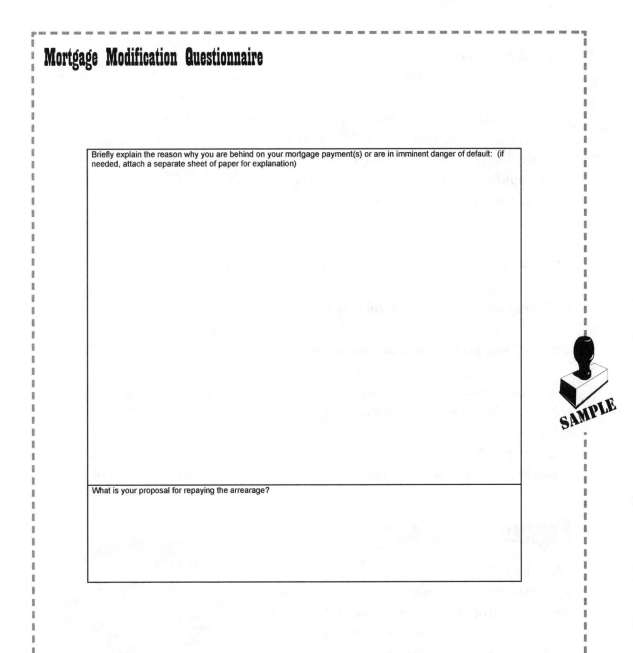

Mortgage Modification Questionnaire

Briefly explain the reason why you are behind on your mortgage payment(s) or are in imminent danger of default: (if needed, attach a separate sheet of paper for explanation)

What is your proposal for repaying the arrearage?

SAMPLE

Lenders will retain all information, some of which may be irrelevant as far as your relationship with them is concerned. They may ask for information such as your current employer and your assets such as savings accounts, certificates of deposit (CDs), stocks, mutual funds and automobiles. Therefore, **while trying to appear as cooperative as possible,** *limit exactly what you disclose, especially regarding your current employer* – **unless you've been at the same job since you applied for the loan.** Otherwise, why tell them where to garnish your wages if there was ever to be a deficiency judgment, for example.

The same premise behind what you were just cautioned about also applies to the rest of your assets and personal information. *If your state allows a lender to sue for a deficiency judgment, why tell them where to go to collect it?* Granted, they will have your original loan application and information, but **you can always move those accounts and protect each possession (if necessary).**

If they can't find it, they can't take it. Listing a single checking account should suffice. **Think twice about acknowledging any other liquid accounts.** As far as other non-liquid assets, such as the oldest used vehicle you own? Sure – tell them about it. For the other newer vehicle or boat you just bought, use your best discretion. *A lender just needs to see that your expenses are slightly more than your income.*

Negotiating With Your Lender

Okay, now that you've shared your story with your lender and answered some of their questions, what's next? Well, **the whole premise behind contacting your lender is to open up a line of communication, so that you can begin negotiating a deal.**

As stated before, they encounter borrowers in your situation on a regular basis so they should be prepared to respond and act swiftly. Remember, *you don't want to lose your home and the lender does not want to have to take it from you!* This mutually shared dilemma almost initially levels the playing field – **especially in today's real estate market, which is pummeling lenders to a pulp.**

So what are your options? Well, *this will all depend on your situation.* **In other words:** Is this a temporary lapse of employment or a problem you know *will be* resolved in the near future…? Or is this a much more complicated and dire situation that will most likely linger for months or years? As you mull over these questions, **an outline of reasonable options is presented below:**

Options for Negotiating Short-Term Financial Problems:

✮ Reinstatement

The **reinstatement period**, as discussed in the previous chapters, is something (despite the laws of your state) that **can actually be negotiated.** *While the laws of most states will give you every right to reinstate if you pay all fees owed, most lenders will entertain a deal.* In other words, **present them with what you can afford to pay to save your loan!**

As you are likely aware, *lenders make their money off interest.* If you are two months behind, consider offering to pay just the interest owed on those two months in exchange for the lender reporting your loan as current.

Unfortunately, it's difficult to play hardball with anyone at this point, but *a good sob story – plus hinting that you are prepared to let your home go – may get your lender to give a little.* And as long as this is your first time dealing with their collections department, this is a reasonable presentation to make.

★ Forbearance

A *forbearance* **is where the lender will agree to allow you to stop making your payments for a brief period of time** – *so long as you agree to reinstate the loan by a specific date*.

This tactic will most certainly involve convincing the lender that you have the means to accomplish what you claim (i.e., a company bonus is on the way, your lottery winnings are paid the first of the year, your hit movie will be released next fall, your inheritance is still in probate…). **But be prepared** – *they may ask for some type of documentation to support your offer!*

★ Repayment Plan

This option differs from the previous two because **instead of dealing with large lump sums, you actually offer to start making whole monthly payments again,** *while adding a little extra each month to make up for those payments you missed*. A lender will usually agree to a constant amount added each month like an extra $100 or at least 10% of your current monthly payment.

Options for Negotiating Long-Term Financial Problems:

★ Mortgage Modification

This option is *where the lender's questionnaire will really play an important part.* If you're faced with a major problem that prevents you from being able to afford your full monthly mortgage obligation, **you can request your lender to modify the terms of your loan – by either adding your missed payments on to your total balance, lowering the interest rate and fixing it** (if an adjustable) **or even**

extending the number of years you have to pay (i.e., if you have 26 years remaining on a 30-year mortgage, extending the time back out to 30 years will reduce your payment).

This is the same principle behind financing a car. You are given a 12- to 72-month option, with the longest always being the lowest. Unfortunately, *the longer loan will ultimately cost you more in interest* – **but at least your monthly payment is more manageable**.

☆ Partial Claim

This option only applies to those loans that have *mortgage insurance* which is insured either by the **Federal Housing Administration (FHA)** or by a private company. **FHA mortgage insurance** is known as **"MI"** and **private mortgage insurance as "PMI."**

Mortgage insurance **is often used when your initial down payment was less than 20% of the sale price.** This insurance is paid by you, but it protects your lender from the lack of down payment in case of foreclosure. **Most conventional lenders will require a *mortgage insurance premium* to be paid, while nonprime lenders can often write loans without it (but your interest rate will be higher).**

Your lender will be able to tell you if your loan has mortgage insurance or not; you can also look on your mortgage statement or coupon book. *If your loan does come with* **mortgage insurance,** *then ask your lender to file a* **partial claim** *– this will grant you a loan* (**paid directly to the lender**) *to bring your mortgage current.*

Mortgage insurance loans backed by FHA are *interest-free,* **but require you to (1) be four or more months behind and (2) be able to demonstrate that you can begin making full payments again.** In addition, *you'll have to agree to sign a promissory note for the loan and have a lien filed against your property until the FHA insurance payout is completely paid off.*

Private mortgage insurance (PMI) companies will have their own terms and guidelines, so you must ask your lender to explain these before deciding which option is best for you.

IMPORTANT: If you know for a fact that **you have an *FHA loan* and your lender is not being very helpful or cooperative**, the **Federal Housing Administration encourages you to call them right away!** Their toll-free number is **(888) 297-8685**. *Despite certain reputations about the "FEDS," this federal department can actually help homeowners!*

Chapter 7

Foreclosure Prevention, Part II: Making the Most Out of Your Money

This Chapter Discusses:

* ★ Stop Paying Nonessential Debt
* ★ Budget Busters
* ★ Liquidating Assets

Communicating with your lender is a great way to get things going – but it's **often not enough.** Most foreclosures are a direct result of *mismanaged finances…* and this chapter can help you to straighten things out. **All it takes is a little** (or maybe a lot of) *self-discipline.* Somewhat like dieting, it's also tough to stomach radical financial change – but when you are faced with losing your home (especially if you have kids or household dependents), *drastic times need drastic changes.* So read this chapter carefully; **all of the material contained here is harvested from ordinary people's real life experiences and industry professionals' expert advice.**

Stop Paying Nonessential Debt

This topic was briefly touched on in **Chapter 2,** for those who could predict their financial future and see the inevitable coming around the bend. *For those of you who are actually experiencing a financial crisis at this time, this is a must!* Even the **Federal Housing Administration** will tell you to *prioritize your spending* – and that's exactly what this chapter does except without sugar coating the concept. *No fluff here;* just the facts, ma'am!

Nonessential debt is defined as **those creditor obligations that are *essentially unnecessary* to maintain a modest existence**. Think about it; what do you *really* need? Food, water, insurance, medication, an education, electricity, transportation, family, friends and a home – *that's about it,* give or take a few other minor things left unmentioned. **So all of that *extra* money you've been spending on payments for credit cards, gasoline cards, personal finance loans and retailer cards needs to stop immediately!**

That's right, stop paying them! – And don't bother to talk to any of those creditors at this time until you reach a point in time where you are **completely** *back on track.* Actually, you should not contact any of those nonessential creditors until you've read the entire *American Credit Repair* volume from this series, because it will give you **Everything U Need to Know...** about the topic, including all the *necessary legal forms* to improve your credit score yourself.

In case you need additional clarification on the difference between an *essential debt and a nonessential debt*, **a list has been provided on the next two pages**…

★ Essential Debt

- **Mortgage (or rent).** Okay, in case you haven't figured this one out already – *you need a place to live.* So unless you have another place lined up, put this as your top priority.

- **Child support.** Not paying child support can get you jail time and/or the revocation of your driver license in some states. Not to mention – many children do depend on it each and every month. Think twice about stopping these payments; you may be hurting more than just your ex-spouse.

- **Utility bills.** These bills should also be at the top of your list. Being without gas, electricity, heating oil, water, or a telephone is just not safe.

- **Car payments.** Unless you are prepared to get to your job on time with public transportation, keep these payments current.

- **Other secured debt.** A debt is secured if a property (referred to as collateral) is used to guarantee its repayment. If you don't make your payments, many states will allow the creditor to repossess the property without first suing you and getting a court judgment. If the property is something you cannot live without, keep those payments current.

- **Auto insurance.** In some states, you can lose your driver license if you are caught driving without insurance.

- **Medical insurance.** If you lose your health insurance, you may have a hard time getting a new policy in the future. If you or your dependents have any preexisting conditions, it's strongly suggested that you hold on to your policy.

- **Taxes.** The government (local, state or federal) is pretty powerful as you may know. Be sure to work out a payment plan so you don't put other assets in jeopardy, such as your bank accounts and wages. The IRS (in particular) can seize almost anything.

- **Children's activities and education.** Do your best to keep your children active and educated. Music lessons, sports, tutors, etc., can have an incredibly positive impact on your child's development and your overall family life.

★ Nonessential Debt

- **Major credit cards.** If you don't pay your Visa, MasterCard, American Express or Discover Card, the worst that could happen is the creditor will sue you. However, initially they refer the debt to a collection agency which can be settled with at a later date.

- **Gasoline and retailer cards.** If the debt is large enough, you may be sued if you stop making your payments. But most of the time, your obligation is usually referred to a collection agency at least for several months.

- **Loans from friends and family.** Catch 'em on the rebound. They should understand unless you've been spending foolishly.

- **Memberships and subscriptions.** Whether it's for magazines, newspapers, fitness centers, etc., you probably don't need them.

- **Student loans.** Only if a federally secured student loan company has threatened to take your tax refund or garnish your wages should you consider honoring some type of payment plan. Otherwise, if you are not being hassled, let 'em go until you get back on your feet.

- **Other unsecured debt.** An unsecured debt has no collateral guaranteeing it. In other words, the creditor must sue you to collect. As with most creditors, the debt is usually assigned to a collection agency, at least initially.

Budget Busters

This is a no-brainer. Dining out, premium cable channels, new cars, Starbucks, the latest electronic gadgets, gambling, weekend trips, top-shelf liquor and too many cigarettes – need we say more? *There is no better time than now to quit everything.*

Despite what you may think, spending a few dollars here or there adds up fast. Here is a list of the most common budget busters:

(Caution: Parental syndrome dead ahead!)

The Most Common Budget Busters:

☆ Dining Out

Restaurant visits (as well as delivery and takeout) are probably ***the best example of excessive spending.*** Eating a meal out just twice a week for a reasonable $30 comes out to $240 a month (this also applies to ordering in pizza). **Now add to that the spouse and kids** – many consumers spend over a thousand dollars a month dining out, which equates to over $10,000 a year. The funny thing is that ***most don't realize it because a debit or credit card is used and small incremental spending disguises the excess***. **It's the grand total that can be a silent killer…** because it's often unseen and rarely ever reconciled.

☆ Designer Coffee Shops

Stop and consider for a moment: Five bucks for a single cup of aromatic coffee? One a day easily adds up to $150 per month. That's over $1,800 a year!!! *Brew your own!*

☆ Cigarettes

Forget about the health debate. Just think about the **cost** that is killing you. *Giving up a pack or two a day could easily keep the lender away!*

☆ Premium Cable/Satellite Channels

Sure, everyone wants their MTV and ESPN, but do you *really* have time to watch all of the premium pay channels? And what about those movies and specials you or your kids are constantly ordering? **Cable bills used to be about $30 a month – and can still be in most markets.** *Just get rid of the premium channels,* which can add $50 or more to your monthly bill. ***Keep the home… or the TV?***

★ Shopping

If you like to shop, *you've got to stop*. What more could you possibly need? This is **directed to both men and women** – whether it's games, clothing, gadgets, accessories or whatnot – *enough is enough!* If you have growing kids, fine. However, **most adults should be equipped with enough threads and gizmos to keep them covered and entertained at least for the duration of these hard times.**

★ Groceries

Sure, everyone needs to eat and the grocery store is the best place to get your food, but have you broken down your grocery bill lately or paid attention to those items that are never used at home? *Some consumers throw out more than they consume!* **Just stop for a second and see what goes to waste versus what is actually used...** and don't forget about using an occasional coupon or two. Just remember – a mere $5 a day is $1,800 a year, so see what you can do with your grocery bill to save at least $35 a week.

These are just examples. *Take a good hard look at your own spending.* Jot down your expenses each week and see where your money goes. You don't have to spend a lot of money to play, relax or eat well... **For those of you who have kids, do your best to keep them involved in extracurricular activities** – including educational and recreational ones, as best you can. As far as you and your spouse go, take a brief break with the family once in a while (*everyone needs one!*) – just budget for it and *be sure you always know where you stand financially.*

Once again, it's the whole concept of being prepared. **Before you spend, plan ahead. Know exactly how much money you have and what bills are coming up next.** *Otherwise, don't dip into your pocket until you've done your math*. And don't forget to save as much as you can for those rainy (or stormy) days...

Liquidating Assets

Garage sale, anyone? That's right – sell, sell, sell!
If you don't need it, get rid of it. If you have a chance
to negotiate with your lender and need extra cash, don't
overlook all the useless stuff you own.

Second to your useless stuff (if you've got it) is ***your savings***. However, **unless
you've tightened your belt and are prepared to sustain yourself, it will do you no
good to deplete your savings accounts** – otherwise, ***hold on to as much cash as
possible and try not to tell the world where you are keeping it...***

**Here's a breakdown of the most common types of assets and suggested actions
pertaining to each of them:**

The Most Common Assets and What You Should Do With Them:

☆ Personal Belongings

The garage sale overture was serious. ***Anything that's rarely or
never used, sell!*** Furniture, old appliances, consumer electronics,
bicycles, Beanie Babies, Cabbage Patch dolls, antiques **(although
family heirlooms, you should probably keep),** old clothing, etc...
You get the point.

☆ Recreational Toys

Fun is grand, but boats, wave runners, motorcycles, ATVs, bicycles,
etc., are expensive and ***may be able to bring in enough cash to
stabilize your situation.*** This is when it's good to encourage your
friends to buy their own or maybe even buy yours from you.

★ Collectibles

Items of considerable personal or financial value need to be considered carefully. If it's part of a life-long passion or a promise to your child, hold onto it as long as you can. But if you forgot that you had that coin, stamp, baseball or doll collection, etc., then by all means, *sell it to help save your home!*

★ Savings Accounts

Cash accounts (including CDs) **should be touched only if you have first tightened your belt on spending.** *Cash is king and should be kept to the very end!* **Cash gives you the ability to finance another home, secure an apartment or feed your family should you lose your job.** *So before your savings accounts are entirely spent, sell something…*

★ Stocks and Bonds

The *approach to savings accounts also applies to securities.* However, **you must consider the tax consequences** and the position of each stock and bond – *some may be worth holding on to for a little while longer.* If you determine it's best to sell them, **make sure they are not tied into your retirement plan.**

★ Retirement Accounts

As much as there is a need for immediate cash at this point, *all retirement accounts should be off limits!* This includes **any account you have consistently designated for retirement purposes**, regardless of whether it's a 401k or IRA.

Cash accounts (including money market funds) can be retirement accounts if your intention has always been to use them only when you retire, not as a short term reserve This is a mind set that you need to maintain. *If you are at the point of no return, let the house go and move on. You never want to jeopardize your life as a retiree!* Ask any senior citizen.

For those of you who are currently retired and are facing foreclosure, **strip your budget down as much as possible** and be sure you've **contacted your lender** and the **Federal Housing Administration** (or applicable government agency) for guidance. You can also reference the enclosed **CD-ROM** for web links to various agencies and programs listed under *Foreclosure Prevention Resources.*

Do *not* take the advice of any company who claims they can help you out of foreclosure *if they are looking for something in return.* As mentioned earlier, more information about foreclosure scams is discussed in **Chapter 10**.

If you can get your hands on a single sheet of paper and a pencil, that's all it takes to get you focused. The concept is simple; it's effort and self-discipline that can often save your home – and a paper and pencil will help get you there! Silly as it may sound, it gets you to focus instead of running around in a state of panic.

Even in times of great hardship due to the loss or injury of a spouse or family member, you need to take a deep breath and a moment to strategize your financial return – *map out your spending habits* **and then orchestrate a solution** *one dollar at a time.*

Remember: *Every dollar a day saved is $30 a month (or $365 a year).* A basic calculation, yes, but a very effective approach that can have an accumulative effect and may help you save your home…

Chapter 8

Foreclosure Prevention, Part III:
When Keeping Your Home Is Not an Option

This Chapter Discusses:

- ★ **Listing Your Home for Sale**
- ★ **Selling Short**
- ★ **Assumable Loans**
- ★ **Deed in Lieu of Foreclosure**

It could happen... As stated earlier, there will be no sugar coating in this volume – **you may have to face facts and let go of your home!** Just don't dilly-dally around to make this determination, because time stops for no one. ***The earlier you can sever the emotional attachment, the better your chances are of avoiding foreclosure.*** **And as long as you've tried your best, nothing greater can be expected of you...**

Now, **there are several options available to you when leaving your home** – *all of which should actually be attempted simultaneously (and even if you are still trying to keep it).* Using the tactics mentioned in earlier chapters can't hurt. **Go ahead and throw everything you have –** *even* **the kitchen sink – toward as many solutions as possible and see**

what sticks! You never know when you may just get a bite from somewhere unexpected, giving you an opportunity to save your home instead of giving it up.

Listing Your Home for Sale

This area was briefly touched on in **Chapter 2**, for those who aren't delinquent, but could feel a financial crunch. **If you were not able to predict your situation and are now delinquent, consider listing your home for sale with a licensed real estate agent as soon as possible.**

This doesn't mean you should give up negotiating with your lender and strategizing your financial return! **You simply need to be prepared for the worst and – even though you may not want to move –** *it's better to sell it than to have it taken.*

> ➤ *Why use a real estate agent to sell your home?*

The main benefit of contracting with a real estate agent is that **your home is immediately listed in the** *MLS (Multiple Listing Service) system.* **The MLS advertises your listing to other real estate agents,** *thereby giving your home the best possible marketing exposure so you have a better chance of selling.*

The overwhelming majority of homes throughout the United States are bought and sold through this system – *not by owner or even the real estate agent's own marketing strategy.* In addition, *most real estate agents* are competent enough to handle the details of your situation to *ensure the deal is negotiated appropriately.* **You should focus on other financial tactics or personal issues that may be occurring at this time.**

And by the way, **don't worry about the agent's fee at this point.** *It's worth it, although you should not agree to pay more than 5% in commission.* This figure appears to be pretty common especially among **RE/MAX** agents. (*Never accept 7%* – there are plenty of competent real estate professionals that can just as easily sell your home at 5% or even 6% max – if the market justifies a premium.)

Don't be greedy – *set a fair market price for your home.* Remember, your time is limited and if you're trying to go for the gold, you may mistakenly sit for too long. **You want to get rid of your home quickly without giving it away, so be prepared to lower your price to entice buyers.** As of this edition, you may even find that the local market is so distressed that buyers will offer far less than you anticipated. **If your real estate agent tells you that your home may not be able to attract more than what is owed**, you may need to consider the following concept of *selling short*.

Selling Short

When local market conditions are upside down and/or your time is running out, you should try to entice buyers by selling your property for less than what you owe. This is going to ring especially true for someone who originally purchased the home with little or no down.

The practice of selling your home for less than your loan balance is called *"selling short"* or the *"short sale."*

A *short sale* involves the same steps as any other real estate transaction – except your real estate agent (in this case) **must make sure the contract is written and accepted by both parties with the following contingency:** *The lender and all other lien holders attached to the property must agree to release the lien (or their liens) for less than what is owed.*

Your real estate agent should be willing to approach your lender and anyone else who has an interest in the property in order to negotiate a settlement offer. After all, the agent gets a commission if the home sells, period.

Now, this maybe a shocker. ***It's a fact that many lenders have agreed to accept as little as half of the outstanding loan balance. It all depends on the lender's willingness to settle and its own assessment of current market conditions.*** If a lender weighs its options of an expensive foreclosure in a poor or slow moving market,

50%

they would be foolish to turn down a reasonable offer of an immediate payoff – even though it's less than its initial expectations. **But don't think you can do this in advance!** As much as this volume advocates being prepared, *the short sale tactic can only be attempted when you are* **at least** *two months behind.*

By the way, this is how real estate investors make a fortune in the foreclosure market – *they buy homes from desperate borrowers who are racing against the clock to sell their property.* **Short sales are good for borrowers, but** *great* **for investors!** It's not a scam; it's a benefit to both parties. **And as soon as you get back on your feet, you** *could* **do the same and start buying short sales.**

Assumable Loans

You may have heard of one party *"assuming"* **another's loan before.** It's not the easiest tactic, but *it works, especially if interest rates have risen.* If you have a loan that is *assumable*, **a buyer** (in accordance with the lender's provisions) **can purchase your property and** *assume* **the existing terms of your loan.** In this case, the buyer would take over your payments and finish paying off the loan for whatever years remain until he or she decides to sell the property. Even if rates have gone up, the original rate stays the same for the new buyer.

This approach is obviously not too enticing to a potential new buyer if the loan has an adjustable rate or a *"balloon"* **ready to mature** (a balloon loan requires you to make one large final payment at the end of its term instead of continuing to make smaller installments). *But… if you have a fixed rate that's not double digits, you may have a shot.*

It will be up to the lender to permit the assumption. Even if the loan did not have an assumable clause, **the lender** *may* **still consider your proposal**. Once again, if the market is slow, it may be in everyone's best interest (especially the lender) to work out a deal and get this property sold. *Upon closing, the lender will provide you with a written release stating that you are no longer responsible for any future payments.*

Deed in Lieu of Foreclosure

It's exactly as it sounds. **The lender agrees to take possession of your home without foreclosing.** You simply give it to them if they are willing to accept it. *Many experts recommend this approach as a last resort only when all other attempts have failed – but that's only if you don't want to sell your home.*

If you've decided early on that **you don't want to make an effort to hold on to your property,** then *this should be at the top of your list,* **along with selling your property** – because the lender will usually require your home to be on the market for at least 90 days. **A** *deed in lieu of foreclosure* **is best when you're not able to find a buyer and only have one loan, with no other liens attached to the property.**

Sure, your credit will take a hit, but if the lender is willing to take possession of the property without foreclosing, *give it to them!* Why drag out the process, the headaches and the escalating fees any further?

By the way, **when they say a** *deed in lieu of foreclosure* **is a less damaging remark on your credit file than an actual foreclosure remark, that is not the case.** *The impact is pretty much the same.* In other words – a repossession is a repossession. Voluntary or not, your negative payment history will still be reported on your credit report. And even though a specific remark will be there to distinguish between the two, this subtle distinction is seldom recognized by creditors when you apply for mortgages, car loans, credit cards, etc.

Fortunately, time heals all derogatory remarks on a credit file – so don't worry about your credit now – *just get back on your feet and learn to manage your cash as best as possible!* **Your credit score should be the least of your worries.** Plus, as promised, the *American Credit Repair* volume will be there for you when you are ready to learn how to play the credit game and take charge of your remaining debt.

Chapter 9

Foreclosure Prevention, Part IV: Loan Counseling and Free Assistance

---

This Chapter Discusses:

★ **HUD Approved Housing Counselors**

★ **FHA Disaster Relief**

★ **Non-FHA Disaster Relief**

★ **Servicemembers Civil Relief Act (SCRA)**

★ **FHASecure Program**

★ **Lender Help Lines**

★ **EUNTK.com**

Thankfully, there *is* help out there to assist you when you are losing your home. This assistance isn't necessarily always in the form of a check, but you can still get help. **Many programs and organizations have been established to offer** *free advice and counseling.* These are people with whom you can share your story and hope that someone may have a great idea  or solution to your problem. **If you are able to use any of the contacts in this chapter, go for it!** Even though this volume will try to provide you with **Everything U Need to Know...,** everyone's situation is a little unique. The benefit of contacting a professional is to have your specific issues reviewed and then addressed accordingly.

HUD Approved Housing Counselors

As mentioned earlier, you can contact the **Federal Housing Administration (FHA)** directly. The FHA may refer you to an organization in your area that has been approved by them or by the **Department of Housing and Urban Development (HUD).** *Exercise a little caution, however,* **because some of these organizations are actually consumer credit counseling services that may try to have you sign up with them.**

It's been suggested that you keep your discussion focused on the other remedies mentioned in previous chapters, because traditional *consumer credit counseling services can only benefit a limited number of circumstances.* If nothing more, you can listen to their advice and determine the best course of action for yourself.

Initially, you want to find an organization to help you handle your mortgage issues, not credit card issues. *There are plenty that actually specialize only in housing assistance.* The list of services they offer includes: **pre-foreclosure assistance, homebuyer education programs**, **renters' assistance** and **services for the homeless.** *These are the types of organizations you should contact instead of your traditional consumer credit counselor.* However, it never hurts to listen to any of them! *All it takes is that one spark of creativity to guide you in the right direction.*

To find out more about the local organizations approved by **HUD,** visit the **Everything U Need to Know...** website at **www.EUNTK.com**.

FHA Disaster Relief

If there was ever a legitimate exception to the rule, *this is it.* New Orleans, Malibu, Tornado Alley, the entire state of Florida… and the list goes on and on – **wherever disaster can strike, there is always an exception for your primary residence!**

When a natural or man-made event has damaged your home or affected your ability to pay for it and the *President of the United States declares it to be a disaster area, your lender must provide relief.*

The **disaster relief options described below** were obtained directly from the **FHA.** *If you are at risk of losing your home because of a disaster, your lender must stop or delay initiation of foreclosure for 90 calendar days.*

Lenders may also waive late fees for borrowers who have become delinquent on their loans. *Just follow the four steps below* to see if help may be available to you. **Contact your lender for further information and to find out if you are eligible for relief.**

Disaster Relief Options for Loans Guaranteed by the FHA:

★ Step 1: Answer Four Basic Questions

- Did my *expenses rise* or *income fall?*
- Were these changes in my finances *caused directly or substantially by the disaster?*
- Have I *missed any mortgage payments?*
- Am I *without other resources*, such as **insurance settlements,** to catch up?

If you answered "yes" to all of these questions – but you don't have an FHA-insured loan – see the next section on Non-FHA Disaster Relief. *If you have an FHA-insured loan, please continue reading.*

⭐ Step 2: See If and How You Can Participate in FHA Disaster Relief

The next step is to *determine if you are one of the affected borrowers,* as described below. **You must be in one of three basic groups in order to qualify for a moratorium on foreclosure**:

- ◆ You or your family *live within the geographic boundaries of a Presidentially declared disaster area*; you are automatically covered by a 90-day foreclosure moratorium.
- ◆ You are a *member of a household in which someone is missing, deceased or injured directly due to the disaster*; you qualify for a moratorium.
- ◆ Your *financial ability to pay your mortgage debt was directly or substantially affected by a disaster*; you qualify for a moratorium.

If Your FHA Loan Was Current Before the Disaster But Now You Can't Make Your Next Month's Payment

This special program is designed to help borrowers who are at risk of imminent foreclosure, so a moratorium won't apply to your situation. However, if your inability to pay your loan resulted from the disaster, your lender may waive any late fees normally charged and let you know about other options. Also, **if you foresee ongoing problems in making your mortgage payments resulting from changes in your financial status,** *you should contact your lender immediately!*

How Can This FHA Disaster Relief Help Me?

HUD has instructed FHA lenders to use reasonable judgment in determining who is an *"affected borrower."* Lenders are required to reevaluate each delinquent loan until reinstatement or foreclosure and to identify the cause of default. *Contact your lender to let them know about your situation.* Some of the actions that your lender may take are listed on the next page.

- During the term of a **moratorium**, *your lender will not refer your loan to foreclosure if you were affected by a disaster*.
- Your lender will evaluate you for *any available loss mitigation assistance to help you retain your home.*
- Your lender may enter into a *special forbearance plan* – **or execute a** *loan modification* **or a** *partial claim* – if these actions are likely to help you reinstate your loan.
- If saving your home is *not* feasible, **lenders have some flexibility in using the** *pre-foreclosure sales program* **or may offer to accept a** *deed in lieu of foreclosure.*

★ Step 3: Take Action to Qualify for Relief

A foreclosure moratorium applies only to borrowers who are delinquent on their FHA loan. *If you are current on your loan payments, then you should continue to make them.* When contacting your lender for further instructions, please be prepared to provide them information about disability or other insurance that may be available to assist you in making your payments.

FHA lenders will automatically stop all foreclosure actions against families with delinquent loans on homes within the boundaries of a Presidentially declared disaster area.

If you were physically or financially impacted by a disaster and are in default or foreclosure, contact your lender immediately to request assistance!

Borrowers who were injured or whose income relied on individuals who were injured or died in the disaster will be asked for documentation, such as medical records or death certificates, if available. Your lender will ask you for financial information to help evaluate what assistance can be provided to reinstate your loan.

FHA Loans Already in Foreclosure

It is very important that you notify your lender to be sure that they realize you are an affected borrower! Your lender may request supporting documentation and use it to determine if you meet the relief criteria. **Once identified as an affected borrower, foreclosure action may be stopped for the duration of the moratorium period.**

★ Step 4: If Your Lender is Unable to Assist You

HUD is confident that your mortgage lender will make every attempt possible to assist you. If you are not satisfied after discussing possible relief actions with your lender, please *call a HUD approved counseling agency* toll-free at **(800) 569-4287** or *call HUD's National Servicing Center* at **(888) 297-8685**.

Non-FHA Disaster Relief

If your home loan is not FHA-insured, your lender will likely have some disaster relief plan in place. Expect each policy to differ from lender to lender, but *count on some offer of an extended grace period or temporary deferment of foreclosure* as long as you *live in the disaster area – not next to one!* When disaster strikes, the **Federal Emergency Management Agency (FEMA)** publishes all zip codes that are declared as being federal disaster areas and rest assured, your lender will check this list to verify your claim.

If you qualify and your lender grants you a grace period or deferment, they will **usually also waive any late payments and additional interest**. This way, you can rest assured that all you have to worry about is resuming where you left off, instead of back-peddling to catch up on hefty fines and penalties.

And **you should not have to worry about the effect on your credit report.** *Most lenders will continue to report your account status as it was before the disaster occurred.* **But as a precaution, don't hesitate to ask them or remind them about your credit file, so that your score isn't negatively impacted as a result of the hardship caused by the disaster.** You should also *have your lender clarify the length of your grace period and whether any additional or long-term solutions may be available as well…*

Servicemembers Civil Relief Act (SCRA)

This section applies to *military personnel*. Most of the information provided in this section is obtained directly from the **Federal Housing Administration** and is deemed to be reliable as of the release of this edition.

If you or your spouse is on active military duty, *you may qualify for a reduction in your interest rate –* which would, consequently, lower your payment.

➢ *Who is eligible?*

The provisions of the *Servicemembers Civil Relief Act (SCRA)* **apply to active duty military personnel who had a home loan prior to enlistment** *or* **prior to being ordered to active duty.**

This includes members of the *Army, Navy, Marine Corps, Air Force, Coast Guard*; commissioned officers of the *Public Health Service* and the *National Oceanic and Atmospheric Administration* **engaged in active service;** *reservists* **ordered to report for military service;** people ordered to *report for induction (training) under the* **Military Selective Service Act;** and *guardsmen* **called to active service** *for more than 30 consecutive days*. **In limited situations,** *dependents of servicemembers* **are also entitled to protection.**

➤ *Am I entitled to debt payment relief?*

The **SCRA** *limits the interest that may be charged on mortgages incurred* (or acquired) *by a servicemember* (including debts incurred jointly with a spouse) *before he or she entered into active military service*.

Mortgage lenders must – at your request – reduce the interest rate to *no more than 6% per year during the period of active military service* **and recalculate your payments to reflect the lower rate.** This provision **applies to both conventional** *and* **government-insured mortgages**.

➤ *Is the interest limitation automatic?*

No. *You must ask for this temporary interest rate reduction by submitting a* **written request** *to your lender and including a copy of your* **military orders.** The request may be submitted **as soon as the orders are issued,** but *no later than 180 days after the date of your release* **from active duty military service.**

➤ *Am I eligible even if I can afford to make my payments?*

If a mortgage lender believes that military service has not affected your ability to repay your mortgage, they have the right to ask a court to grant relief from the interest rate reduction. **This is not very common**.

➤ *What if I still can't afford to pay even at the reduced rate?*

Your mortgage lender may let you stop paying the principal amount due on your loan during active duty service. **Lenders are not required to do this** – but they will generally try to work with you.

Additionally, *most lenders have other programs to assist borrowers who can't make their mortgage payments*. If this is the case for you or your spouse at any time before or after active duty service, *contact your lender immediately and ask about loss mitigation options*.

If you have an *FHA insured loan* and are having difficulty making mortgage payments, you may *also* be eligible for a special forbearance and other loss mitigation options.

➤ *Am I protected against foreclosure?*

Mortgage lenders may not foreclose while you are on active duty or within 90 days after military service *without court approval.* In court, the lender would be required to show that your ability to repay the debt was not affected by your military service.

➤ *What information do I need to provide to my lender?*

When you contact your mortgage lender, you should **provide the following information**:

- ♦ **Notice** that you have been **called to active duty**
- ♦ A **copy of the orders from the military,** notifying you of your activation
- ♦ Your **FHA case number**
- ♦ **Evidence** that the *debt precedes your activation date*

HUD has reminded FHA lenders of their obligation to follow the SCRA. If notified that a borrower is on active military duty, **the lender *must* advise the borrower or representative of the adjusted amount due, provide adjusted coupons or billings – and ensure that the adjusted payments are not returned as insufficient payments.**

➤ *Will my payments change later? Will I need to pay back the interest rate "subsidy" at a later date?*

The change in interest rate is not a subsidy. *Interest in excess of 6% per year that would otherwise have been charged is forgiven.* However, the reduction in the interest rate and monthly payment amount *only applies during the period of active duty.* **Once the period of active military service ends, the interest rate will revert to the original interest rate,** *with payments recalculated accordingly.*

➤ *How long does the benefit last?*

Interest rate reductions are only for the period of active military service. **Other benefits** – such as *postponement* (delaying) of monthly principal payments on the loan and *restrictions* on foreclosure – **may begin immediately upon assignment to active military service** and *end on the third month following the term of active duty assignment.*

➤ *How can I learn more about this relief program?*

Servicemembers who have questions about the *SCRA* **or the protections to which they may be entitled can contact their** *unit judge advocate* **or** *installation legal assistance officer.* **Dependents** of servicemembers can also contact or visit *local military legal assistance offices* where they reside. **A legal assistance office locator for each branch of the armed forces is available online at www.EUNTK.com.**

FHASecure Program

On January 1, 2008, the *Federal Housing Administration (FHA)* **started helping families avoid foreclosure, by enhancing its refinancing program.** Under the new *FHASecure* **plan**, the **FHA** *will allow those families with strong credit histories who had been making timely payments before their loans were adjusted to a higher rate – but who are now in default – to refinance at a fixed rate.*

In addition, the **FHA** also implements *risk-based mortgage insurance (MI) premiums* that **match a borrower's credit worthiness with the** *mortgage insurance premium* **they pay** (*i.e., the better your credit, the less you pay*). This risk-based pricing structure went into effect on January 1, 2008. The combination of *FHASecure* and *risk-based mortgage insurance premium pricing* is **intended to bring stability to the real estate market** – by helping to break the cycle of foreclosures and depreciating property values.

The *FHASecure program* **operates under the same guidelines** as the **FHA**'s existing *mortgage insurance program*. **Eligible borrowers are required to meet strict underwriting guidelines and pay a mortgage insurance premium**, which offsets the risk to the **FHA**'s insurance fund.

FHASecure – like all **FHA** products – **is underwritten to ensure you have the ability to repay the loan** *and will require escrow for taxes and insurance*. The **FHA** *has never permitted and will not include* **pre-payment penalties** *or* **teaser rates** (introductory interest rates that change within a few months after the loan is funded). **Volatile mortgages such as these are partially to blame for the current mortgage crisis!**

FHASecure Requirements

☆ **To qualify for FHASecure, you must meet the following five criteria:**

- **A history of on-time mortgage payments** before the teaser rates expired and loans reset
- **Interest rates must have reset between June 2005 and December 2008**
- **Three percent cash or equity** in the home
- A **sustained history of employment**
- **Sufficient income** to make the mortgage payment

For more information about *FHASecure* and other products, call **(800) CALL-FHA.**

Lender Help Lines

Most of the major lenders in the United States have toll-free assistance help lines if you are delinquent on your mortgage – whether it is due to a disaster or a personal financial crisis. *The following page provides a convenient reference of many of the major lenders and their toll-free help lines.* In case these numbers have changed since the publication of this edition, **don't hesitate to contact your lender's customer service department (listed on your statement or coupon book)** and ask to be directed to a representative that may be able to help you.

An excerpt from the Department of Housing and Urban Development (HUD):

"The federal government and the mortgage industry have partnered to assist those homeowners who have been negatively impacted by recent changes in the economy, or are concerned about the future. The mortgage lenders listed on the next page are voluntarily participating in this special effort. If your lender is listed here, you can help protect your home by contacting them immediately!"

HUD's "Help for Homeowners" Lenders

Bank of America	(800) 846-2222
Chase Home Finance	(800) 848-9136
Citimortgage	(800) 926-9783
Countrywide	(800) 763-1255
HSBC Mortgage Corporation	(800) 338-6441
Irwin Mortgage Corporation	(888) 444-6446
James B. Nutter & Company	(800) 315-7334
Midland Mortgage	(800) 552-3000
Mortgage Services	(800) 449-8767
National City Mortgage	(800) 367-9305
Nationwide Advantage Mortgage	(800) 356-3442, Ext. 6002
Principal Residential Mortgage	(800) 367-6448
SunTrust Mortgage	(800) 443-1032, Option 2
Wells Fargo Mortgage	(800) 766-0987
Wendover Financial Services	(888) 934-1081
Washington Mutual Home Loans	(866) 926-8937

EUNTK.com

 Much of the pertinent information referenced in any of the **"Everything U Need to Know..."** volumes is provided online, in case you need to find out more about a particular reference or topic. **EUNTK** is simply the acronym for **Everything U Need to Know...** and is easy to remember once you begin frequenting the website.

In addition to reference materials, **EUNTK.com** also has **links to other volumes in the series** and provides **online forums** – where you can *discuss your individual situation, ask questions and offer your advice and experience to others for free*!

Chapter 10

Foreclosure Prevention Scams:
Homeowner Beware

This Chapter Discusses:

★ **Crooked Counselors and Negotiators**

★ **Equity Skimming**

★ **"Predatory" Lenders**

★ **Steps You Should Take to Protect Your Home**

---

oreclosure... It happens all the time and it is terribly unfortunate... The primary motivation for introducing this *American Foreclosure* volume is because many homeowners in this current real estate market are *desperately* looking for answers. **In such a vulnerable situation, you are willing to talk to (and often follow) almost** *anyone* **who appears to have a solution.**

Sadly, **most foreclosure solutions solicited through the mail and by phone are** *absolutely useless* **and should be outlawed.** *These persons and companies are motivated to do one thing –* take your money – *and it doesn't matter at what cost.* **They could care less about you and your family –** *so beware and read this chapter carefully!*

Crooked Counselors and Negotiators

This section does not necessarily refer to those *consumer credit counseling organizations* **that offer noble educational services. The crooked counselors and negotiators are the ones who will try to charge you** *any way they can* **for work that** *you should be doing* **– which is talking to your lender!** *You don't need anyone to get on the phone with your lender unless it's a licensed real estate professional – or perhaps a HUD approved counselor.*

Don't be coaxed into any quick fixes! By all means, if you have the time, you can always listen – *but don't do anything that involves a fee or the deed to your home without consulting with a real estate agent, a HUD approved counselor or an attorney.*

Now, this book is not implying that every company or individual who approaches you will try to deceive you – *but beware of the many that will!* **If you** *ever* **have any questions about what someone is proposing,** *call HUD* toll-free at **(800) 569-4287** to **contact an approved foreclosure counselor** *for free advice*.

Equity Skimming

Scam! In case that wasn't clear enough, it was meant to read as: *SCAM!* **This is** *the biggest SCAM* **in the real estate industry.** As soon as that **Notice of Default** or complaint is filed, you are going to appear popular… And every rodent and weasel will wiggle their way out of their holes to come find you! Most of the time, it's through the U.S. Postal Service – but more are beginning to pick up the phone to call you (some will even show up at your front door in person).

However, these scam artists are not to be confused with honest investors that have legitimate offers to buy your home – as discussed later in **Chapter 12**. It is important to learn the distinction between a scam such as *equity skimming* and an honest offer to purchase your home – just in case a reasonable one is presented to you.

Equity skimming (as defined by **HUD**) is a type of scam where **a "buyer" approaches you offering to either repay your loan or sell your property as long as you sign over the deed and move out – *usually leaving you with the debt and no house!*** That's right – *you* would still be responsible for making your loan payments, while someone else owns your house. A brilliant little scam, isn't it?

Never, *ever,* sign an agreement or a *quit-claim deed* that relinquishes your rights in your home *without getting a satisfaction of your loan in return.* In plain words: **Don't sell your house *unless your lender will be completely satisfied* – either by being paid in full or by agreeing to accept a *short sale* offer.** In case you are unfamiliar with a ***"quit-claim deed,"*** it is a one- or two-page **legal instrument used to get the homeowner to give up any and all rights to his or her property. The deed, itself, is not bad or illegal –** *so long as it is used in a legitimate purchase.*

A sample of a *quit-claim deed* appears on the next page.

If you ever knowingly sign a **quit-claim deed,** *you* will *lose your home – unless you're able to hire an attorney to fight a long-winded battle, trying to show why the transaction was fraudulent.* There have been cases that drag on for years, so read before you sign. Better yet, **don't sign at all unless you consult with an attorney or a real estate agent who represents you –** *not* **the other side!**

Quit-Claim Deed

Instructions:
1. Insert your IMAGE or LOGO (optional)
2. Complete QUIT-CLAIM FIELDS
3. REPLACE ALL of this text with YOUR contact info
4. Click on 'PRINT FORM' when finished

Everything U Need to Know...

Click here to insert image/logo

Quit-Claim Deed

QUIT-CLAIM DEED

THIS QUIT-CLAIM DEED, is executed _____ by _____, hereinafter referred to as "Grantor(s)", whose address is _____, _____, _____ County, _____, hereinafter referred to as "Grantee(s)", whose address is _____ _____, _____ County, _____;

WITNESSETH, that the Grantor(s), for and in consideration of the sum of $ _____ in hand paid by the said Grantee(s), the receipt whereof is hereby acknowledged, does hereby remise, release and quit-claim unto the Grantee(s), all right, title, interest, and claim which the Grantor(s) has in and to the following property located at _____, _____ County, _____;

TO HAVE AND HOLD the same, together with all and singular the appurtenances thereunto, of all interest, equity and claim whatsoever the Grantor(s) may have, either in law or equity, for the proper use, benefit and behalf of the Grantee(s) forever.

IN WITNESS WHEREOF, the Grantor(s) has signed and sealed these presents on _____.

Signature of grantor(s): _____

Signature of grantee(s): _____

NOTARY PUBLIC

STATE OF _____)

COUNTY OF _____)

The foregoing instrument was acknowledged before me this _____ day of _____, 20 _____, by the Grantor referred to above.

_____
Notary Public Signature

_____
Notary Public Printed

_____
My commission expires

This form provided by USLandlord.com

SAMPLE

One final word on *equity skimming* – **these bandits may even try to throw a little cash your way to bring your mortgage current.** *Don't be tempted by meager amounts of money if it means losing your home right from under you!* **Either hold on to your home or sell it to someone who legitimately wants to buy it!**

"Predatory" Lenders

These are the folks you also want to avoid at all costs! The job of the *"predatory" lender* is **to write loans with terms you can't afford to pay and which eventually lead you to lose the equity in your home.** It would be nice to believe that most mortgage lenders and brokers have your best interests in mind. However, there's an overwhelming number of *"predatory" lenders* that *will try to take advantage of you, especially when you are behind in your payments.*

Ironically, predatory lending is not adequately addressed under any federal law or statute (at least at the time of this edition). Therefore, *you have to turn to your individual state to see how predatory lending is defined.*

➤ *Whom do predatory lenders target?*

Predatory lenders target elderly and low-income homebuyers, minorities and women, people with less-than-perfect credit, and people who know very little about home loans and mortgages. These lenders usually tell you that you can get loans with very low monthly payments, refinance your existing mortgage or take out a loan or second mortgage to help pay for expenses like medical costs and home-improvement work. **There are legitimate loans that can help with these things but be sure to research your lender's standing with your state's Department of Banking and Finance**

and ask your lender questions. A reputable lender will not mind or hesitate to answer all your questions. *If in doubt, review your documents with a trusted advisor before signing anything.*

★ How to Spot a Predatory Lender

- **Predatory lenders usually offer loans with** *high interest rates* **and** *many fees* (including broker fees, administration fees, loan commitment fees and even credit life insurance, to name a few).

- **Be suspicious of anyone who offers you a** *"bargain loan"* – whether they mail or email you an offer, call you on the phone or come to your door. *Avoid promises of "No Credit? Bad Credit? No Problem!" and beware of offers that are only "good for a very short time."*

- **Avoid lenders who encourage you to borrow more than you need or more than the value of the home**. *Beware of terms that change at the last minute* or offer next-day approval contingent upon prepayments or up-front fees.

If you do come across one of these predatory lenders, *don't hesitate to report them to your state's Attorney General or Department of Banking and Finance.* You may even call the **Mortgage Bankers Association** toll-free at **(800) 348-3931** to find out what steps to take in order to file a complaint. **It's bad enough to be down on your luck, but when somebody tries to kick you while you're down...** *that's criminal!*

Steps You Should Take to Protect Your Home

All of the topics discussed in this chapter can be handled as long as you educate yourself and scrutinize every detail. Scam artists create documents and contracts, hoping that you will never take the time to read all of the fine print. **It's not unusual for consumers to be so compulsive and anxious that they forget to think about the consequences of signing a legal document.**

A simple checklist is provided below to help you *think before you sign.*
Granted, times are tough and *you need the best solution possible* (you may even need
a miracle), but **times could get much** *worse* **if you forget to stop and pay attention
to what you are doing!**

Before You Sign Anything, Consider the Following:

☆ Beware of "Easy Money"

You should *be suspect of someone telling you, "Your credit doesn't
matter."* **If a solicitation for a loan sounds too good to be true,
it probably is** – so get all of the terms in writing and be sure to
scrutinize them carefully!

☆ Shop Around

Talk to several lenders to find the best loan for your situation.
**A proposed loan may not seem predatory until you compare it
against an offer made by at least one other lender.**

☆ Understand the Terms

Compare loan terms from different lenders. Understand the best
loan terms available in the marketplace and compare the *annual
percentage rate (APR)* of loans from different lenders. **The** *APR*
**takes into account both the interest rate and the points and fees
of the loan.** If you need assistance, just **contact a local housing
counselor** approved by **HUD**.

☆ Ask About Prepayment Penalties

You should know if the loan being offered has a *prepayment penalty*
**(a fee required to be paid by you if you sell, pay off or refinance
the property before the expiration of a specific time frame** –
usually between one and five years after getting the loan).

★ Make Sure All Documents Are Accurate

Be cautious of someone who *offers to falsify any documents to qualify you for a loan, especially your proof of income.* **You should** *never* **falsify information or sign documents with information you know to be fraudulent!** This is not to be confused with legitimate loan programs that permit you to estimate (or state) your income without having to provide proof.

★ Make Sure All Documents Are Complete

You should *not sign documents that have missing or incorrect dates or blank fields.* **Be wary of promises that a lender will** *"fix it later"* **or** *"fill it in later."* There are very important state and federal lending laws that require certain disclosures and documents to be signed within a specific time frame, demonstrating that a borrower was duly informed of his or her rights within so many days. Unscrupulous lenders will attempt to leave the dates blank so they can go back and retroactively put whatever date would make it appear as if they complied with these laws.

★ Be Careful About Up-Front Fees

You should *question any fee you are asked to pay up-front!* **The only fees** you may be expected to pay when applying for a loan are **for an appraisal and a credit report (and possibly a survey of your property).** *Nothing else* will ever be expected of you by a legitimate lender.

Beware if you are told that *single-premium (pre-paid) credit insurance* **is required to get a loan or that purchasing it will improve your chances of being approved.** Review every fee and compare different lenders' fees to ensure you receive the most competitive loan terms.

⭐ Beware of the Bait and Switch

Ask for a **Good Faith Estimate (GFE) – a written estimate detailing all points, fees and closing costs.** The loan may not seem problematic until you get to the closing table. *If any fees or charges differ from what was previously disclosed, refuse to sign anything until you are satisfied with all the loan terms.*

⭐ Be Truthful

Don't let anyone talk you into making false or incorrect statements on your application paperwork! They may tell you it's not a big deal, but it is – *it's fraud and can result in legal action!* **There is absolutely no sense in financing or refinancing a home you can't afford to keep**.

⭐ Understand the Costs and What is Covered

Mortgage loan terms typically *include the actual amount you're borrowing, private mortgage insurance premiums and closing costs.* **Make sure your loan is not** *"packed"* **with premium credit insurance add-ons that you don't understand** *or* **want (like** *credit life insurance* – a type of insurance which pays off your loan balance should you die). You'd be better off with a regular 20-, 30- or 40-year term life policy that's adequate to cover the mortgage while allowing extra money for your spouse and children.

The bottom line is that *if you don't understand what you're signing, then don't sign it.* Regardless of how desperate times may be, **stop and ask to take the unsigned document(s) to someone you can trust to help you understand it better**. If the persons or company you are dealing with will not allow you ample time to review those documents, then something fishy may be up. *No reputable person or company would deny you such an opportunity.*

Finally, never sign a blank document – *you will be bound by whatever you sign!* So *never* accept someone telling you, "We'll fill that in later." **Always cross out blank sections or put "N/A" (for "not applicable") in their place!**

Once again, **most of the foreclosure solutions** being pitched by an individual or company *either are* a scam *or can be* **performed by yourself** without having to pay a substantial premium for someone else to do the work for you. However, if you and your trusted support group are convinced that you've been presented with a unique, sensible and legitimate chance to save your home, then by all means give it a shot... you may have *finally* found that winning lottery ticket.

Chapter 11

How to Delay or Stop Foreclosure: Fast-Acting Legal Tactics

This Chapter Discusses:

★ Filing a Lawsuit (Temporary Restraining Order/Injunction)
★ Filing Bankruptcy

I f you want (or need) to stay in your home as long as possible or believe you have sufficient evidence to refute your lender's right to foreclose – there are essentially *two primary tactics that may be used to fight the non-judicial process* and one to fight the judicial process. However, most of the time, these are not permanent solutions. *As you'll discover in this chapter, unless you have a good defense against your*

lender or can demonstrate a legitimate need for filing bankruptcy (and have a good source of income), you will only be delaying what is to be the inevitable loss of your home. But if your intention is to only delay the process (not to completely stop it), then these tactics are a sure thing.

If you are able to retain an attorney, there are a few other options you can try, but **you will find these two to be at the forefront of courtroom foreclosure prevention**...

Filing a Lawsuit (Temporary Restraining Order/Injunction)

This tactic *only applies to non-judicial foreclosures* and **involves filing a lawsuit against your lender. This tactic is extremely difficult to accomplish on your own.** Therefore, it's imperative you *hire a real estate attorney experienced in the area of foreclosures.* But just in case you decide to defend yourself by suing your lender, the information provided in this section will help you decide whether you are in a position to use such a tactic.

To begin with, *this is not an easy task and will require* you and your attorney to assemble *proof that something may have gone wrong somewhere, somehow* (e.g., a defective promissory note, a defective deed of trust or mortgage, there was some type of fraud committed by the lender, the amount owed is inaccurate or a law was violated somewhere along the way).

In order to begin filing a lawsuit to enjoin (prevent) foreclosure, **you must file a motion asking the court for an** *injunction (court order)* **to stop the lender from foreclosing, until the issues you allege have been resolved.** Each state law will vary, but most promulgate the court to issue a *temporary restraining order (TRO)*, but there is a catch: **the request alone will not automatically stop foreclosure proceedings –** *you must also convince the court of three points:*

The Three Points You Must Make to Get a Temporary Restraining Order

☆ Point 1: You Will Be Irreparably Harmed

While this may seem obvious, *you must tell the court that losing your only home would be detrimental to you and your family.* As long as this is not a second home or investment property, this should be an *easy* point to make.

☆ Point 2: A Monetary Award Would Be Insufficient

In other words, if your lender is permitted to continue with foreclosing on your home and you ultimately win your case against them – but the house is then long gone – *a monetary award would not replace the expenses of losing your primary residence, including emotional damage it will cause.*

☆ Point 3: You Have a Reasonable Chance of Prevailing

No court will make the effort to stop a foreclosure proceeding if you're unable to **somehow** *demonstrate that you have an affirmative defense to block your lender's actions.* Fortunately, **because this is only an emergency hearing,** *you won't have to reveal all your evidence and testimony until trial.* **For now, your written claims simply have to be adequate.**

A *TRO* **can be issued quite quickly** – usually within 24 hours – and **may remain in effect for up to four weeks** – or until the court schedules a preliminary hearing to review your evidence and testimony during which the lender presents its side of the story.

The court may require you (in exchange for a **TRO**) *to post a bond* in an effort to protect the lender while the foreclosure proceedings are delayed. **Bonds can be purchased from a bonding or insurance company for 10% of the amount required by the court.** The bond guarantees that the lender will be compensated for lost interest and legal fees if you lose your case and fail to pay them. **Your lender will likely request the court to set the bond as high as possible** – *but you can always argue there is sufficient equity* (if true) *in the property to cover any losses that may result from these proceedings.*

CAUTION

To further perpetuate the delay of your foreclosure, **your next step is to attend a preliminary hearing, during which you must ask for a *temporary injunction*. The *same three points* considered at the emergency hearing for the TRO will be reviewed again – *but this time, the court will get the chance to review more of the evidence from both sides.*** So if you're lucky, the court will continue to agree with you and grant a temporary injunction to stop foreclosure proceedings and schedule a trial date. ***This could then delay the foreclosure for months, if not years.***

However, if the court determines that your defense has no merit, *the TRO will be removed and the lender may proceed with selling your home.* And if – by some miracle – you make it all the way to trial and actually prevail, **a *permanent injunction* would be ordered by the court to put an end to the foreclosure once and for all.**

Now if you are actually considering suing your lender, ***you need to carefully plan the date to file the lawsuit.*** **If you file *too soon* after receiving a *Notice of Default*,** your lender will have ample time to combat your case and continue foreclosure proceedings with very little or no delay. On the other hand – **if you file *too late,*** the court may consider your motion to be simply a stall tactic without merit, and ***may immediately deny your request.***

Filing Bankruptcy

This tactic is by far the easiest way to stall either a judicial or non-judicial foreclosure – but we must preface this section by telling you that *bankruptcy is not an effective alternative for most people when it comes to playing the game of credit and resolving your debts!* Once again, if you need credit assistance, reference the *American Credit Repair* volume, because this section suggests this option only as a means of stalling foreclosure.

So if you need to stay in your home beyond the normal time it takes a lender to foreclose, *this* is how to do it – *just make sure you have an attorney help you, not a paralegal or form company.* You can hire a competent bankruptcy attorney for only a few hundred dollars.

As soon as you file bankruptcy, a federal court will issue what is called an *Order of Relief* – **a federal court order requiring all of your creditors (including your mortgage lender) to immediately stop any collection activity and foreclosure proceedings they have pending against you.**

A *bankruptcy trustee* will then be appointed by the court to determine **(1) if filing bankruptcy is appropriate for you** – chances are they will agree – and **(2) how to divvy up your property and income to satisfy your creditors** (this will depend on what type of bankruptcy you file – as discussed further on in this section).

Fortunately, bankruptcy can be filed with two pieces of paper in an emergency situation. You are then allowed **15 days** to provide the remaining paperwork – or your case will be dismissed. *If you follow through with the remaining papers, you may be able to delay foreclosure for several months or years* (or even *permanently*).

There are essentially four types of bankruptcy available to an individual – they are **Chapters 7, 11, 12** and **13**. Once again, **this is where an attorney would be beneficial** – because a separate 400-page volume could easily be written for each type of bankruptcy! **The following is a brief introduction to the popular types of bankruptcy and** *how they may or may not help you* **fight foreclosure**:

How Each Type of Bankruptcy Affects Foreclosure Proceedings

☆ Chapter 7

This is **the** *most traditional* **form of bankruptcy** – *which requires your nonessential assets to be liquidated*. This form is generally *not a good maneuver for stalling a foreclosure* – because if there is equity in your property, the trustee will want to sell the property to pay your creditors. And if there is no equity to begin with, the trustee will want the lender to proceed with foreclosure. **The best you could probably do is stall foreclosure** *for a couple of weeks or maybe a few months, if you're lucky.*

☆ Chapter 11

This type of bankruptcy is *for high-net-worth individuals and corporations.* With that being said, *it is also very complicated* – involving high filing fees, legal fees and even substantial quarterly fees that must be paid to the *U.S. Trustees Office*. If your secured debts total more than **$922,000** and your unsecured debts more than **$307,000**, then discuss this with an attorney. The plus to **Chapter 11** is that **you get to act as your own bankruptcy trustee to manage your real estate** – *but you are expected to negotiate with your creditors to pay them in whole or in part.*

☆ Chapter 12

This type of bankruptcy *only applies to a family farmer.* It was introduced in 1986 to help prevent the loss of small farms to foreclosure. **Chapter 12** allows you to keep your farm and make reasonable rent payments to your lender while in bankruptcy, which can last from 3 to 5 years. These rent payments are based on comparables in your community. Even if your real estate market is severely distressed (causing the comparable monthly rent to be significantly lower than your loan payment), the lender must accept this monthly payment for the entire duration of the bankruptcy.

☆ Chapter 13

For most people, *this is the best chance of stalling or stopping the foreclosure process if you can keep your finances in order.* **Chapter 13** allows you 3 or 5 years to pay off as much debt as possible *without having to sell your assets*. **The main requirement is that you cannot be a high-net-worth individual.** Your secured assets must be less than **$922,000** and your unsecured assets less than **$307,000**. In order to keep your lender at bay, **you *must* be able to begin making current payments almost immediately.** In addition, *you must also pay the amount past due.* The court will give you a payment plan that could range anywhere from 6 to 36 months to satisfy all of the missed payments and lender fees. *If you fail to honor the court's payment plan, the lender will most likely be permitted to foreclose.*

Now that you've been introduced to the concept of bankruptcy, it cannot be stressed enough that *you would be wise to retain an attorney if you are contemplating filing.* Don't let a paralegal or form company (or book, for that matter) sell you on the idea that you can "do-it-yourself." While you may be competent to handle many difficult situations, **the extraordinary complexity of foreclosure only adds to your financial and personal risk.** So don't do this *Pro Se* (Latin for "on one's own behalf").

Even though you are involved in a court proceeding, bankruptcy requires a lot of negotiating with your creditors as well as the court-appointed trustee and the court, itself. In addition, you have to be able to understand and argue the convoluted bankruptcy code and legal loopholes – *so get yourself some help from a trusted bankruptcy attorney*.

You have now reached the point in this book where you are going to learn **the other side of the story** – *as it pertains to investors*. However, **if you're a homeowner –** *don't stop reading just yet!* The remaining chapters in this volume are a **treasure trove of information** that can **help you improve your own personal strategy for** *preventing foreclosure.*

Bankruptcy and lawsuits – and the other prevention tasks – are no walk in the park, so **understanding an investor's point of view and their tactics is critical to knowing all of your options and how to negotiate them to the best of your ability.** Not to mention, you'll be able to better recognize a bad deal or scam when one is presented to you. *So keep an open mind –* **because you may be able to use this knowledge to your advantage, both as a homeowner and as a potential future investor.**

Chapter 12

Buying Foreclosures, Part I:
Pre-Foreclosures

This Chapter Discusses:

★ **Finding Pre-Foreclosures**
★ **Researching Pre-Foreclosures**
★ **Contacting the Homeowner**
★ **Negotiating a Sales Contract**
★ **Financing Pre-Foreclosures**

If you're just getting to this chapter after reading all of the previous ones, great! You are ready to proceed. But **if you jumped ahead because you are not facing foreclosure and are anxious to learn how to invest,** *it's important to first understand the entire foreclosure process and the timeline of events before you break out your checkbook.*

So, it's to your benefit to at least read **Chapters 3, 4 and 5** before you tackle this one. **These three chapters will supply you with the essential terms and insight to help develop and improve your investment strategy** *– and even humanize the whole experience, by providing a little understanding and compassion toward those who are facing foreclosure.*

Finding Pre-Foreclosures

In most states, the property owner has the right of redemption before his or her property is auctioned off to the highest bidder. A *pre-foreclosure property* is one that can be *purchased anytime prior to the foreclosure auction* conducted by the sheriff, trustee or professional auctioneer. **The most difficult part with a pre-foreclosure** is contacting and negotiating with the homeowner *prior to the auction taking place*. It's important to get up-to-date pre-foreclosure data, so that you can act as quickly as possible.

Frequent trips to the county recorder's office will be necessary – unless you want to pay to use a reliable service who reports timely **Notice of Defaults** and *Lis Pendens*. Such a service will usually cost less than **$50 per month** to subscribe. There's plenty of information and special promotional offers on the **EUNTK.com website** – as well as included **on the enclosed CD-ROM**, should you want to try such a service *for free.* Otherwise, contact your local courthouse or sheriff for more information on how to go about obtaining pre-foreclosure data for your area.

Researching Pre-Foreclosures

After you locate a pre-foreclosure, it's *always* necessary to do some preliminary research before you approach the homeowner. Your checklist should include three necessary steps to help you decide **whether the property may be a viable investment opportunity.** Regardless of whether your intention is to **renovate and resell the property** (also called **"flipping"**) or to **rent it out and become a landlord**, *all three of these steps are still important…*

Three Steps to Researching Pre-Foreclosures

★ Step 1: Confirm Pre-Foreclosure Status

Unless you are living at the county recorder's office everyday, **you can never be sure a property is still involved in foreclosure proceedings.** Remember – a homeowner has the right to reinstate or redeem the property – so before you waste any of your precious time, *contact the trustee or attorney assigned to the property to ask if its status is still an active, pending foreclosure.* While they cannot share personal or specific information with you, they can disclose whether the property has since been reinstated or redeemed. **If it** *hasn't,* **then proceed to the next step.**

★ Step 2: Perform a Field Review

This is a common procedure used in the mortgage industry **if a lender becomes a little leery about the true existence or condition of a property**. So they order a field review through an independent appraiser – **which basically means they conduct a drive-by to visually assess the property and the neighborhood.** *You should do the same to determine if the property is or has the potential of meeting or exceeding your expectations.* And you never know… the property owner or a neighbor could be outside at the time – providing you an opportunity to strike up a casual conversation, which may yield some **valuable information…!**

★ Step 3: Perform a Comparable Market Analysis (CMA)

In addition to visually assessing the property, **you must crunch some numbers to see if your first impression rings true.** A *comparable market analysis (CMA)* is **when you compare other properties that have recently sold in the area – and are similar in style, type, size and condition – to the pre-foreclosure you are considering.** *This will give you a realistic idea of its value or potential value.*

(Step 3: Continued)

You can start analyzing a property in this manner by getting a hold of *recent sale activity.* **This can be accomplished** *for free* **if you take the time to pull the** *property tax records* **or** *establish a give-and-take relationship with a local real estate agent or property appraiser* **– who may let you utilize their research services** *in exchange* **for hiring them to work on your sales transactions.** And of course, there are always services you can hire to provide this type of analysis.

Instead of just researching your own sales data and property tax records, **USHomeValue.com provides valuation reports that are actually** *performed by licensed professionals* **and** *usually contain the original mortgage information* – so you know where the property at least *started* in terms of equity.

The problem with most of the services in the real estate industry is that they only provide an *automated computer assessment –* **which has a** *high margin of error and often no mortgage information.* As of 2008, **full reports** from **USHomeValue.com** were priced at **$29.95** for registered users (*registration is free*) – and **data-only reports** are **significantly less,** *although these are not performed by licensed professionals.*

A sample of a USHomeValue.com report has been provided on the next three pages for your review. Once again, **this service is optional**. *Any licensed real estate professional should be able to do the same for you* – it just takes a little "give and take…"

It is generally accepted by most real estate investors that **your goal should be to pay 20% less than the fair market value of the property.** So if you perform a CMA and determine the value to be $100,000, your offer should not exceed $80,000. However, this varies depending upon its condition and marketability.

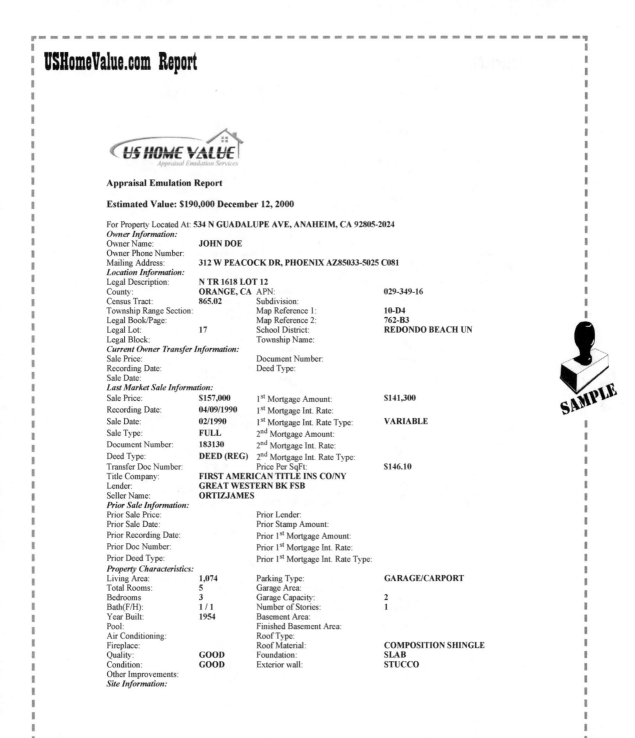

USHomeValue.com Report

Appraisal Emulation Report

Estimated Value: $190,000 December 12, 2000

For Property Located At: 534 N GUADALUPE AVE, ANAHEIM, CA 92805-2024

Owner Information:

Owner Name:	**JOHN DOE**
Owner Phone Number:	
Mailing Address:	**312 W PEACOCK DR, PHOENIX AZ85033-5025 C081**

Location Information:

Legal Description:	**N TR 1618 LOT 12**		
County:	**ORANGE, CA**	APN:	029-349-16
Census Tract:	**865.02**	Subdivision:	
Township Range Section:		Map Reference 1:	**10-D4**
Legal Book/Page:		Map Reference 2:	**762-B3**
Legal Lot:	**17**	School District:	**REDONDO BEACH UN**
Legal Block:		Township Name:	

Current Owner Transfer Information:

Sale Price:		Document Number:	
Recording Date:		Deed Type:	
Sale Date:			

Last Market Sale Information:

Sale Price:	**$157,000**	1st Mortgage Amount:	**$141,300**
Recording Date:	**04/09/1990**	1st Mortgage Int. Rate:	
Sale Date:	**02/1990**	1st Mortgage Int. Rate Type:	**VARIABLE**
Sale Type:	**FULL**	2nd Mortgage Amount:	
Document Number:	**183130**	2nd Mortgage Int. Rate:	
Deed Type:	**DEED (REG)**	2nd Mortgage Int. Rate Type:	
Transfer Doc Number:		Price Per SqFt:	**$146.10**
Title Company:	**FIRST AMERICAN TITLE INS CO/NY**		
Lender:	**GREAT WESTERN BK FSB**		
Seller Name:	**ORTIZJAMES**		

Prior Sale Information:

Prior Sale Price:		Prior Lender:
Prior Sale Date:		Prior Stamp Amount:
Prior Recording Date:		Prior 1st Mortgage Amount:
Prior Doc Number:		Prior 1st Mortgage Int. Rate:
Prior Deed Type:		Prior 1st Mortgage Int. Rate Type:

Property Characteristics:

Living Area:	**1,074**	Parking Type:	**GARAGE/CARPORT**
Total Rooms:	**5**	Garage Area:	
Bedrooms	**3**	Garage Capacity:	**2**
Bath(F/H):	**1 / 1**	Number of Stories:	**1**
Year Built:	**1954**	Basement Area:	
Pool:		Finished Basement Area:	
Air Conditioning:		Roof Type:	
Fireplace:		Roof Material:	**COMPOSITION SHINGLE**
Quality:	**GOOD**	Foundation:	**SLAB**
Condition:	**GOOD**	Exterior wall:	**STUCCO**
Other Improvements:			

Site Information:

Everything U Need to Know...

USHomeValue.com Report

Land Use:	**SFR**	Acres:	**0.14**		
Flood Zone:	**X**	Lot Area:	**6,113**		
Flood Panel:	**0602130014F**	Lot Width/Depth:	**59.00 x 102.00**		
Flood Panel Date:	**01/03/1997**	Zoning:	**R-1**		
Tax Information:					
Assessed Value:	**$180,000**	Tax Exemption:			
Land Value:	**$137,548**	Property Tax:	**$1,910.64**		
Improvement Value:	**$42,452**	Tax Area:	**01001**		
Assessed Year:	**2001**	Tax Year:	**2001**		

SAMPLE

Comp#:	**1**			Distance From Subject: **0.15 (miles)**	
Address:	**645 N GUADALUPE, ANAHEIM CA 92805-1939 C030**				
Owner Name:	**BARNS ALEX**				
Seller Name:	**HESTER ROBERT & LINDA**				
APN:	**029-102-14**	Map Reference 1:	**10-E3**	Total Living Area:	**1,145**
County:	**ORANGE, CA**	Map Reference 2:	**726-B5**	Total Rooms:	**6**
Subdivision:	**ANAHEIM EXT**	Census Tract:	**865.02**	Bedrooms:	**3**
Sale Price:	**$185,000**	Prior Sale Price:		Bath(F/H):	**1 /**
Sale Date:	**12/20/2000**	Prior Sale Date:		Year Built:	**1948**
Recording Date:	**01/18/2001**	Prior Recording Date:	**04/16/1998**	Air Conditioning:	
Document Number:	**72315**	Acres:	**0.30**	Fireplace:	
1st Mortgage Amount:	**$129,950**	Lot Area:	**13,104**	Pool:	
Cash Down:		Number of Stories:	**1**	Roof Material:	
Total Assessed Value:	**$40,526**	Land Use:	**SFR**	Parking:	**GARAGE/CARPORT**

Comp#:	**2**			Distance From Subject: **0.3 (miles)**	
Address:	**926 E EASTWOOD DR, ANAHEIM CA 92805-2137 C030**				
Owner Name:	**BRYSON** THOMAS & SHARRON				
Seller Name:	**BYRD YVONNE**				
APN:	**029-301-12**	Map Reference 1:	**10-J6**	Total Living Area:	**1,123**
County:	**ORANGE, CA**	Map Reference 2:	**726-B4**	Total Rooms:	**6**
Subdivision:		Census Tract:	**864.05**	Bedrooms:	**3**
Sale Price:	**$205,000**	Prior Sale Price:	**$161,500**	Bath(F/H):	**1 /**
Sale Date:	**12/28/2000**	Prior Sale Date:		Year Built:	**1953**
Recording Date:	**01/23/2001**	Prior Recording Date:	**09/18/1992**	Air Conditioning:	
Document Number:	**92641**	Acres:	**0.17**	Fireplace:	**1**
1st Mortgage Amount:	**$180,000**	Lot Area:	**7,245**	Pool:	
Cash Down:		Number of Stories:	**1**	Roof Material:	**COMP SHINGLE**
Total Assessed Value:	**$165,000**	Land Use:	**SFR**	Parking:	**GARAGE/CARPORT**

Comp#:	**3**			Distance From Subject: **0.3 (miles)**	
Address:	**762 E BELMONT AVE, ANAHEIM CA 92805-1527 C015**				
Owner Name:	**BRUBAKES JAMES & MARILYN**				
Seller Name:	**ALBERTS MICHAEL & KIMBERLY**				
APN:	**029-302-16**	Map Reference 1:	**10-E5**	Total Living Area:	**1,253**
County:	**ORANGE, CA**	Map Reference 2:	**726-B4**	Total Rooms:	**6**
Subdivision:		Census Tract:	**864.04**	Bedrooms:	**3**
Sale Price:	**$207,000**	Prior Sale Price:	**$175,000**	Bath(F/H):	**2 /**
Sale Date:	**11/08/2000**	Prior Sale Date:		Year Built:	**1955**
Recording Date:	**11/27/2000**	Prior Recording Date:	**03/15/1993**	Air Conditioning:	
Document Number:	**72160**	Acres:	**0.14**	Fireplace:	**1**

USHomeValue.com Report

1st Mortgage Amount:	$165,000	Lot Area:	6,180	Pool:	
Cash Down:		Number of Stories:	1	Roof Material:	**COMP SHINGLE**
Total Assessed Value:	$185,443	Land Use:	SFR	Parking:	**GARAGE/CARPORT**

Comp#:	**4**			Distance From Subject:	**0.4 (miles)**
Address:	**1613 E ADELE ST, ANAHEIM CA 92805-3307 C008**				
Owner Name:	**GARCIA, LOUIS & MARCELA**				
Seller Name:	**HILL BRADLY**				
APN:	**031-301-12**	Map Reference 1:	**10-D5**	Total Living Area:	**1,249**
County:	**ORANGE, CA**	Map Reference 2:	**726-B3**	Total Rooms:	**5**
Subdivision:		Census Tract:	**864.05**	Bedrooms:	**3**
Sale Price:	**$195,000**	Prior Sale Price:	**$92,500**	Bath(F/H):	**1 / 1**
Sale Date:	**12/11/2000**	Prior Sale Date:		Year Built:	**1952**
Recording Date:	**01/25/2001**	Prior Recording Date:	**03/02/1990**	Air Conditioning:	**WINDOW**
Document Number:	**927186**	Acres:	**0.15**	Fireplace:	**1**
1st Mortgage Amount:	**$172,000**	Lot Area:	**6,615**	Pool:	
Cash Down:		Number of Stories:	**1**	Roof Material:	**COMP SHINGLE**
Total Assessed Value:	**$148,354**	Land Use:	**SFR**	Parking:	**GARAGE/CARPORT**

Up to 10 comparable sales will be included.

Contacting the Homeowner

As stated at the beginning of this chapter, **the most difficult part of pre-foreclosure investing is *initiating contact with the homeowner* – and then**, as discussed in the following section, ultimately **negotiating the deal**. *Now is the time* to **really think about using a *real estate agent*** to take the anxiety and burden off of your hands – *by having them contact the homeowner for you.* **Just make sure** you've **done your homework** and are **prepared to buy the property!**

Before making contact, **you (or your agent) may want to check if the homeowner has already listed the property for sale in the local *MLS system*.** If you do not have an agent or access to *MLS*, conducting a search on **Realtor.com** is often just as effective. *It's quite possible the home may already be listed*, since the first thing homeowners will try to do (***especially** if they have a good amount of equity*) is to attempt to sell the property.

If the property is listed for sale with another agent, your wiggle room for bargaining may appear to be restricted initially to accommodate their commission and serve the interests of the homeowner – *but this is not always the case.* Remember – **the homeowner has a limited amount of time** and **you may have all the time in the world** to **Git 'R Done** *on your own terms!*

Fortunately for you, **many homeowners do not bother to formally list their home for sale** (*even though they should* for their own benefit!). So **this is the most difficult part – contacting the homeowner.** *But the reward is often higher* – as there will be no listing agent commission to deal with. **You just have to *convince the homeowner*** that – **under the circumstances** – you have a *great deal* to offer them!

Many organizations and experts suggest contacting the homeowner by mail first. *However, because there is so much mail being received by the homeowner at this point, you really want to* **personalize the experience** *and* **get him or her on the phone** or at least leave a handwritten note at the front door.

> *Before you call the homeowner, make sure their phone number is not listed in the* **National Do Not Call Registry** – which was enacted to stop telemarketers from calling consumers. And yes, **due to the nature of your business**, *you (even as a sole proprietor) are bound by this consumer protection service,* governed by the **Federal Trade Commission (FTC).**
>
> **In order to check a homeowner's number, you need to** *register as a telemarketer* – **by visiting the following website operated by the FTC: http://telemarketing.donotcall.gov**. Registration is **free** for anyone who wants to subscribe to receive up to five area codes. If you require more, each additional area code will cost $62 a year. Despite what others may tell you, **always** *be on the safe side and operate your real estate ventures* in accordance with *all* laws!

If you are able to get the homeowner on the phone (or at least leave them a message), **your goal is to communicate very clearly – without sounding like a used car salesperson** – that *you're interested in buying his or her home and would like to work out a mutually beneficial arrangement.* With the many scam artists preying on pre-foreclosures, you have to put yourself in the homeowner's shoes and understand his or her skepticism.

Be sure to be *very clear* **and emphasize that you want to** *buy* **the property** – *not steal it with a* **quit-claim deed** *or a* **bait and switch maneuver**. If leaving a message, **never** *mention the word* "foreclosure" *or the phrase* "losing your home" – *because you never know who may intercept the message!* Have you ever let your answering machine pick up a call while you have guests over – or, maybe, you haven't told the kids yet? **Once again, put yourself in the homeowner's shoes!**

If the homeowner has not already listed his or her home for sale, expect the first response to be, "I do not want to sell." This is when you need to reassure him or her that, while you understand and respect his or her position, *it's always better to sell than to lose your home* – **especially when all other attempts have failed.**

Don't ever push the homeowner! You must be patient and be prepared to sit and wait while your idea is mulled over. As long as you are willing to offer a fair price that would (at a minimum) release the homeowner from his or her financial obligations with the lender, **the owner may be more interested to sell as the day of the auction gets closer.**

By the way, *you don't necessarily have to make a killing*. The price you decide on should be **enough to cover any renovation or repairs needed plus whatever your desired profit margin is to compensate you for your effort, time and risk** – this is something only you can decide.

On the flip side, **it's *always* a good feeling to see the homeowner leave with a little cash, as opposed to merely a satisfaction of the loan.** Use your best judgment. Obviously, it's your money, so you come first – **just be fair**, *so that you can prosper and still feel good about your actions at the end of the day!*

If the homeowner continues to refuse your offer, **you may still have a chance to purchase the property at the *foreclosure auction*.** Refer to **Chapter 13** for more information on auctions.

Negotiating a Sales Contract

Well, if you've made it to this point, then congratulations would be in order – because **getting the homeowner to a final agreement is tough**.

Before signing the final paperwork, **you need to set up an appointment to perform a walk-through of the property, to make sure you are** *absolutely convinced* **this is a good deal for you.** If necessary, you can always adjust the figure you had in mind, but **expect most homes to need at least minor repairs –** *and don't expect the homeowner to make any of them for you!* **The homeowner will most likely require your agreement to be an** *"as is" contract.* If you are uncomfortable with assessing repairs yourself, **be sure to bring someone along** *who is qualified* **to evaluate the home's condition** – so your idea of a good bargain doesn't turn into a money pit.

Once again, **a** *real estate agent* can help you tremendously regarding this whole transaction. But **if you are determined to go it alone,** *then you must seek a* **title company** *or* **title attorney** *to assist you with the* **sales contract forms.**

Title companies and **attorneys** will gladly give you these forms **for free,** *as long as you intend on using them for the title work, escrow and closing matters.* By the way, **depending upon your offer and the remaining amount of the loan,** *you may need to contact the homeowner's lender to negotiate a settlement* (i.e., a **"short sale,"** as discussed in **Chapter 8**) in order to get their approval.

Many lenders will settle for less than what is owed. If this is the case, **be sure to have your offer to purchase contingent upon the lender's complete satisfaction of the homeowner's loan and any other liens that may be filed against it.**

If the loan happens to be *assumable* (as discussed in **Chapter 8**) and interest rates have gone up, you may want to seriously consider bringing the loan current and *assuming* **the homeowner's interest rate and payments** for the rest of the loan term.

Just remember – *homeowners are more likely to work with you when you are willing to work with them!* One way of extending a helping hand is to **allow them to stay in the property** (for example, *rent free for 30 days*), **giving them additional time to coordinate a move to a different property.** You could even let them stay for longer and charge them a reasonable amount of rent by having them sign a lease agreement. *Just be good-natured and flexible*, so you can feel better about the money you are making off of others' hardships!

Financing Pre-Foreclosures

Luckily, *pre-foreclosures* **can be financed – just like any other property**. Even if the foreclosure auction is just around the corner, the homeowner's lender will likely be glad to work with you if you express a serious interest to purchase the property. The main point to address here is that *you need to be prepared* **well before** *you begin looking for a* **pre-foreclosure**.

If you haven't established a relationship with a local lender, *this should supercede* all *other steps discussed* – **because you need** *someone you can trust* to accurately review your credit, income and assets, in order to pre-qualify you. *Otherwise, all of your time and effort will be wasted!*

Many loan officers are inexperienced when it comes to processing applications for investment property (known in the lending industry as *"non-owner occupied property"*). So **don't hesitate to ask the lender** (a dozen times, if necessary) **to make sure he or she is pre-qualifying you for** *non-owner occupied property* – unless you actually intend on purchasing the pre-foreclosure as your primary residence. This way, everything should move a little smoother. But, regardless – *be sure to have* ALL *of your financial statements, lease agreements and tax returns* (and whatever else the lender will require of you) *all set and ready to go...*

Some lenders may have a problem financing a property that needs repairs in excess of $1,000. So be sure to discuss the property's condition with your loan officer. If necessary (and with the homeowner's permission), *you may have to make some of the repairs before the lender will approve your loan.*

The last thing you want **is to stumble upon a great opportunity – only to have your lender tell you that** *you* (or the property) *don't qualify,* on account of some ridiculous minor underwriting stipulation that may ultimately kill your deal!

Chapter 13

Buying Foreclosures, Part II:
Foreclosure Auctions

This Chapter Discusses:

★ Finding Foreclosure Auctions
★ Researching Foreclosure Auctions
★ Financing Foreclosure Auctions
★ Placing a Bid
★ Taking Possession

As you've learned, **once a home is foreclosed, it is scheduled to be sold by public auction.** Whether it's conducted by the sheriff, trustee or professional auctioneer, *your approach to a foreclosure auction varies radically from direct dealings with an often bewildered and anxious homeowner*. The auction is a game played by a public gathering of investors eager to get the best deal, while simultaneously trying to outbid one another. Ironic, isn't it? The wise investor is worried about spending too much – when the only way to win ownership of the foreclosure is to be the highest bidder.

Finding Foreclosure Auctions

Foreclosure auctions (also known as *trustee sales* and *foreclosure sales*) **can be found by contacting your county courthouse.** Depending on your state, a *Notice of Sale* can be posted by the sheriff, trustee, professional auctioneer – or whomever the court appoints. You may want to review **Chapter 5** to refresh your memory about the normal course of events frequented in your state and the parties involved. **You'll often find notices posted in your *local newspaper* or *at the county courthouse*, since each state requires the public to be notified.** And in today's market, there's usually an auction conducted somewhere nearby and in the near future.

On the other hand – if it's more convenient – **you can subscribe to an *online service* to keep you apprised of activity in almost *every area* of the United States.** And **unlike pre-foreclosures**, *auctions are easier to pursue,* **because the auction date is publicized several weeks in advance** – giving you more than ample time to prepare. (Some states even have auctions occurring regularly each month, on a specific day of the week – see **Chapter 5**.) **Everything U Need to Know...** has a special promotion on the **EUNTK.com** website, as well as **on the enclosed CD-ROM**, if you want to review such a service *for a free trial period*.

Researching Foreclosure Auctions

When you learn of a **foreclosure auction** happening in your area, **it's always necessary to research the property *before* you consider placing a bid. Similar to pre-foreclosure research, there are *three basic steps* that should be added to your checklist** to give you an idea as to whether the property may be a viable investment opportunity.

Three Steps to Researching Foreclosure Auctions

★ Step 1: Confirm Auction Status and Bidding Terms

While a **Notice of Sale** is intended to be accurate, *proceedings may be interrupted or postponed* (for example, the homeowner could have reinstated the loan or the auction date could be pushed back for administrative reasons – among others). **You can easily check the status of a particular property** *by contacting the person or department identified* on the **Notice of Sale**. This step ensures you do not waste your time or resources. **If you do fail to check ahead of time, a change in status or delay would also be posted at the location where the auction was scheduled to be conducted.**

It's also necessary to confirm the manner in which bids will be accepted and how the winning purchase price must be settled. *Count on* **cash** *or* **certified funds** *to be required.* **However, you may not have to pay the entire amount due until 30 days later.** If you're lucky, you just have to bring a 5% or 10% deposit to secure your bid. See **Chapter 5** for special notes about **common bidding procedures in each state**. *Please be aware that the terms of each auction may differ – so always be sure to call first for clarification.*

★ Step 2: Perform a Field Review

This step is particularly important when it comes to foreclosure auctions. *You need to drive by the subject property to perform a visual assessment of its condition as well as the neighborhood to see if the property meets or exceeds your expectations.* And if the trustee or court will be scheduling a public walk-through, *be sure to take advantage of that opportunity to assess the interior* – because that might be your only chance! **Auctions** – as you would expect – **are sold "as is,"** so there is no recourse against the auctioneer (or previous homeowner) should you buy a lemon.

(Step 2: Continued)

Many investors who bid on foreclosure auctions do so blindly. *If you are given a chance to see, open your eyes and go look!* And if you're ever in the area at other times and a neighbor happens to be working out in the yard, grab a shovel and start digging for information. **By striking up a friendly conversation about your interest in buying a house in the area, you may learn the inside scoop on desirability, criminal activity, proposed community changes, etc.**

★ Step 3: Perform a Comparable Market Analysis (CMA)

As with any investment opportunity, *you need to determine the potential value of the property to be auctioned.* As mentioned in the previous chapter on pre-foreclosures, **a** *comparable market analysis (CMA)* **is when you take a look at other properties that have recently sold and are similar in style, type, size and condition to the property you are considering.**

Once again, *establishing a mutually beneficial relationship with a real estate agent or property appraiser would be an* **ideal** *way of analyzing your prospects for free.* If not, then **USHomeValue.com** will be able to assist you for a **reasonable fee**. You may refer back to **Chapter 12** to view a **sample report**.

Financing Foreclosure Auctions

Hopefully, you've heeded the advice in the previous section – *by finding out the bidding terms ahead of time so you are prepared.* At the very best, you will have to bring 5% or 10% down and have 30 days to pay the remaining balance. If this is possible and the unit is vacant (or the occupants are cooperative enough to allow an appraisal), **you may be able to use a lender to finance the deal – but don't count on it**. *Most auctions require the winning bid to be* **paid in full** *within 24 hours!*

If your local auction allows you 30 days, then *be sure to get pre-qualified well in advance* – so the last thing your lender needs is a **Certificate of Sale** and an **Appraisal**. *All other items required to underwrite the file should be easily obtainable* (e.g., **title search**, your **financials** and your **credit score**).

Granted, **lining up financing prior to an auction is a gamble,** because you will be one of many trying for the same real estate. But if this is your only way of paying for the property, you don't have much of a choice. **Since most auctions will not have an appropriate time frame to accommodate traditional lenders, try lining up some investment capital with friends, family or entrepreneurs** who have some extra cash *in exchange for offering them a partnership percentage or even a private repayment plan.* This will undoubtedly take some good selling on your part to convince them of your expertise. But don't get discouraged – **there are plenty of cash investors out there;** you just need to network a little to meet them.

Placing a Bid

A couple of business days before the auction, you should call the trustee or the auctioneer to confirm *one last time* **that the auction has not been canceled or postponed.** With a bit of luck, your hard work has a chance of paying off if the homeowner hasn't reinstated or redeemed the property. *Don't worry if there is a delay; the auction may simply be rescheduled.*

On the day of the auction, don't be late! **This is a** *serious competition* **and if you are doing this for the first time, you want to arrive early to register –** *at least 30 minutes before* the real estate rodeo is scheduled to begin. Then try to get yourself acclimated, by talking with other bidders (your competitors) – don't be surprised if there are some unfriendly folk there who don't take to strangers too kindly.

Chances are there will be multiple properties auctioned off the same day, so keep your eye on the action as it occurs and don't let your emotions get the best of you. *If the bidding escalates beyond what your research told you was an acceptable bidding range, then put your arm down!*

Taking Possession

Okay, so you've won – *now what?* **If you are the winning bidder**, the person in charge of the auction will most likely give you a *Certificate of Sale* or *Deed*, depending on the type of foreclosure and your state's requirements. **In some jurisdictions, the title to the property can be transferred immediately or in a couple of days** – while others require you to wait for the court to review and confirm the sale (known as a *confirmation period*).

Once again, see **Chapter 5** for an overview of your state's common procedures and then ask the auctioneer or the county courthouse for specific information. **Don't forget** – *some states allow for a redemption period even after you've paid for the property*. For example, **the state of Alabama allows the homeowner to redeem the property** *up to a year after the sale*! So *review your state's redemption period before you start spending a considerable amount of time and/or money.*

One final note about taking possession: *If the homeowner does not vacate and the state does not evict them, you may have to contact the county courthouse, sheriff or a local attorney to help you do the evicting.* **Hopefully, you won't have to do this** – because all it takes is for a disgruntled homeowner to forget to stop the clogged toilet or faucet from running and your home becomes worthless! For this reason alone, *you never want to take matters into your own hands and/or get confrontational with the homeowner or other occupants* (e.g., tenants) – **leave that up to the sheriff.**

Chapter 14

Buying Foreclosures, Part III:
Real Estate Owned Properties (REOs)

This Chapter Discusses:

★ **Finding REOs**

★ **Researching REOs**

★ **Contacting the Lender**

★ **Negotiating a Sales Contract**

★ **Financing REOs**

A *Real Estate Owned property (REO)* – also called a *"bank-owned property"* – is one where **the lender has taken possession of a home, by either negotiating a deal with the homeowner before the auction** (i.e., the lender accepted a *deed in lieu of foreclosure*) **or being the highest bidder at the auction.**

Remember (as stated in **Chapter 4**) – **the lender typically receives credit for the total amount of the foreclosure judgment.** So if the loan balance was high, other bidders at the auction probably won't bid enough to cover the lender's outstanding balance. *The lender then has the right to bid the full amount of its credit to buy the home so it can sell it on its own.*  However, if the lender's loan was guaranteed by either the **Department of Housing and Urban Development (HUD)** or the **Department of Veterans Affairs (VA),** *then that government agency would coordinate the sale.*

In either case, an **REO** is not nearly as great a deal as a pre-foreclosure or foreclosure auction, because the lender needs to recoup its expenses during and after foreclosure – which may include legal fees, liens against the property, repairs, etc. As a result, **the lender will often hire a real estate agency to sell the property as close to market value as possible.**

On the plus side, **REO**s are **much easier to negotiate and acquire than any other type of foreclosure.** And if you do your homework, you can still find a good buy!

Finding REOs

Most **Real Estate Owned** properties **can easily be located for free by contacting a local real estate agent, because most of them will be listed in the** *MLS system.* Another way of finding **REO**s is to contact the **REO** (or *asset management*) department of a local bank or lender to obtain a list of their available properties – count on each lender's level of cooperation to vary. **They may even simply refer you to their own real estate agent.**

Again, if it's more convenient for you, **you can subscribe to an online service to keep you apprised of activity in almost every area of the United States.** The **same type of service** discussed for **pre-foreclosures** and **foreclosure auctions** will also include **REO**s. **Just remember, third-party services are offered only as a matter of convenience.** *All foreclosure listings can be obtained on your own as long as you put forth the time and effort to contact the respective local sources.* But for those willing to pay for the data, **Everything U Need to Know...** has a special promotion on the **EUNTK.com** website, as well as **on the enclosed CD-ROM,** if you want to try such a service *for free*.

Researching REOs

Your approach to reviewing a **Real Estate Owned** property **should be the same as buying any property listed by a real estate agent in the *MLS system*.** This will involve **similar steps to those used when investigating pre-foreclosures and auctions.** There are ***three basic steps*** to help you decide whether the property may be a viable investment opportunity.

Three Steps to Researching REOs

☆ Step 1: Confirm the Listing Status

This is easy to do. **You or your own real estate agent should call the listing agent or lender and confirm that the property is still for sale, whether there are any pending offers on the table and if it is vacant.** It would be a shame to learn of a listing and perform extensive research and analysis – only to learn that the property was sold weeks ago. **MLS** data is not updated automatically; it must be updated manually by the listing agent who may sometimes forget to change a listing's status.

☆ Step 2: Perform a Field Review

Not only is your time precious, but so is the time of others – and **the last thing you want to do is wear out your welcome with the REO agent, lender… or even your own agent.** In order to get results, you need to ***present yourself as a professional investor*** who isn't shooting blanks or grasping at straws, trying to find a property.

So ***before you schedule an appointment to see an REO listing, you should perform a field review*** (a visual assessment of the property and the neighborhood) to ensure the property has the potential to meet or even exceed your expectations.

(Step 2: Continued)

Since all **REO**s *should* **be vacant property** (you should confirm this, as stated in **Step 1**), ask the neighbors or carefully *take a peek in one of the front windows* – just be sure you're not wearing your dark hooded jacket or black leather trench coat with matching ski mask and duffle bag!

Once again, if a neighbor happens to be working out in the yard, grab a shovel and start digging for information. **By striking up a friendly conversation about your interest in buying a house in the area, you may learn the inside scoop on desirability, criminal activity, proposed community changes, and more.**

☆ Step 3: Perform a Comparable Market Analysis (CMA)

As with any investment opportunity, **you need to determine the potential value of the property to be auctioned.** As mentioned in the previous chapters on pre-foreclosures and auctions, **a *comparable market analysis* is when you take a look at other properties that have recently sold – and are similar in style, type, size and condition to the property you are considering.**

It's worth saying this again: *Establish a mutually beneficial relationship with a real estate agent or property appraiser, so you can analyze your prospects for free.* There is **no need to pay for this type of research**, as long as you don't wear out your welcome. **There isn't a real estate agent or appraiser that will turn you down as long as you bring them a little business on occasion.** Nonetheless, if you prefer to go at it alone, then **USHomeValue.com** is your best bet. *See* **Chapter 12 for a sample report.**

Contacting the Lender

This will actually be the second time you or your real estate agent will be contacting the lender or its agent – *but this time you are contemplating submitting an offer.* You may even want to consider putting a little money in escrow to back up your posturing. And – by all means – *make sure you are pre-qualified and ready to buy!* Otherwise, bid *adieu* to your reputation if you fail to deliver…

The **purpose of your second call** should be *to arrange an appointment to walk through and inspect the property.* If necessary, **bring along someone who is qualified to assess a property's condition and estimate the cost of any needed repairs** (e.g., a general contractor). **If you don't have much renovation experience, you'll definitely want to get a reliable estimate to accurately calculate how much you can afford to spend.**

Negotiating a Sales Contract

Now that you've walked through the property and are convinced it's a good buy, **you or your agent need to begin negotiating the terms of the sales contract with the lender or its agent.** *A real estate agent is strongly recommended at this point to handle the negotiations* – unless you feel skilled and knowledgeable enough to hammer out the terms of your own legal contract.

If the lender indicates the property is still subject to a *redemption period,* **ask to see if you can still submit an offer to purchase contingent upon the expiration of the homeowner's right to redeem – or if you can at least put some money down to secure your position in line.** This should only delay your closing by a few weeks (at worst, a few months), depending on the foreclosure laws of your state. *The important thing is to try and reserve your place in line!*

The lender or its **REO** agent should be motivated to work with you at this point, because their primary goal is to sell the property to recover a considerable loss that is escalating everyday. **Just be prepared to accept the property *"as is"*** – which means the lender will not offer *any* guarantee or warranty regarding the property's condition. *As long as you've inspected the property carefully, this shouldn't be much of a concern...*

Many investors, such as yourself, prefer to buy homes direct from the lender – because it tends to be a more reliable process than pre-foreclosures or auctions. And as long as you're willing to buy without requiring the lender to be subject to numerous conditions, you'll probably be able to negotiate a pretty good bargain.

If you're lucky, the lender's inventory of **REOs** *will be high* – motivating them to sell more readily at a *below-market price*. Fortunately, an **REO is a non-performing asset** which means it doesn't make money just sitting there. Therefore, this is *not* something a lender wants to sit on for too long.

At the end of the deal (if you have any money left or resources available), **let the lender or its agent know you are always looking for properties to purchase and encourage them to *keep you in front of the line.*** Remember – there are plenty of other investors just like you, waiting in the wings!

Financing REOs

As you've probably guessed, *financing Real Estate Owned property* **is no different than financing any other property.** You should **contact a local lender to get pre-qualified,** in order to be prepared to submit a contract well before you bother contacting the lender or its agent.

Pre-qualification letters are usually good for 60-90 days – **unless you've neglected to pay your bills recently.** In case you're unfamiliar with how to obtain the best possible financing, reference the *American Mortgage* volume to learn the tricks of the trade regarding credit corrections, income, assets and more...

As it's been stated before, but worth mentioning again: **If you haven't established a relationship with a local lender, this should be paramount!** *You are only as good as your financial backing.* **Without a solid source of money, you might as well forget investing in foreclosures!**

This means that you'll need an **experienced and productive loan officer** whom you can trust to get the job done. Otherwise, all of your time and effort will be wasted! Unfortunately, **many loan officers are inexperienced when it comes to originating** *investment* (non-owner occupied) *property loans. So be sure you clarify your intentions and ask questions along the way!*

The *last* thing you want is to endeavor to prospect all the way to a *promising goldmine…* only to find – after expending much blood, sweat and tears – that you can't stake your claim in the end!

Conclusion

So, there you have it… The world of the *American Foreclosure* – from both sides of the story. Ideally, you've found the information you sought to discover, *as well as gaining an understanding of the perspective from the other side of the field.*

If you are facing imminent foreclosure, it's not always enough to know what steps you can take to prevent losing your home – *half of the game is* **knowing the laws and forces that are working against you.** And, similarly, **as an investor, it's both prudent and empathetic to understand just what your potential profit may be** *costing* **you and the homeowner.**

The important thing is for both sides to understand **the totality of the foreclosure process** – and while this volume can't possibly address *every individual situation*, we hope it has given you the overview you need and has provided sufficient additional resources, which can steer you to the help you need…

If you ever need further advice or assistance, you can *always* **check out the official website for this entire book series** at EUNTK.com – where you'll find discussion forums, laws and statutes, other related subjects within the series, and a whole lot more… Remember, **this site is free** – and you can't beat that *for the absolute easiest way there is to learn* "Everything U Need to Know…"

Wherever you may stand – **preventing** *or* **buying** – we wish you the best of luck and hope **this volume has helped empower you with** *the knowledge you will need to succeed.* **Just remember that when there's a homeowner on the other end of your deal** – *it's more than about a piece of property and your personal profit margin* – **and if you can** *successfully* **communicate with the other side,** *you've already won half the battle!*

Government Publications:
Resources to Help Avoid Foreclosure

This Appendix Includes:

★ **HUD Brochure: How to Avoid Foreclosure**

★ **Congressional Office Manual**

★ **FTC Facts for Consumers**

The following publications contained in this appendix are intended to show how and with what tools the federal government is advising consumers who are faced with the possibility of losing their home. While this *American Foreclosure* volume may disagree with some of the government's recommendations and its failure to be candid with homeowners about their realistic options and alternatives regarding foreclosure, these documents are worth reading so that you can extract the bits and pieces that may be of use to you.

As stated earlier, it can never hurt to listen to the advice and recommendations of others – just be sure you take the time to carefully consider all of your options and ask as many questions as you need to in order to feel comfortable about your decision. If your goal is to save your home no matter what the cost, then be sure the solution also provides you enough room (financially) to enjoy living there.

HUD Brochure: How to Avoid Foreclosure

U.S. Department of Housing and Urban Development

HOW TO AVOID FORECLOSURE

This booklet explains how property owners can avoid losing their homes because of delinquent payments.

Este folleto explica a los propietarios de casas como evitar perder su hogar debido al incumplimiento en los pagos. Para información en español llame a la entidad que le dió el préstamo.

www.hud.gov

hud

Q: WHAT HAPPENS WHEN I MISS MY MORTGAGE PAYMENTS?

Foreclosure may occur. This is the legal means that your lender can use to repossess (take over) your home. When this happens, you must move out of your house. If your property is worth less than the total amount you owe on your mortgage loan, a deficiency judgment could be pursued. If that happens, you not only lose your home, you also would owe HUD an additional amount.

Both foreclosures and deficiency judgments could seriously affect your ability to qualify for credit in the future. So you should avoid foreclosure if possible.

Q: WHAT SHOULD I DO?

1. DO NOT IGNORE THE LETTERS FROM YOUR LENDER. If you are having problems making your payments, call or write to your lender's Loss Mitigation Department without delay. Explain your situation. Be prepared to provide them with financial information, such as your monthly income and expenses. Without this information, they may not be able to help.
2. Stay in your home for now. You may not qualify for assistance if you abandon your property.
3. Contact a HUD-approved housing counseling agency. Call **1-800-569-4287** or **TDD 1-800-877-8339** for the housing counseling agency nearest you. These agencies are valuable resources. They frequently have information on services and programs offered by Government agencies as well as private and community organizations that could help you. The housing counseling agency may also offer credit counseling. These services are usually free of charge.

Q: WHAT ARE MY ALTERNATIVES?

You may be considered for the following:

<u>Special Forbearance.</u> Your lender may be able to arrange a

1

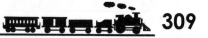

repayment plan based on your financial situation and may even provide for a temporary reduction or suspension of your payments. You may qualify for this if you have recently experienced a reduction in income or an increase in living expenses. You must furnish information to your lender to show that you would be able to meet the requirements of the new payment plan.

Mortgage Modification. You may be able to refinance the debt and/or extend the term of your mortgage loan. This may help you catch up by reducing the monthly payments to a more affordable level. You may qualify if you have recovered from a financial problem and can afford the new payment amount.

Partial Claim. Your lender may be able to work with you to obtain a one-time payment from the FHA-Insurance fund to bring your mortgage current.

You may qualify if:
1. your loan is at least 4 months delinquent but no more than 12 months delinquent;
2. you are able to begin making full mortgage payments.

When your lender files a Partial Claim, the U.S. Department of Housing and Urban Development will pay your lender the amount necessary to bring your mortgage current. You must execute a Promissory Note, and a Lien will be placed on your property until the Promissory Note is paid in full.

The Promissory Note is interest-free and is due when you pay off the first mortgage or when you sell the property.

Pre-foreclosure sale. This will allow you to avoid foreclosure by selling your property for an amount less than the amount necessary to pay off your mortgage loan.

2

You may qualify if:

1. the loan is at least 2 months delinquent;

2. you are able to sell your house within 3 to 5 months; and

3. a new appraisal (that your lender will obtain) shows that the value of your home meets HUD program guidelines.

<u>Deed-in-lieu of foreclosure.</u> As a last resort, you may be able to voluntarily "give back" your property to the lender. This won't save your house, but it is not as damaging to your credit rating as a foreclosure.

You can qualify if:

1. you are in default and don't qualify for any of the other options;

2. your attempts at selling the house before foreclosure were unsuccessful; and

3. you don't have another FHA mortgage in default.

Q: HOW DO I KNOW IF I QUALIFY FOR ANY OF THESE ALTERNATIVES?

Your lender will determine if you qualify for any of the alternatives. A housing counseling agency can also help you determine which, if any, of these options may meet your needs and also assist you in interacting with your lender. Call **1-800-569-4287** or **TDD 1-800-877-8339**.

Q: SHOULD I BE AWARE OF ANYTHING ELSE?

Yes. Beware of scams! Solutions that sound too simple or too good to be true usually are. If you're selling your home without professional guidance, beware of buyers who try to rush you through the process. Unfortunately, there are people who may try to take advantage of your financial difficulty. Be especially alert to the following:

3

<u>Equity skimming.</u> In this type of scam, a "buyer" approaches you, offering to get you out of financial trouble by promising to pay off your mortgage or give you a sum of money when the property is sold. The "buyer" may suggest that you move out quickly and deed the property to him or her. The "buyer" then collects rent for a time, does not make any mortgage payments, and allows the lender to foreclose. Remember, signing over your deed to someone else does not necessarily relieve you of your obligation on your loan.

<u>Phony counseling agencies.</u> Some groups calling themselves "counseling agencies" may approach you and offer to perform certain services for a fee. These could well be services you could do for yourself for free, such as negotiating a new payment plan with your lender, or pursuing a pre-foreclosure sale. If you have any doubt about paying for such services, call a HUD-approved housing counseling agency at **1-800-569-4287** or **TDD 1-800-877-8339.** Do this before you pay anyone or sign anything.

Q: ARE THERE ANY PRECAUTIONS I CAN TAKE?

Here are several precautions that should help you avoid being "taken" by a scam artist:

1. Don't sign any papers you don't fully understand.

2. Make sure you get all "promises" in writing.

3. Beware of any contract of sale or loan assumption where you are not formally released from liability for your mortgage debt.

4. Check with a lawyer or your mortgage company before entering into any deal involving your home.

5. If you're selling the house yourself to avoid foreclosure, check to see if there are any complaints against the prospective buyer. You can contact your state's Attorney

4

General, the State Real Estate Commission, or the local District Attorney's Consumer Fraud Unit for this type of information.

Q: WHAT ARE THE MAIN POINTS I SHOULD REMEMBER?

1. Don't lose your home and damage your credit history.

2. Call or write your mortgage lender immediately and be honest about your financial situation.

3. Stay in your home to make sure you qualify for assistance.

4. Arrange an appointment with a HUD-approved housing counselor to explore your options at **1-800-569-4287** or **TDD 1-800-877-8339.**

5. Cooperate with the counselor or lender trying to help you.

6. Explore every alternative to keep your home.

7. Beware of scams.

8. Do not sign anything you don't understand. And remember that signing over the deed to someone else does not necessarily relieve you of your loan obligation.

Act now. Delaying can't help. If you do nothing, YOU WILL LOSE YOUR HOME and your good credit rating.

Visit our web site at www.hud.gov.

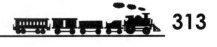

hud

U.S. Department of Housing and Urban Development
Office of Single Family Housing
451 Seventh Street, SW
Washington D.C. 20410-3000

May 2001
HUD-PA-426-H

04344

Congressional Office Manual

CONGRESSIONAL OFFICE MANUAL
RESOURCES TO HELP HOMEOWNERS AVOID FORECLOSURE

Government and Nonprofit Resources: *A number of federal and state agencies and nonprofit organizations have developed foreclosure prevention programs to help homeowners who are having trouble with their home loans. The following organizations offer free or low-cost foreclosure prevention programs to eligible homeowners:*

U.S. Department of Housing and Urban Development (HUD)

HUD provides a variety of resources for homeowners at risk of foreclosure. The Department funds free housing counseling services throughout the country. HUD-approved counselors can help homeowners understand the law and their options, organize their finances, and represent borrowers in negotiations with their lenders if this assistance is needed.

Telephone: 1-800-569-4287

Find HUD-Approved Housing Counseling Agencies in your State:
http://www.hud.gov/offices/hsg/sfh/hcc/hcs.cfm?weblistaction=summary

Additional HUD resources for avoiding foreclosure:
http://www.hud.gov/foreclosure/index.cfm

State Attorneys General

Homeowners who suspect that they have been a victim of fraud, misleading information, or other deceptive practices, should contact their state Attorney General's office. These offices investigate complaints and sue lenders and other mortgage originators for alleged illegal behavior. In addition, several state Attorneys General have been instrumental is setting up multi-agency foreclosure prevention task forces that provide financial resources and proactive intervention for homeowners facing or at risk of foreclosure.

Find your state Attorney General's office:
http://www.naag.org/attorneys_general.php

State Housing Finance Agencies

State Housing Finance Agencies administer a wide range of affordable housing and community development programs. A number of state HFAs have partnered with other entities (including nonprofit counseling agencies, local governments, state housing departments and lenders) to provide comprehensive foreclosure prevention and mitigation strategies.

Find your state housing finance agency:
http://www.ncsha.org/section.cfm/4/39/187

NeighborWorks

NeighborWorks is a national network of more than 240 community-based nonprofit organizations (located in 50 states) created by Congress to provide financial support, technical assistance, and training for community revitalization efforts. NeighborWorks provides a variety of resources for preserving homeownership in the face of rising foreclosure rates including *HOPE for Homeowners*, a toll-free national hotline that offers free foreclosure prevention and counseling advice from a third party, HUD-certified, not-for-profit network of counseling agencies dedicated to helping homeowners avoid foreclosure. NeighborWorks has teamed up with the Homeownership Preservation Foundation and the Financial Services Roundtable to provide this service.

HOPE for Homeownership **Hotline** (in English and Spanish): 1-888-995-HOPE

Find a HUD-certified NeighborWorks organization:
http://www.nw.org/network/nwdata/hudhousing.asp

Information on the Center for Foreclosure Solutions:
http://www.nw.org/network/neighborworksProgs/foreclosuresolutions/default.asp

National Community Reinvestment Coalition (NCRC)

NCRC is a national coalition of more than 800 non-profit organizations that seek to increase the flow of private capital into underserved communities. NCRC's Consumer Rescue Fund works with victims of predatory lending to provide mediation, refinancing or renegotiation of mortgages. Refinancing services are currently available in the states of: Alabama, Arizona, California, Florida, Georgia, Illinois, Indiana, Maryland, Massachusetts, Nevada, New York, North Carolina, Ohio, Pennsylvania, Rhode Island, Texas and Wisconsin.

NCRC's Information and CRF Services line: 202-628-8866

Website for the CRF: http://www.fairlending.com/

National Council of LaRaza (NCLR)

NCLR is the largest national Hispanic civil rights and advocacy organization in the United States. NCLR's Homeownership Network of 42 community-based organizations provide home ownership counseling and can intervene between borrowers facing financial crisis and the lenders and/or mortgage servicer.

Contact NCLR's: 202-785-1670

NCLR's Website: www.nclr.org

Neighborhood Assistance Corporation of America (NACA)

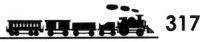

NACA is a national non-profit advocacy and homeownership organization. NACA's Refinance Program offers new loans to eligible homeowners with unaffordable mortgages. NACA's *Home Save* program gives counseling and financial assistance to eligible homeowners who are at risk of foreclosure.

NACA's Information and Refinancing Services line: 1-888-302-NACA

Website: https://www.naca.com/program/homesaveProgram.jsp

Government Sponsored Enterprise Resources: GSEs also provide excellent resources for Congressional offices seeking to aid constituents facing or at risk of foreclosure:

Fannie Mae

Fannie Mae's *HomeStay Initiative* provides flexible mortgage products that help homeowners with blemish credit histories refinance as well as counseling and foreclosure prevention services. In addition, Fannie Mae has worked with three state housing finance agencies (Massachusetts, New York, and Ohio) to develop refinancing programs to assist homeowners who are facing foreclosure or have a mortgage product that may no longer be suitable to their financial situation. Fannie has designed a product that allows eligible at-risk homeowners to refinance into 30-year fixed rate mortgage loan.

Information on *HomeStay Initiative*: https://www.efanniemae.com/homestay

Information on other Fannie Mae refinancing initiatives: contact state HFA agencies in MA, NY and OH.

Freddie Mac

Freddie Mac helped to develop and fund *Don't Borrow Trouble,* a comprehensive consumer awareness and foreclosure prevention campaign. In addition, Freddie Mac has partnered with national non-profit organizations, counseling agencies and several lenders on a foreclosure-avoidance initiative designed to reach out to delinquent borrowers early on and provide appropriate counseling through trusted intermediaries to help avoid foreclosure.

Information on *Don't Borrow Trouble*: http://www.dontborrowtrouble.com/

Legal Resources: In addition to the resources above, some homeowners may want to retain an attorney to help them navigate the legal system:

National Association of Consumer Advocates

The National Association of Consumer Advocates (NACA) is a nationwide organization of more than 1000 attorneys who represent and have represented hundreds of thousands of consumers victimized by fraudulent, abusive and predatory business practices. NACA attorneys have represented thousands of victims of predatory lending practices. The legal services are provided by legal service lawyers and private practice attorneys who provide free or low-cost legal representation.

Contact NACA: 202-452-1989

Find an attorney: http://members.naca.net/findanattorney.php

(Prepared by Financial Services Committee, Majority Staff)

FTC Facts for Consumers

FTC FACTS for Consumers

Mortgage Payments Sending You Reeling?

Here's What to Do

The possibility of losing your home because you can't make the mortgage payments can be terrifying. Perhaps you are one of the many consumers who took out a mortgage that had a fixed rate for the first two or three years and then had an adjustable rate. Or maybe you're anticipating an adjustment, and want to know what your payments will be and whether you'll be able to make them. Or maybe you're having trouble making ends meet because of an unrelated financial crisis.

Regardless of the reason for your mortgage anxiety, the Federal Trade Commission (FTC), the nation's consumer protection agency, wants you to know how to help save your home, and how to recognize and avoid foreclosure scams.

KNOW YOUR MORTGAGE

Do you know what kind of mortgage you have? Do you know whether your payments are going to increase? If you can't tell by reading the mortgage documents you received at settlement, contact your loan servicer and ask. A loan servicer is responsible for collecting your monthly loan payments and crediting your account.

Here are some examples of types of mortgages:

- Hybrid Adjustable Rate Mortgages (ARMs): Mortgages that have fixed payments for a few years, and then turn into adjustable loans. Some are called 2/28 or 3/27 hybrid ARMs: the first number refers to the years the loan has a fixed rate and the second number refers to the years the loan has an adjustable rate. Others are 5/1 or 3/1 hybrid ARMs: the first number refers to the years the loan has a fixed rate, and the second number refers to how often the rate changes. In a 3/1 hybrid ARM, for example, the interest rate is fixed for three years, then adjusts every year thereafter.

- ARMs: Mortgages that have adjustable rates from the start, which means your payments change over time.

- Fixed Rate Mortgages: Mortgages where the rate is fixed for the life of the loan; the only change in your payment would result from changes in your taxes and insurance if you have an escrow account with your loan servicer.

If you have a hybrid ARM or an ARM and the payments will increase — and you have trouble making the increased payments, find out if you can refinance to a fixed-rate loan. Review your contract first, checking for prepayment penalties. Many ARMs carry prepayment penalties that force borrowers to come up with thousands of dollars if they decide to refinance within the first few years of the loan. If you're planning to sell soon after your adjustment, refinancing may not

Facts for Consumers

be worth the cost. But if you're planning to stay in your home for a while, a fixed-rate mortgage might be the way to go. Online calculators can help you determine your costs and payments.

IF YOU ARE BEHIND ON YOUR PAYMENTS

If you are having trouble making your payments, contact your loan servicer to discuss your options as early as you can. Most loan servicers are willing to work with customers they believe are acting in good faith, and those who call them early on. The longer you wait to call, the fewer options you will have. After you've missed three or four payments and your loan is in default, most loan servicers won't accept a partial payment of what you owe. They will start foreclosure unless you can come up with the money to cover all your missed payments, plus any late fees.

AVOIDING DEFAULT AND FORECLOSURE

If you have fallen behind on your payments, consider discussing the following foreclosure prevention options with your loan servicer:

Reinstatement: You pay the loan servicer the entire past-due amount, plus any late fees or penalties, by a date you both agree to. This option may be appropriate if your problem paying your mortgage is temporary.

Repayment plan: Your servicer gives you a fixed amount of time to repay the amount you are behind by adding a portion of what is past due to your regular payment. This option may be appropriate if you've missed only a small number of payments.

Forbearance: Your mortgage payments are reduced or suspended for a period you and your servicer agree to. At the end of that time, you resume making your regular payments as well as a lump sum payment or additional partial payments for a number of months to bring the loan current. Forbearance may be an option if your income is reduced temporarily (for example, you are on disability leave from a job, and you expect to go back to your full time position shortly). Forbearance isn't going to help you if you're in a home you can't afford.

Loan modification: You and your loan servicer agree to permanently change one or more of the terms of the mortgage contract to make your payments more manageable for you. Modifications can include lowering the interest rate, extending the term of the loan, or adding missed payments to the loan balance. A loan modification may be necessary if you are facing a long-term reduction in your income.

Before you ask for forbearance or a loan modification, be prepared to show that you are making a good-faith effort to pay your mortgage. For example, if you can show that you've reduced other expenses, your loan servicer may be more likely to negotiate with you.

Selling your home: Depending on the real estate market in your area, selling your home may provide the funds you need to pay off your current mortgage debt in full.

Bankruptcy: Personal bankruptcy generally is considered the debt management option of last resort because the results are long-lasting and far-reaching. A bankruptcy stays on your credit report for 10 years, and can make it difficult to obtain credit, buy another home, get life insurance, or sometimes, even get a job. Still, it is a legal procedure that can offer a fresh start for people who can't satisfy their debts.

If you and your loan servicer cannot agree on a repayment plan or other remedy, you may want to investigate filing Chapter 13 bankruptcy. If you have a regular income, Chapter 13 may allow you to keep property, like a mortgaged house or car, that you might otherwise lose. In Chapter 13, the court approves a repayment plan that allows you to use your future income toward payment of your debts during a three-to-five-year period, rather than surrender the property. After you have made all the payments under the plan, you receive a discharge of certain debts.

To learn more about Chapter 13, visit **www.usdoj.gov/ust**; it's the website of the U.S. Trustee Program, the organization within the U.S.

Department of Justice that supervises bankruptcy cases and trustees.

If you have a mortgage through the Federal Housing Administration (FHA) or Veterans Administration (VA), you may have other foreclosure alternatives. Contact the FHA (**www.fha.gov**) or VA (**www.homeloans.va.gov**) to discuss your options.

CONTACTING YOUR LOAN SERVICER

Before you have any conversation with your loan servicer, prepare. Record your income and expenses, and calculate the equity in your home. To calculate the equity, estimate the market value less the balance of your first and any second mortgage or home equity loan. Then, write down the answers to the following questions:

- What happened to make you miss your mortgage payment(s)? Do you have any documents to back up your explanation for falling behind? How have you tried to resolve the problem?

- Is your problem temporary, long-term, or permanent? What changes in your situation do you see in the short term, and in the long term? What other financial issues may be stopping you from getting back on track with your mortgage?

- What would you like to see happen? Do you want to keep the home? What type of payment arrangement would be feasible for you?

Throughout the foreclosure prevention process:

- Keep notes of all your communications with the servicer, including date and time of contact, the nature of the contact (face-to-face, by phone, email, fax or postal mail), the name of the representative, and the outcome.

- Follow up any oral requests you make with a letter to the servicer. Send your letter by certified mail, "return receipt requested," so you can document what the servicer received. Keep copies of your letter and any enclosures.

- Meet all deadlines the servicer gives you.

- Stay in your home during the process, since you may not qualify for certain types of assistance if you move out. Renting your home will change it from a primary residence to an investment property. Most likely, it will disqualify you for any additional "workout" assistance from the servicer. If you choose this route, be sure the rental income is enough to help you get and keep your loan current.

CONSIDER GIVING UP YOUR HOME WITHOUT FORECLOSURE

Not every situation can be resolved through your loan servicer's foreclosure prevention programs. If you're not able to keep your home, or if you don't want to keep it, consider:

Selling Your House: Your servicers might postpone foreclosure proceedings if you have a pending sales contract or if you put your home on the market. This approach works if proceeds from the sale can pay off the entire loan balance plus the expenses connected to selling the home (for example, real estate agent fees). Such a sale also would allow you to avoid late and legal fees and damage to your credit rating, and protect your equity in the property.

Short Sale: Your servicers may allow you to sell the home yourself before it forecloses on the property, agreeing to forgive any shortfall between the sale price and the mortgage balance. This approach avoids a damaging foreclosure entry on your credit report. You still may face a tax liability on the amount of debt forgiven. Consider consulting a financial advisor, accountant, or attorney for more information.

Deed in Lieu of Foreclosure: You voluntarily transfer your property title to the servicers (with the servicer's agreement) in exchange for cancellation of the remainder of your debt. Though you lose the home, a deed in lieu of foreclosure can be less damaging to your credit than a foreclosure. You will lose any equity in

Facts for Consumers

the property, and you may face an income tax liability on the amount of debt forgiven. A deed in lieu may not be an option for you if other loans or obligations are secured by the property on your home.

HOUSING AND CREDIT COUNSELING

You don't have to go through the foreclosure prevention process alone. A counselor with a housing counseling agency can assess your situation, answer your questions, go over your options, prioritize your debts, and help you prepare for discussions with your loan servicer. Housing counseling services usually are free or low cost.

While some agencies limit their counseling services to homeowners with FHA mortgages, many others offer free help to any homeowner who is having trouble making mortgage payments. Call the local office of the U.S. Department of Housing and Urban Development (**www.hud.gov**) or the housing authority in your state, city, or county for help in finding a legitimate housing counseling agency nearby. Or consider contacting the NeighborWorks® Center for Foreclosure Solutions at 888-995-HOPE or **www.nw.org**. The Center is an initiative of NeighborWorks America.

BE ALERT TO SCAMS

Scam artists follow the headlines, and know there are homeowners falling behind in their mortgage payments or at risk for foreclosure. Their pitches may sound like a way for you to get out from under, but their intentions are as far away from honorable as they can be. They mean to take your money. Among the predatory scams that have been reported are:

- The foreclosure prevention specialist: The "specialist" really is a phony counselor who charges outrageous fees in exchange

for making a few phone calls or completing some paperwork that a homeowner could easily do for himself. None of the actions results in saving the home. This scam gives homeowners a false sense of hope, delays them from seeking qualified help, and exposes their personal financial information to a fraudster.

- The lease/buy back: Homeowners are deceived into signing over the deed to their home to a scam artist who tells them they will be able to remain in the house as a renter and eventually buy it back. Usually, the terms of this scheme are so demanding that the buy-back becomes impossible, the homeowner gets evicted, and the "rescuer" walks off with most or all of the equity.

- The bait-and-switch: Homeowners think they are signing documents to bring the mortgage current. Instead, they are signing over the deed to their home. Homeowners usually don't know they've been scammed until they get an eviction notice.

FOR MORE INFORMATION

To learn more about mortgages and other credit-related issues, visit **www.ftc.gov/credit** and **MyMoney.gov**, the U.S. government's portal to financial education.

The FTC works for the consumer to prevent fraudulent, deceptive, and unfair business practices in the marketplace and to provide information to help consumers spot, stop, and avoid them. To file a complaint or to get free information on consumer issues, visit **www.ftc.gov** or call toll-free, 1-877-FTC-HELP (1-877-382-4357); TTY: 1-866-653-4261. The FTC enters Internet, telemarketing, identity theft, and other fraud-related complaints into Consumer Sentinel, a secure online database available to hundreds of civil and criminal law enforcement agencies in the U.S. and abroad.

Internal Revenue Service (IRS): Income Tax Implications of Foreclosure

This Appendix Includes:

* ★ IRS Press Release
* ★ Questions and Answers on Home Foreclosure and Debt Cancellation
* ★ Mortgage Forgiveness Debt Relief Act of 2007

The following publications contained in this appendix pertain to the most recent changes in the U.S. tax code, which have a direct impact on your personal tax return should you ever face foreclosure. The information presented is intended as a cursory overview and should *not* be relied upon solely without consulting with a Certified Public Account (CPA) or your tax advisor. Either of these can provide you with specific information about exactly how a foreclosure would affect *your* tax return.

While you'd think that – once your home is foreclosed upon – that would be the end of it, a foreclosure may still unexpectedly and unfortunately come back to haunt you with an additional tax burden – dependent on your personal situation and on what the lender may do at the end of their fiscal year.

IRS Press Release

Special Web Section Unveiled for Homeowners Who Lose Homes;
Foreclosure Tax Relief Available to Many

IR-2007-159, Sept. 17, 2007

WASHINGTON — The Internal Revenue Service unveiled a special new section today on IRS.gov for people who have lost their homes due to foreclosure. The IRS also reassured homeowners that, although mortgage workouts and foreclosures can have tax consequences, special relief provisions can often reduce or eliminate the tax bite for financially strapped borrowers who lose their homes.

The new section of IRS.gov includes a variety of information, including a worksheet designed to help borrowers determine whether any of the foreclosure-related relief provisions apply to them. For those taxpayers who find they owe additional tax, it also includes a form they can use to request a payment agreement with the IRS. . In some cases, eligible taxpayers may qualify to settle their tax debt for less than the full amount due using an offer-in-compromise.

The IRS urges struggling homeowners to consider their options carefully before giving up their homes through foreclosure.

Under the tax law, if the debt wiped out through foreclosure exceeds the value of the property, the difference is normally taxable income. But a special rule allows insolvent borrowers to offset that income to the extent their liabilities exceed their assets.

The IRS cautions that under the law, relief may be limited or unavailable in some situations where, for example, part or all of a home was ever used for business or rented out.

Borrowers whose debt is reduced or eliminated receive a year-end statement (Form 1099-C) from their lender. By law, this form must show the amount of debt forgiven and the fair market value of property given up through foreclosure. Though the winning bid at a foreclosure auction is normally a property's fair market value, it may not necessarily reflect its true value in some cases.

The IRS urges borrowers to check the Form 1099-C carefully. They should notify the lender immediately if any of the information shown on their form is incorrect. Borrowers should pay particular attention to the amount of debt forgiven (Box 2) and the value listed for their home (Box 7).

The IRS also reminds lenders of their obligation to provide accurate information on the Form 1099-C. By law, the lender must send a copy of this form to the IRS. IRS follow-up contacts with taxpayers involved in foreclosure are based largely on the information reported on this form, and whether it conflicts with information provided by the taxpayer on their federal income tax return.

The IRS normally initiates these follow-up contacts by sending the borrower a notice. The tax agency urges borrowers with questions to call the phone number shown on the notice. The IRS also urges borrowers who wind up owing additional tax and are unable to pay it in full to use the installment agreement form, normally included with the notice, to request a payment agreement with the agency.

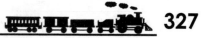

Questions and Answers on Home Foreclosure and Debt Cancellation

Questions and Answers on Home Foreclosure and Debt Cancellation

Update Feb. 4, 2008 — The Mortgage Forgiveness Debt Relief Act of 2007 generally allows taxpayers to exclude income from the discharge of debt on their principal residence. Debt reduced through mortgage restructuring, as well as mortgage debt forgiven in connection with a foreclosure, qualify for this relief.

This provision applies to debt forgiven in 2007, 2008 or 2009. Up to $2 million of forgiven debt is eligible for this exclusion ($1 million if married filing separately). The exclusion doesn't apply if the discharge is due to services performed for the lender or any other reason not directly related to a decline in the home's value or the taxpayer's financial condition.

The amount excluded reduces the taxpayer's cost basis in the home. More information on claiming this exclusion will be available soon.

The questions and answers, below, are based on the law prior to the passage of the Mortgage Forgiveness Debt Relief Act of 2007.

1. What is Cancellation of Debt?

If you borrow money from a commercial lender and the lender later cancels or forgives the debt, you may have to include the cancelled amount in income for tax purposes, depending on the circumstances. When you borrowed the money you were not required to include the loan proceeds in income because you had an obligation to repay the lender. When that obligation is subsequently forgiven, the amount you received as loan proceeds is reportable as income because you no longer have an obligation to repay the lender. The lender is usually required to report the amount of the canceled debt to you and the IRS on a Form 1099-C, Cancellation of Debt.

Here's a very simplified example. You borrow $10,000 and default on the loan after paying back $2,000. If the lender is unable to collect the remaining debt from you, there is a cancellation of debt of $8,000, which generally is taxable income to you.

2. Is Cancellation of Debt income always taxable?

Not always. There are some exceptions. The most common situations when cancellation of debt income is not taxable involve:

- Bankruptcy: Debts discharged through bankruptcy are not considered taxable income.
- Insolvency: If you are insolvent when the debt is cancelled, some or all of the cancelled debt may not be taxable to you. You are insolvent when your total debts are more than the fair market value of your total assets. Insolvency can be fairly complex to determine and the assistance of a tax professional is recommended if you believe you qualify for this exception.
- Certain farm debts: If you incurred the debt directly in operation of a farm, more than half your income from the prior three years was from farming, and the loan was owed to a person or agency regularly engaged in lending, your cancelled debt is

generally not considered taxable income. The rules applicable to farmers are complex and the assistance of a tax professional is recommended if you believe you qualify for this exception.

- Non-recourse loans: A non-recourse loan is a loan for which the lender's only remedy in case of default is to repossess the property being financed or used as collateral. That is, the lender cannot pursue you personally in case of default. Forgiveness of a non-recourse loan resulting from a foreclosure does not result in cancellation of debt income. However, it may result in other tax consequences, as discussed in Question 3 below.

3. I lost my home through foreclosure. Are there tax consequences?

There are two possible consequences you must consider:

- Taxable cancellation of debt income. (Note: As stated above, cancellation of debt income is not taxable in the case of non-recourse loans.)
- A reportable gain from the disposition of the home (because foreclosures are treated like sales for tax purposes). (Note: Often some or all of the gain from the sale of a personal residence qualifies for exclusion from income.)

Use the following steps to compute the income to be reported from a foreclosure:

Step 1 - Figuring Cancellation of Debt Income *(Note: For non-recourse loans, skip this section. You have no income from cancellation of debt.)*

1. Enter the total amount of the debt immediately prior to the foreclosure._____
2. Enter the fair market value of the property from Form 1099-C, box 7. _____
3. Subtract line 2 from line 1.If less than zero, enter zero._____

The amount on line 3 will generally equal the amount shown in box 2 of Form 1099-C. This amount is taxable unless you meet one of the exceptions in question 2. Enter it on line 21, Other Income, of your Form 1040.

Step 2 – Figuring Gain from Foreclosure

4. Enter the fair market value of the property foreclosed. For non-recourse loans, enter the amount of the debt immediately prior to the foreclosure _____
5. Enter your adjusted basis in the property.(Usually your purchase price plus the cost of any major improvements.) _____
6. Subtract line 5 from line 4. If less than zero, enter zero.

The amount on line 6 is your gain from the foreclosure of your home. If you have owned and used the home as your principal residence for periods totaling at least two years during the five year period ending on the date of the foreclosure, you may exclude up to $250,000 (up to $500,000 for married couples filing a joint return) from income. If you do not qualify for this exclusion, or your gain exceeds $250,000 ($500,000 for married couples filing a joint return), report the taxable amount on Schedule D, Capital Gains and Losses.

4. I lost money on the foreclosure of my home. Can I claim a loss on my tax return?

No. Losses from the sale or foreclosure of personal property are not deductible.

5. Can you provide examples?

A borrower bought a home in August 2005 and lived in it until it was taken through foreclosure in September 2007. The original purchase price was $170,000, the home is worth $200,000 at foreclosure, and the mortgage debt canceled at foreclosure is $220,000. At the time of the foreclosure, the borrower is insolvent, with liabilities (mortgage, credit cards, car loans and other debts) totaling $250,000 and assets totaling $230,000.

The borrower figures income from the foreclosure as follows:

Use the following steps to compute the income to be reported from a foreclosure:

Step 1 - Figuring Cancellation of Debt Income *(Note: For non-recourse loans, skip this section. You have no income from cancellation of debt.)*

1. Enter the total amount of the debt immediately prior to the foreclosure.___$220,000__
2. Enter the fair market value of the property from Form 1099-C, box 7. ___$200,000__
3. Subtract line 2 from line 1.If less than zero, enter zero.___$20,000__

The amount on line 3 will generally equal the amount shown in box 2 of Form 1099-C. This amount is taxable unless you meet one of the exceptions in question 2. Enter it on line 21, Other Income, of your Form 1040.

Step 2 – Figuring Gain from Foreclosure

4. Enter the fair market value of the property foreclosed. For non-recourse loans, enter the amount of the debt immediately prior to the foreclosure. __$200,000__
5. Enter your adjusted basis in the property.(Usually your purchase price plus the cost of any major improvements.) ___$170,000__
6. Subtract line 5 from line 4.If less than zero, enter zero.___$30,000__

The amount on line 6 is your gain from the foreclosure of your home. If you have owned and used the home as your principal residence for periods totaling at least two years during the five year period ending on the date of the foreclosure, you may exclude up to $250,000 (up to $500,000 for married couples filing a joint return) from income. If you do not qualify for this exclusion, or your gain exceeds $250,000 ($500,000 for married couples filing a joint return), report the taxable amount on Schedule D, Capital Gains and Losses.

In this situation, the borrower has a tax-free home-sale gain of $30,000 ($200,000 minus $170,000), because they owned and lived in their home as a principal residence for at least two years. Ordinarily, the borrower would also have taxable debt-forgiveness income of $20,000 ($220,000 minus $200,000). But since the borrower's liabilities exceed assets by $20,000 ($250,000 minus $230,000) there is no tax on the canceled debt.

Other examples can be found in IRS Publication 544, Sales and Other Dispositions of Assets, under the section "Foreclosures and Repossessions".

6. I don't agree with the information on the Form 1099-C. What should I do?

Contact the lender. The lender should issue a corrected form if the information is determined to be incorrect. Retain all records related to the purchase of your home and all related debt.

7. I received a notice from the IRS on this. What should I do?

The IRS urges borrowers with questions to call the phone number shown on the notice. The IRS also urges borrowers who wind up owing additional tax and are unable to pay it in full to use the installment agreement form, normally included with the notice, to request a payment agreement with the agency.

8. Where else can I go to get tax help?

If you are having difficulty resolving a tax problem (such as one involving an IRS bill, letter or notice) through normal IRS channels, the Taxpayer Advocate Service may be able to help. For more information, you can call the TAS toll-free case intake line at 1-877-777-4778, TTY/TDD 1-800-829-4059.

Mortgage Forgiveness Debt Relief Act of 2007

H. R. 3648

One Hundred Tenth Congress
of the
United States of America

AT THE FIRST SESSION

Begun and held at the City of Washington on Thursday,
the fourth day of January, two thousand and seven

An Act

To amend the Internal Revenue Code of 1986 to exclude discharges of indebtedness
on principal residences from gross income, and for other purposes.

Be it enacted by the Senate and House of Representatives of
the United States of America in Congress assembled,

SECTION 1. SHORT TITLE.

This Act may be cited as the "Mortgage Forgiveness Debt
Relief Act of 2007".

**SEC. 2. DISCHARGES OF INDEBTEDNESS ON PRINCIPAL RESIDENCE
EXCLUDED FROM GROSS INCOME.**

(a) IN GENERAL.—Paragraph (1) of section 108(a) of the Internal
Revenue Code of 1986 is amended by striking "or" at the end
of subparagraph (C), by striking the period at the end of subparagraph (D) and inserting ", or", and by inserting after subparagraph
(D) the following new subparagraph:

"(E) the indebtedness discharged is qualified principal
residence indebtedness which is discharged before January
1, 2010.".

(b) SPECIAL RULES RELATING TO QUALIFIED PRINCIPAL RESI-
DENCE INDEBTEDNESS.—Section 108 of such Code is amended by
adding at the end the following new subsection:

"(h) SPECIAL RULES RELATING TO QUALIFIED PRINCIPAL RESI-
DENCE INDEBTEDNESS.—

"(1) BASIS REDUCTION.—The amount excluded from gross
income by reason of subsection (a)(1)(E) shall be applied to
reduce (but not below zero) the basis of the principal residence
of the taxpayer.

"(2) QUALIFIED PRINCIPAL RESIDENCE INDEBTEDNESS.—For
purposes of this section, the term 'qualified principal residence
indebtedness' means acquisition indebtedness (within the
meaning of section 163(h)(3)(B), applied by substituting
'$2,000,000 ($1,000,000' for '$1,000,000 ($500,000' in clause (ii)
thereof) with respect to the principal residence of the taxpayer.

"(3) EXCEPTION FOR CERTAIN DISCHARGES NOT RELATED TO
TAXPAYER'S FINANCIAL CONDITION.—Subsection (a)(1)(E) shall
not apply to the discharge of a loan if the discharge is on
account of services performed for the lender or any other factor
not directly related to a decline in the value of the residence
or to the financial condition of the taxpayer.

"(4) ORDERING RULE.—If any loan is discharged, in whole
or in part, and only a portion of such loan is qualified principal
residence indebtedness, subsection (a)(1)(E) shall apply only
to so much of the amount discharged as exceeds the amount

H. R. 3648—2

of the loan (as determined immediately before such discharge) which is not qualified principal residence indebtedness.

"(5) PRINCIPAL RESIDENCE.—For purposes of this subsection, the term 'principal residence' has the same meaning as when used in section 121.".

(c) COORDINATION.—

(1) Subparagraph (A) of section 108(a)(2) of such Code is amended by striking "and (D)" and inserting "(D), and (E)".

(2) Paragraph (2) of section 108(a) of such Code is amended by adding at the end the following new subparagraph:

"(C) PRINCIPAL RESIDENCE EXCLUSION TAKES PRECEDENCE OVER INSOLVENCY EXCLUSION UNLESS ELECTED OTHERWISE.—Paragraph (1)(B) shall not apply to a discharge to which paragraph (1)(E) applies unless the taxpayer elects to apply paragraph (1)(B) in lieu of paragraph (1)(E).".

(d) EFFECTIVE DATE.—The amendments made by this section shall apply to discharges of indebtedness on or after January 1, 2007.

SEC. 3. EXTENSION OF TREATMENT OF MORTGAGE INSURANCE PREMIUMS AS INTEREST.

(a) IN GENERAL.—Subclause (I) of section 163(h)(3)(E)(iv) of the Internal Revenue Code of 1986 (relating to termination) is amended by striking "December 31, 2007" and inserting "December 31, 2010".

(b) EFFECTIVE DATE.—The amendment made by this section shall apply to amounts paid or accrued after December 31, 2007.

SEC. 4. ALTERNATIVE TESTS FOR QUALIFYING AS COOPERATIVE HOUSING CORPORATION.

(a) IN GENERAL.—Subparagraph (D) of section 216(b)(1) of the Internal Revenue Code of 1986 (defining cooperative housing corporation) is amended to read as follows:

"(D) meeting 1 or more of the following requirements for the taxable year in which the taxes and interest described in subsection (a) are paid or incurred:

"(i) 80 percent or more of the corporation's gross income for such taxable year is derived from tenant-stockholders.

"(ii) At all times during such taxable year, 80 percent or more of the total square footage of the corporation's property is used or available for use by the tenant-stockholders for residential purposes or purposes ancillary to such residential use.

"(iii) 90 percent or more of the expenditures of the corporation paid or incurred during such taxable year are paid or incurred for the acquisition, construction, management, maintenance, or care of the corporation's property for the benefit of the tenant-stockholders.".

(b) EFFECTIVE DATE.—The amendment made by this section shall apply to taxable years ending after the date of the enactment of this Act.

H. R. 3648—3

SEC. 5. EXCLUSION FROM INCOME FOR BENEFITS PROVIDED TO VOLUNTEER FIREFIGHTERS AND EMERGENCY MEDICAL RESPONDERS.

(a) IN GENERAL.—Part III of subchapter B of chapter 1 of the Internal Revenue Code of 1986 (relating to items specifically excluded from gross income) is amended by inserting after section 139A the following new section:

"SEC. 139B. BENEFITS PROVIDED TO VOLUNTEER FIREFIGHTERS AND EMERGENCY MEDICAL RESPONDERS.

"(a) IN GENERAL.—In the case of any member of a qualified volunteer emergency response organization, gross income shall not include—

"(1) any qualified State and local tax benefit, and

"(2) any qualified payment.

"(b) DENIAL OF DOUBLE BENEFITS.—In the case of any member of a qualified volunteer emergency response organization—

"(1) the deduction under 164 shall be determined with regard to any qualified State and local tax benefit, and

"(2) expenses paid or incurred by the taxpayer in connection with the performance of services as such a member shall be taken into account under section 170 only to the extent such expenses exceed the amount of any qualified payment excluded from gross income under subsection (a).

"(c) DEFINITIONS.—For purposes of this section—

"(1) QUALIFIED STATE AND LOCAL TAX BENEFIT.—The term 'qualified state and local tax benefit' means any reduction or rebate of a tax described in paragraph (1), (2), or (3) of section 164(a) provided by a State or political division thereof on account of services performed as a member of a qualified volunteer emergency response organization.

"(2) QUALIFIED PAYMENT.—

"(A) IN GENERAL.—The term 'qualified payment' means any payment (whether reimbursement or otherwise) provided by a State or political division thereof on account of the performance of services as a member of a qualified volunteer emergency response organization.

"(B) APPLICABLE DOLLAR LIMITATION.—The amount determined under subparagraph (A) for any taxable year shall not exceed $30 multiplied by the number of months during such year that the taxpayer performs such services.

"(3) QUALIFIED VOLUNTEER EMERGENCY RESPONSE ORGANIZATION.—The term 'qualified volunteer emergency response organization' means any volunteer organization—

"(A) which is organized and operated to provide firefighting or emergency medical services for persons in the State or political subdivision, as the case may be, and

"(B) which is required (by written agreement) by the State or political subdivision to furnish firefighting or emergency medical services in such State or political subdivision.

"(d) TERMINATION.—This section shall not apply with respect to taxable years beginning after December 31, 2010.".

H. R. 3648—4

(b) CLERICAL AMENDMENT.—The table of sections for such part is amended by inserting after the item relating to section 139A the following new item:

"Sec. 139B. Benefits provided to volunteer firefighters and emergency medical responders.".

(c) EFFECTIVE DATE.—The amendments made by this section shall apply to taxable years beginning after December 31, 2007.

SEC. 6. CLARIFICATION OF STUDENT HOUSING ELIGIBLE FOR LOW-INCOME HOUSING CREDIT.

(a) IN GENERAL.—Subclause (I) of section 42(i)(3)(D)(ii) of the Internal Revenue Code of 1986 (relating to certain students not to disqualify unit) is amended to read as follows:

"(I) single parents and their children and such parents are not dependents (as defined in section 152, determined without regard to subsections (b)(1), (b)(2), and (d)(1)(B) thereof) of another individual and such children are not dependents (as so defined) of another individual other than a parent of such children, or.".

(b) EFFECTIVE DATE.—The amendment made by this section shall apply to—

(1) housing credit amounts allocated before, on, or after the date of the enactment of this Act, and

(2) buildings placed in service before, on, or after such date to the extent paragraph (1) of section 42(h) of the Internal Revenue Code of 1986 does not apply to any building by reason of paragraph (4) thereof.

SEC. 7. APPLICATION OF JOINT RETURN LIMITATION FOR CAPITAL GAINS EXCLUSION TO CERTAIN POST-MARRIAGE SALES OF PRINCIPAL RESIDENCES BY SURVIVING SPOUSES.

(a) SALE WITHIN 2 YEARS OF SPOUSE'S DEATH.—Section 121(b) of the Internal Revenue Code of 1986 (relating to limitations) is amended by adding at the end the following new paragraph:

"(4) SPECIAL RULE FOR CERTAIN SALES BY SURVIVING SPOUSES.—In the case of a sale or exchange of property by an unmarried individual whose spouse is deceased on the date of such sale, paragraph (1) shall be applied by substituting '$500,000' for '$250,000' if such sale occurs not later than 2 years after the date of death of such spouse and the requirements of paragraph (2)(A) were met immediately before such date of death.".

(b) EFFECTIVE DATE.—The amendment made by this section shall apply to sales or exchanges after December 31, 2007.

SEC. 8. MODIFICATION OF PENALTY FOR FAILURE TO FILE PARTNERSHIP RETURNS; LIMITATION ON DISCLOSURE.

(a) EXTENSION OF TIME LIMITATION.—Section 6698(a) of the Internal Revenue Code of 1986 (relating to failure to file partnership returns) is amended by striking "5 months" and inserting "12 months".

(b) INCREASE IN PENALTY AMOUNT.—Paragraph (1) of section 6698(b) of such Code is amended by striking "$50" and inserting "$85".

H. R. 3648—5

(c) LIMITATION ON DISCLOSURE OF TAXPAYER RETURNS TO PART-NERS, S CORPORATION SHAREHOLDERS, TRUST BENEFICIARIES, AND ESTATE BENEFICIARIES.—

(1) IN GENERAL.—Section 6103(e) of such Code (relating to disclosure to persons having material interest) is amended by adding at the end the following new paragraph:

"(10) LIMITATION ON CERTAIN DISCLOSURES UNDER THIS SUB-SECTION.—In the case of an inspection or disclosure under this subsection relating to the return of a partnership, S cor-poration, trust, or an estate, the information inspected or dis-closed shall not include any supporting schedule, attachment, or list which includes the taxpayer identity information of a person other than the entity making the return or the person conducting the inspection or to whom the disclosure is made.".

(2) EFFECTIVE DATE.—The amendment made by this sub-section shall take effect on the date of the enactment of this Act.

(d) EFFECTIVE DATE.—The amendments made by subsections (a) and (b) shall apply to returns required to be filed after the date of the enactment of this Act.

SEC. 9. PENALTY FOR FAILURE TO FILE S CORPORATION RETURNS.

(a) IN GENERAL.—Part I of subchapter B of chapter 68 of the Internal Revenue Code of 1986 (relating to assessable penalties) is amended by adding at the end the following new section:

"SEC. 6699. FAILURE TO FILE S CORPORATION RETURN.

"(a) GENERAL RULE.—In addition to the penalty imposed by section 7203 (relating to willful failure to file return, supply information, or pay tax), if any S corporation required to file a return under section 6037 for any taxable year—

"(1) fails to file such return at the time prescribed therefor (determined with regard to any extension of time for filing), or

"(2) files a return which fails to show the information required under section 6037,

such S corporation shall be liable for a penalty determined under subsection (b) for each month (or fraction thereof) during which such failure continues (but not to exceed 12 months), unless it is shown that such failure is due to reasonable cause.

"(b) AMOUNT PER MONTH.—For purposes of subsection (a), the amount determined under this subsection for any month is the product of—

"(1) $85, multiplied by

"(2) the number of persons who were shareholders in the S corporation during any part of the taxable year.

"(c) ASSESSMENT OF PENALTY.—The penalty imposed by sub-section (a) shall be assessed against the S corporation.

"(d) DEFICIENCY PROCEDURES NOT TO APPLY.—Subchapter B of chapter 63 (relating to deficiency procedures for income, estate, gift, and certain excise taxes) shall not apply in respect of the assessment or collection of any penalty imposed by subsection (a).".

(b) CLERICAL AMENDMENT.—The table of sections for part I of subchapter B of chapter 68 of such Code is amended by adding at the end the following new item:

"Sec. 6699. Failure to file S corporation return.".

H. R. 3648—6

(c) EFFECTIVE DATE.—The amendments made by this section shall apply to returns required to be filed after the date of the enactment of this Act.

SEC. 10. MODIFICATION OF REQUIRED INSTALLMENT OF CORPORATE ESTIMATED TAXES WITH RESPECT TO CERTAIN DATES.

The percentage under subparagraph (B) of section 401(1) of the Tax Increase Prevention and Reconciliation Act of 2005 in effect on the date of the enactment of this Act is increased by 1.50 percentage points.

Speaker of the House of Representatives.

Vice President of the United States and President of the Senate.

Bonus CD-ROM:
The American Foreclosure Resource Center

System Requirements:

★ **Windows 2000, XP or Vista (with CD-ROM Drive)**
★ **Adobe Reader (Version 7 or Higher - Available as a Free Download)**
★ **Internet Connection (Recommended)**

The enclosed CD-ROM is outfitted with real estate forms, rental agreements and publications, as well as many other invaluable foreclosure prevention and investing resources *[some forms and agreements may need to be modified (or amended) to accommodate new or existing laws in your state]*. Each form comes equipped with fields that can be highlighted and then hovered with your mouse to reveal pop-up instructions. You can even personalize each form and agreement with your contact information and logo *(see the illustrations on the following pages)*.

Installation Instructions

Insert the CD into your CD-ROM drive and follow the onscreen instructions. If the installation process does not automatically begin, click the **START** button, then click **RUN** and type in the following: **D:\americanforeclosure.exe** and click **OK** to begin following the onscreen instructions. *(If the location of your CD-ROM begins with a letter other than **D**, you must replace it with the proper drive letter.)*

Terms of Use

All copyrighted forms are provided for your personal use only and may not be redistributed or sold.
Note: The contents of this CD-ROM are not intended as a substitute for the advice of an attorney.

How to Personalize a Real Estate Form

Instructions:
1. Insert your IMAGE
2. Enter 'PROPE
3. REPLACE ALL of this te
4. Click on 'PRINT FORM' whe

Highlight instructions to delete or replace with your contact information

Everything U Need to Know...

Click here to insert image/logo

Insert a logo or image from your computer to display on the top right of your form

Forms with landlord required fields can be completed onscreen before printing

Your personalized information cannot be saved - so be sure to print multiple copies for future use

Applicant Information			
Property address applying for: **1002 Nor_**			
Name:			
Date of birth:		SSN:	
Current address:			
City:			ZIP Code:
Own Re			How long?
Previous			
City:			ZIP Code:
Owned			How long?
Employmen			
Current employer:			
Employer address:			How long?
City:	State		ZIP Code:
Phone:			
Position:			
Emergency Conta			
Name of a person not residi			
Address:			
City:	State		Phone:
Relationship:			
References			
Name:	Address:		Phone:

The End Result

JOHN Z. DOE RENTAL PROPERTY LLC
2008 Western Avenue
Anytown, USA 12345
PH (555) 555-1212
FX (555) 555-1313

JZD
Rental Property LLC

Residential Rental Application

Applicant Information

Property address applying for: 1002 North Canyon Rd , Unit #3, Anytown, USA 12345

Name:		
Date of birth:	SSN:	Phone:
Current address:		
City:	State:	ZIP Code:
Own Rent (Please circle)	Monthly payment or rent:	How long?
Previous address:		
City:	State:	ZIP Code:
Owned Rented (Please circle)	Monthly payment or rent:	How long?

Employment Information

Current employer:		
Employer address:		How long?
City:	State:	ZIP Code:
Phone:	E-mail:	Fax:
Position:	Hourly Salary (Please circle)	Annual income:

Emergency Contact

Name of a person not residing with you:			
Address:			
City:	State:	ZIP Code:	Phone:
Relationship:			

References

Name:	Address:	Phone:

Have you ever been convicted of a crime? (yes / no) If so, please explain all offenses including where, when and why:

Have you ever been evicted? (yes / no) If so, please explain where, when and why:

I acknowledge that falsification or omission of any information on this rental application may result in the immediate dismissal or retraction of an offer of tenancy. I hereby voluntarily consent to and authorize the AmerUSA Corporation ("AmerUSA"), acting as the landlord's designated screening organization for the above referenced rental property, to obtain my consumer report and render a credit decision. I further authorize all persons and organizations that may have information relevant to this research to disclose such information to the landlord's authorized agent, AmerUSA. I hereby release the landlord and its authorized agent, AmerUSA, from all claims and liabilities of any nature in connection with this research, results and decision. A photocopy of this authorization will be considered valid. I understand that I have specific prescribed rights as a consumer under the federal Fair Credit Reporting Act ('FCRA') and have received a copy of those rights titled "FCRA Summary of Rights."

Signature of applicant:	Date:

This form provided by USLandlord.com

Index

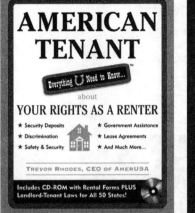
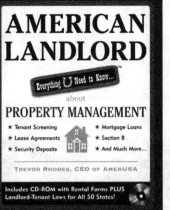
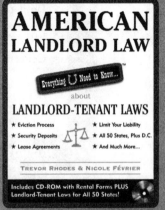